# THE REBEL LEAGUE

## THE SHORT AND UNRULY LIFE OF THE WORLD HOCKEY ASSOCIATION

# ED WILLES

McCLELLAND & STEWART

**Library and Archives Canada Cataloguing in Publication**

Willes, Ed
    The rebel league : the short and unruly life of the World Hockey
Association / Ed Willes.

Includes index.
ISBN 13: 978-0-7710-8949-7 (pbk.). – ISBN 10: 0-7710-8949-X (pbk.)
ISBN 10: 0-7710-8947-3 (bound)

    1. World Hockey Association – History.    I. Title.

GV847.8.W67W54 2004        796.962'64        C2004-902521-X

We acknowledge the financial support of the Government of Canada
through the Book Publishing Industry Development Program and that of
the Government of Ontario through the Ontario Media Development
Corporation's Ontario Book Initiative. We further acknowledge the
support of the Canada Council for the Arts and the Ontario Arts Council
for our publishing program.

Typeset in Bembo by M&S, Toronto
Printed and bound in the United States of America

McClelland & Stewart,
a division of Random House of Canada Limited,
a Penguin Random House company
www.penguinrandomhouse.ca

6 7 8 9    18 17 16 15

This book is dedicated to: the memory of Doug Michel, John Bassett, and Al Smith; the hockey fans of Winnipeg, Quebec, and Hartford; and that little bit of the WHA that lives inside all of us.

# CONTENTS

# ACKNOWLEDGEMENTS

There are several people I'd like to thank for their immeasurable contribution to this book. My wife, Kathy, for making all things possible. J.P. and Robert, for their inspiration. Ed and Bernice Willes, for their unwavering support. Owen and Pat Kealey, for all their help. Warren, Graham, and Domenic, for their friendship. And all the Willeses and all the Kealeys, for the bonds of family.

On a professional level, I'd like to extend a sincere thank-you to Vivienne Sosnowski, Malcolm Kirk, Wayne Moriarty, Paul Chapman, and Erik Rolfsen at the *Vancouver Province*; Kevin Paul Dupont of the *Boston Globe*, who interviewed Derek Sanderson, Gerry Cheevers, and John McKenzie; Jason Kay and Mark Brender at *The Hockey News*, for providing invaluable resource material; Jim Matheson and Terry Jones in Edmonton, Philippe Cantin and Michael Farber in Montreal, and Roy MacGregor in Ottawa, for their pro bono proofreading; and Jim Coleman, Dave Anderson, George Vecsey, Stephen Brunt, Cam Cole, Al Maki, and Al Strachan, for sending the elevator back down.

I n 1978-79, the last season of the World Hockey Association's rich seven-year life, Quebec Nordiques coach Jacques
Demers had to dress for a pre-game warmup to ensure his
team met the league's minimum player requirement.

Demers, who coached four different WHA teams without
ever being fired, doesn't see anything odd in that. The year
before, Demers, then coach of the Cincinnati Stingers, had to
bail Frankie Beaton of the Birmingham Bulls out of jail in
Cincinnati after Beaton was arrested on a three-year-old
warrant. His reaction is the same. No big deal. Demers started
his WHA coaching career in Chicago, where the Cougars played
out of the Chicago Amphitheater, a dank, decrepit old barn that
was located near the stockyards and tended to smell of rotting
animal flesh. The old coach still regards it as the luckiest break
of his life.

"We did what we had to do to survive," says Demers, who
would go on to coach in the NHL for fourteen years and win a

Stanley Cup with the Montreal Canadiens in 1993. "That was one thing about the WHA, we were all trying to pull together for the league."

If there's a theme that runs through the history of the WHA, it's survival. Players, coaches, and owners were all stakeholders in the grand adventure – Dennis Sobchuk, who played in both leagues, says the biggest difference between the NHL and the WHA was that in the NHL you never saw the owners, in the WHA you drank with them – and all were committed to doing whatever was necessary to keep the league alive. It didn't matter if a payroll was missed. It didn't matter if the franchise folded. It didn't matter if bills went unpaid and the sheriff was at the door.

In the WHA you just tried to make it to the next game.

"It was a way of life with us," says Gerry Pinder, who played five-plus seasons in the WHA. "We knew we'd taken some risks coming into the new league. But it wasn't a panic situation, because we felt like pioneers. We were doing something no one else was prepared to do."

It's interesting to note, then, how that same theme of survival has continued to run through the lives of so many of the WHA's players and hockey men long after the league folded. Bill Goldthorpe, who lived like Stagger Lee, was shot and wounded, he says, while trying to protect a woman. While he was in the hospital convalescing, his father died. Upon his release, Goldthorpe went back to school, took accounting and computer-programming courses, and now works as a construction foreman in San Diego.

In the summer of 1998, the hot-water heater exploded in the Pointe-du-Chene, New Brunswick, home Gordie Gallant shared with his partner, Debbie McFadden. Gallant, who also served in the Canadian army, suffered burns to 80 per cent of his body while saving McFadden and her seven-year-old son, and went into a coma. Given the last rites on two different occasions, he spent five months in the burn unit at the Moncton hospital and underwent nine operations. Today, he's back playing oldtimers hockey.

In December 1999, Paul Shmyr was diagnosed with cancer of the throat and given three months to live. Instead of accepting the death sentence, he started networking with other cancer patients and was led to a hospital on Staten Island that offered an aggressive treatment called stereotactic radiation. The sessions were paid for in large part by the NHL Emergency Fund and the NHL Alumni Association. In the fall of 2003, Shmyr celebrated his return to the Vancouver Canucks' oldtimers. "I tell the guys on the oldtimers team it's costing them a lot to keep me around," Shmyr said at the time. "But it's worth it because I make the power play go."

Shmyr passed away shortly before this book was published. The treatments bought him five years and he was fighting right until the end. Cancer is pretty tough, he'd say, but it's never fought a Shmyr. "Everywhere he went, the guys liked him," said Al Hamilton, Shmyr's teammate in Edmonton. "He had a great sense of humour and everything was a lot of fun when he was around. But he was also as tough as they come and he absolutely maximized his abilities."

There are many more stories like this. Derek Sanderson hit rock bottom after his WHA adventure but rebounded and now, remarkably, is an investment consultant to other athletes. André Lacroix runs a rink in downtown Oakland where one of his jobs is organizing hockey leagues for inner-city kids. Gary Smith, the hero of the Winnipeg Jets' last Avco Cup run, lost his beloved brother Brian, an Ottawa sportscaster, when he was shot by a crazy man. Gary Smith has been a single parent to his wheelchair-bound son, Marshall, since 1987. He's also been paying off Revenue Canada for the last twenty-some years.

This is what Smith says about his life: "I have my health. I have a lot of good friends. And I have a lot of fun. There's not much I'm missing."

One final thing to remember as you read the story that follows. Former Edmonton and Indianapolis owner Nelson Skalbania was relating the tale of how he signed Wayne Gretzky to his first pro contract on his private jet. Gretzky had earlier told me that, when it came to filling out the name of the team he'd play for, he had to write down both Indianapolis and Houston because Skalbania owned the former and was looking into buying the latter. When asked about this, Skalbania said, "No, that's not the way I remember it. I already owned Indianapolis. I owned half of Edmonton. Why would I want to buy Houston?" I pointed out to Skalbania that this is one of the problems encountered in piecing together events that are twenty-five and thirty years old. The truth sometimes becomes obscured.

"The truth is someone's memory," he said.

Here, then, is what the men of the WHA remember.

# CHAPTER I

# "They knew nothing about hockey. Absolutely zero."

I t certainly wasn't unusual that Steve Durbano had been kicked out of the game that night at the Winnipeg Arena during the 1977-78 season. Nor, by the standards of the World Hockey Association, was it unusual that an inebriated fan knocked on the Birmingham Bulls' dressing-room door after the game and demanded to see Durbano. Nor was it unusual that the fan took a swing at the Bulls' defenceman when he came to the door with a towel wrapped around his waist.

But even for the WHA, what followed next was unusual.

Bulls head coach Glen Sonmor, who was in the hallway, saw the fracas developing and rushed into the Bulls' dressing room. "Durby's in trouble," Sonmor yelled. "Everyone outside." The Bulls, who never had to be asked twice to join in a brawl, sprang into action, and with Durbano's assailant beating a hasty retreat they poured into the corridor.

There was just one problem. Most of the players had been preparing for their post-game showers and hadn't bothered to cover up when Sonmor sounded the alarm. A horde of naked hockey players combed the area looking for the fan amid a stunned group of Jets supporters. The search was finally abandoned. The fan had escaped. And the Bulls, unperturbed, turned and marched back to their locker room, laughing and joking among themselves as the Winnipeggers watched, dumbfounded. "It was a little exciting for a while," says Sonmor. "I remember [Bulls forward] Frankie Beaton said one of the fans was making fun of his equipment [not the hockey variety] and he was going to get him. But he was joking."

If you were looking for a metaphor for the WHA, you could do worse than a story about a bunch of naked hockey players running around like madmen while the rest of the world wondered just what the hell they were doing.

Dave Hanson was part of the Birmingham crew and a year removed from his role as one of the Hanson brothers in the epic movie *Slap Shot*. Hanson, who played parts of three seasons in the WHA and has a few similar stories to tell, has an eighteen-year-old son, Christian, who's considered an NHL prospect. When asked if he's ever told his boy about life in the WHA, Hanson says, "Maybe one day I'll sit down with him, have a beer, and tell him about our league. But not yet. It's hard for anyone who's playing today to relate to some of the things that went on. I guess it was a different time."

Oh, it was a different time all right. And a different league. The WHA survived for seven riotous seasons, produced twenty-seven teams, give or take the Miami Screaming Eagles, and, in its time, stuck a bottle of seltzer down the pants of the staid, established National Hockey League even as it revolutionized the game.

It brought major-league hockey to a series of new and sometimes improbable markets. It made rich men poor and poor hockey players rich. At its best, it helped pioneer the speed-and-skill Euro-game, which remains the best part of the modern NHL. At its worst, well, you will read about the New Jersey Knights.

It's now largely forgotten – three of the four teams that survived to the merger have since moved, the Edmonton Oilers being the sole remaining link to the WHA – but its impact on the game is immeasurable. The rebels broke down the NHL's monopoly on hockey and liberated a generation of players who were chained to a brutal system. It made a broad commitment to European players when the NHL believed they were too soft to play in North America. It challenged and defeated the NHL's reserve clause in the courts.

But mostly it left behind a legacy that strains the bounds of credulity. Did a seventeen-year-old Wayne Gretzky really write out his own contract with the Indianapolis Racers on a charter flight to, where else, Edmonton? Did Gordie Howe really attempt to rip Roger Cote's nose off his face? Did Ogie Oglethorpe really exist? How about San Diego Bev? Did they really zip Frankie Beaton into that equipment bag to escape the long arm of the law?

"When you hear POWs talk about their experiences, they always talk about the funny things that happened," says Harry Neale, who coached in six of the WHA's seven seasons. "You think, How can that be? They must have seen some terrible things. Well, it's the same thing with the WHA. If you survived it, you just remember the funny things."

Yes, they can laugh now, because it all happened in a time and a place long ago and far away. It all happened in the WHA, and it all started with a plan. It was quite a plan.

It had to be.

Dennis Murphy has always said the idea to start up the World Hockey Association just popped into his head one day in late 1970 while he was flying to Los Angeles, which, given what would follow, seems appropriate. Murphy, at the time, was the general manager of the American Basketball Association's Miami Floridians, his fourth posting in that league in four years, and he was growing tired of the constant travel and uncertainty of his position. Four years before his hockey brainstorm, he'd started up the ABA after he tried to put together an American Football League franchise in Orange County. He was also involved in World Team Tennis, Roller Hockey International, and the International Basketball Association, for players six-foot-four and under.

Dennis Murphy never lacked for ambition or imagination or, for that matter, gall. Still, if he was tired of the travel and uncertainty of the ABA, you'd never guess it from his next course of action.

Murphy, a self-confessed sports fanatic, had been a political operator before he went about the business of changing the world of sports forever. He'd been the mayor of Buena Park, California, the home of Knott's Berry Farm, and a fundraiser for California governor Pat Brown. He was also a loyal alumnus of the University of Southern California, where, among other things, he'd struck up a friendship with former USC quarterback Jim Hardy and former USC assistant coach Al Davis.

In 1965, Hardy was intent on putting an AFL franchise in Orange County, and he had the support of Davis, who was the owner-operator of the Oakland Raiders. The deal was eventually killed by the AFL–NFL merger, but the AFL, which began play in 1960, remains the single greatest success story involving a rebel league, and in many ways it would provide the blueprint for Murphy's subsequent ventures. The AFL went to war against an established league that operated on its own outdated principles and hindered the growth of its sport. The industry's supply was not keeping up to demand, and that created opportunities beyond the traditional markets for a new generation of sporting entrepreneurs. Murphy was one of the first men in America to see the landscape change. Following the football merger, he looked around, determined there was only one major basketball league and one major hockey league, and concluded that, if it could work for football, it could work for those two sports as well.

"I knew more about basketball, so we went with the basketball league," Murphy says.

It all sounds so simple now, like a movie where Mickey Rooney turns to Judy Garland and says, "I know! Let's put on a show!" But that's essentially what happened with the ABA.

Through Jim Hardy and his USC connections, Murphy was introduced to former Boston Celtics star Bill Sharman, and Sharman helped guide him through the league's infancy. That original ABA group included Roland Speth, an Orange County real-estate developer, and down the street from Speth's office was the office of a lawyer named Gary Davidson, who'd just started up a practice with his partner and fellow UCLA grad, Don Regan. Speth told Davidson, then in his early thirties, of the deal he was working on with Murphy. Davidson and Regan were young men looking for action. They met with Murphy.

It was like Lenin meeting Trotsky.

"We didn't have any money or any experience, but we were young guys, and even if we lost everything, it wasn't much," says Regan, Davidson's lifelong friend, who was the general counsel for both the ABA and WHA. "We thought a lot of what [Murphy] was saying was crap. But he had Bill Sharman, and some people we knew about, so there was some credibility there. We were looking for something to get involved with, and Dennis had the idea and the vision."

Murphy would become the backroom organizer and consensus builder of the original ABA group, Davidson became the front man, and Regan would perform most of the behind-the-scenes legal work.

Murphy would also join forces with Connie Seredin, a New Yorker who was also working on a new basketball league, and the unlikely alliance went to work. Seed money was raised. Meetings were held. Seredin dropped out. Potential owners were attracted. Some were legitimate. Others were dreaming in technicolor. Murphy originally set the league's franchise fee at $25,000. Mike Storen, the Cincinnati Royals' former business manager, who would go on to manage several ABA teams, talked the fee over with Dick Tinkham, the founder of the Indiana Pacers, and decided it was too steep. Let's not do anything and we'll see what happens, Storen advised. Sure enough, franchise fees went down to $5,000.

George Mikan, a Hall of Fame centre who had a law degree and owned a travel agency in the Twin Cities, would step in and steer the league through its formative stages. He was the ABA's front man and recruited most of its original money. The red, white, and blue ball was his idea. Mikan was also the commissioner, Davidson the president, and the two men clashed. At one point, Mikan tried to suspend Davidson and Davidson tried to suspend Mikan. Finally, at a league meeting, Joe Geary, a money man from Dallas, asked Davidson if he owned any teams or had any money in the league. The meeting recessed. When it reconvened, Davidson was gone and his ABA career was over.

He would, however, take something out of the experience. If you believe history repeats itself, you may want to take note of the similarities between the ABA's startup and the WHA's. There was Murphy's simple idea. There was the leadership group with Murphy, Davidson, and Regan, which had no real money of its own but had some organizational and promotional flair. They also had little credibility in either basketball or hockey, but in both cases they enlisted the aid of men who could open doors for them. Also in both cases, their first order of business was to sign away a huge, charismatic star to a groundbreaking contract. In the ABA it was Rick Barry. In the WHA it would be Bobby Hull.

"The ABA gave us an experience and credibility, and that's an important factor when you're starting up a league," says Davidson.

It was also about *all* they had when they started the WHA. Remarkably, it was enough.

In January of 1971, Murphy contacted Davidson in Los Angeles and told him he was quitting the Floridians. He had a new idea: a hockey league. He drove out to Newport Beach, sat down with his former partner, and each man determined they would throw in five grand and follow much of the ABA model. They'd each take a franchise. They'd scout around for investors. They'd try to land a big star. They'd build a stage in the barn. The difference, of course, was neither Murphy nor Davidson knew a puck from an Eskimo pie, but that didn't seem to bother them one bit.

By the spring, both men were knee-deep in their new venture. Murphy had been talking to a TV pal of his, Bernie Rosen, in Miami, and Rosen advised him that American Hockey League meetings were taking place in the Bahamas. The NHL had just expanded from twelve to fourteen teams, and was contemplating a further expansion. There would be a number of hockey men and potential investors at the meetings. Rosen told Murphy he should go.

Murphy, an engaging sort, arrived in the Bahamas and soon began pressing flesh and ingratiating himself with the hockey community. He passed himself off as a TV reporter to New York Rangers GM Emile Francis and began asking questions about NHL expansion. Soon thereafter, Francis was watching TV in his hotel room when he saw his TV reporter being interviewed by another TV reporter, only his TV reporter was Murphy and he was talking about this new league he was starting. Francis quickly got on the phone to NHL president Clarence Campbell and warned him about it. Campbell was dismissive: he was always dismissive of the WHA. It would cost him and the NHL dearly.

Stateside, meanwhile, Davidson and Regan began looking at the business of hockey and discovered the game was operated by principles and practices that were almost feudal. Hockey players, whose average salary sat around $25,000, were clearly the worst-paid athletes of the four major sports, and minor-leaguers were even worse off, making $10,000 to $12,000 a year. The players were also shackled to their teams by the reserve clause written into the standard player's contract, which automatically extended the life of the contract by one year. Thus, when a player's contract expired, it simply renewed itself, essentially tying that player to his team in perpetuity. The best a player could do was withhold his services and hope for a better deal, but the deck was stacked against him to an absurd, and illegal, extent.

"The weakness of the reserve clause was the legal basis on which we were able to get our league started," says Regan, who would challenge and defeat it in court. "I read the standard player's contract and I thought, This can't be. I sent a contract to two of my friends who were better acquainted with that end of the law. They said, 'It's an interesting document but it's not a contract.' It was like stuff you learn in third-year law."

The birth of the WHA also took place in a sports world, and a society, that was changing dramatically. In 1969, Curt Flood wrote his now-famous letter to baseball commissioner Bowie Kuhn and sued Major League Baseball over its reserve clause. Baseball's first work stoppage took place in 1971. Players' unions were growing more militant, and terms like "free agency" and "salary arbitration" were starting to creep into the sports lexicon. There was also a new figure, the player agent, making his presence felt.

Hockey was impervious to these changes before the WHA's arrival. The NHL Players' Association and its executive director, Alan Eagleson, had made progress in areas such as pensions and insurance, but salaries and players' rights were still stuck somewhere in the late 1950s. Eagleson's relationship with the WHA was, well, curious. The rebel league was the best thing to happen to players since shin pads, but the head of the NHLPA was, at best, patronizing toward the insurgents. During the seven years of the WHA, Eagleson signed only one junior client to the league, forward Danny Arndt, and some fifteen veterans, including Paul Henderson, the hero of 1972, who ended his hockey career with a series of decent paydays in the WHA.

"If it served Al's purposes he'd let his player go," says WHA goalie John Garrett, who was represented by Eagleson. "Otherwise, it was like the league never existed."

"He is a sharp operator but it's difficult to trust his sincerity when you deal with him," Davidson said at the time.

Eagleson, of course, was uncomfortably close to the NHL's owners – he was offered Campbell's job as president in 1976 – and it seemed his mandate was to preserve the status quo instead of advancing the players' cause. And the owners loved the status quo. The NHL didn't have the revenue stream (that is, a national American TV contract) of baseball, basketball, and football, but the sport drew remarkably well and, combined with its meagre labour costs, the owners were making a killing. Davidson estimated the NHL was grossing $50 million a year. The league was a monopoly and it was restrictive, but, with a compliant players' union, they conducted business as they desired. The U.S. Department of Justice had been investigating the NHL for restraint-of-trade practices, but the senior league always managed to avoid prosecution and it seemed they could go on running things their way forever.

Then along came the WHA and ruined their perfect world.

"We felt their weakness was their arrogance and selfishness," says Murphy. "The NHL thought they had it made and, if they ignored us, we'd go away. They could have knocked us out of the box before we even started if they wanted to. But they didn't, and we didn't go away."

The new league, then, had some things in its favour as it started, and it would accumulate more as it took its first unsteady steps. Murphy knew a sportswriter at the *Los Angeles Herald-Examiner* named Walt Marlow, a Canadian by birth who'd worked in Edmonton. During the course of a conversation about the new league, Marlow offered the name of Bill

Hunter, who was the president of the junior Western Canada Hockey League, the general manager of the league's Edmonton Oil Kings, and had some experience fighting the hockey establishment. Hunter sounded like the perfect man for Murphy's project, and Marlow made the call. Hunter was intrigued. He flew out to Orange County to meet with Murphy and his crew, and while he was there, Murphy, Davidson, and Hunter went to a Los Angeles Kings game. At the opening faceoff, Davidson asked Hunter, "What are they doing?" Hunter then turned to Murphy and said, "And this guy is going to be our president?"

"I was impressed with them only as promoters," said Hunter. "They knew nothing about hockey. Absolutely zero."

But they needed each other. Hunter's ongoing war with hockey's power structure had started in the 1960s when he and some fellow junior operators broke away from the Canadian Amateur Hockey Association and established the WCHL, one of the three great junior leagues in Canada. Hunter had also investigated the idea of starting a second pro league out of the old Western Hockey League, a minor-league circuit that had survived in various forms for years. Among his pals were Ben Hatskin, the owner-operator of the junior Winnipeg Jets, and Scotty Munro, the general manager and owner of the Calgary Centennials. On his second trip to California, Hunter brought along Hatskin and Munro. Murphy, Davidson, and Regan hosted the three Canadians at the Balboa Bay Club in a boardroom that overlooked a marina. The Californians faced the wall; Hunter, Hatskin, and Munro faced the marina, where they stared out at about twenty-five luxury yachts and a bevy of young women clad in shorts, T-shirts, and halter tops who were working on the boats. Sort of. The girls were employees of the marina, and Murphy and co. had flipped them a few extra bucks to concentrate their labours on the yachts that faced the boardroom and the three Canadians.

The meetings lasted two days, and Hunter and his group would return home with a deep appreciation for California's charm.

Now that's marketing.

From the start, they formed a strange confederacy: Murphy, the garrulous politician; Davidson, all-California cool with a sharp legal mind and nary a clue about the game; Hunter, Hatskin, and Munro, hockey hard men who lived puck in the frozen north.

Hunter was an original, a proud son of Saskatchewan who flew planes in the Second World War, built successful junior operations in Regina and Edmonton, and took on the most powerful forces in hockey and revelled in the fight. He had made his early living in the media and as a travelling salesman, and you might say it showed. He was a windbag, full of himself, and certain of his path. He also had the imagination to envision things others dared not dream and the ingenuity to turn them into reality. The junior Western Hockey League, the World Hockey Association, the Edmonton Oilers, and Northlands Coliseum (now Rexall Place) are all products of Hunter's immense will.

Ben Hatskin, for his part, was another pioneer with the spirit of the Old West in his blood. His father had emigrated to Winnipeg from Russia in 1911, and Benny, who was born seven years later, quickly took to sports. He played college football in the U.S. on a scholarship when few Canadians were playing south of the border. He came back to Winnipeg, played with the Blue Bombers, and began coaching high-school ball. He also started a stable and raised thoroughbreds. He sold the family's box-making business, invested in real estate, and bought and sold jukeboxes. In the mid-1960s he bought the junior Jets, where his orbit collided with Hunter's and Munro's. Of the threesome, they used to say Munro would think up the ideas, Hunter would sell them, and Benny would pay for them. Munro would be out of the picture by the time the WHA was up and running but that certainly describes Hunter's and Hatskin's role.

The league's first meetings, like the original ABA meetings, were disastrous. Murphy had rounded up some live wires who failed to impress the Canadians, whose standards weren't particularly high. Hunter threatened to quit, then laid down certain conditions instead. He would head up the hockey end of the operation, and Hatskin would look after finances.

For the next year and a half, until Davidson left to form the World Football League, there would be infighting and backbiting among the WHA's executive. But like a dog that can sing, the miracle wasn't that the WHA started well, it's that it started at all. Davidson said the new league should use a fluorescent red puck. Hunter shouted him down. Davidson said the new league should take out the centre red line to speed up play. Hunter rejected that idea. Davidson, Hunter, and Hatskin were all strong-willed people, and it fell to Murphy to smooth things over. "The Canadians didn't like it because I didn't know anything about hockey, but over time we were able to work together," says Davidson. "I was raised in southern California, and I'd never seen a game. I looked like a surfer in those days. But I saw the opportunity that was presented to us."

In June of 1971, Davidson filed the WHA's articles of incorporation in Delaware. From there, it was determined that Hunter and Murphy would hit the road to seek out potential owners, and the two men would spend the next eleven months touring North America in search of live money. Murphy had a list of names from his ABA days, but most of their calls were cold. They'd simply hit a town, talk to the local sports editor or the chamber of commerce about who might be interested in owning a hockey team, then set up their tent and make their pitch. Murphy had this line he loved to use: "Would you rather be known as a guy who sells brassieres in Muskegon or owns a hockey team in Detroit?"

It seemed to resonate with his audience, but Murphy was also telling people what they wanted to hear. Davidson had set down the WHA's business plan, and of course it was foolproof. Individual team payrolls would cost around $750,000, and that would buy you a couple of stars at around $150,000 each. Travel would be $150,000. Throw in $50,000 for equipment, add some other stuff, and you had a budget around $1.25 to $1.5 million. Sure there'd be losses along the way, Davidson admitted, but with his revenue projections, teams should start breaking even by the third year!

"It was easy for me, because I'd done it before with the ABA," says Murphy. "Every town has a high roller, a guy with money who's involved in sports. I'd go into a town and find out who those guys were. Then we'd make our pitch."

They began to make progress. In September, the WHA held its first formal meeting in Los Angeles, and in October they announced they'd operate without the reserve clause in the standard player's contract. Davidson wrote the press release, and it still reads like the players' Emancipation Proclamation: "The reserve clause won't stand up to the scrutiny of . . . players, players associations, the United States Congress, the public and the Supreme Court." In November, they announced their original ten franchises: Hunter had the Alberta Oilers, Hatskin the Winnipeg Jets, and Munro the Calgary Broncos; Murphy would operate the Los Angeles Sharks; Chicago would pass through one ownership group before the Kaiser brothers, who made their money in real estate, stepped in; a group of investors led by scrap-iron king Lou Kaplan would run the Minnesota Fighting Saints, to play in a new rink being built in St. Paul; real-estate developer Herb Martin was in Miami; lawyer Neil Shayne was looking to put a franchise on Long Island; architect

Paul Deneau owned the franchise in Dayton, and Davidson would operate San Francisco.

The WHA's original franchise fee was $25,000. In 1996, the Winnipeg Jets would be sold to a group in Phoenix for $67.5 million.

The NHL, publicly at least, looked at the arrivistes with amusement, then made a move they were confident would squash the bugs scurrying across their tidy floor. The league had just moved into Vancouver and Buffalo for the 1970-71 season, and there were no further expansion plans in their immediate future. But Campbell surprised everyone by announcing his league would have franchises on Long Island and in Atlanta for the 1972-73 season, and they'd take applications for another round of expansion in two more years.

"The board of governors has reassessed its position, and think it is in the best interest to expand now," said Campbell. "I don't suppose it's a coincidence, but we have had these applications on hand for some time. We think it's good business to expand in 1972."

The 1972 expansion succeeded in blocking the new league from Long Island, and it also removed Tom and Bob Cousins, the ABA's Atlanta Hawks' owners, from future WHA plans. But, far from hurting the new league, the NHL's plans to expand again in 1974 were an immense boost to the rebels. Some ten groups made presentations to the NHL for the next phase of expansion, and they included well-heeled and legitimate operators like Nick Mileti in Cleveland and Bill DeWitt, Jr., in Cincinnati. When the NHL awarded its franchises to Washington and Kansas City, Davidson and Murphy nearly tripped over themselves getting to Mileti and DeWitt. San Diego, Houston, and Phoenix were also rejected by the NHL, and all would end up in the WHA.

Mileti, in particular, was perfect for the new league. At one time or another he owned the NBA's Cavaliers, baseball's Indians, and the AHL's Barons. He was, even by 1970s standards, a flash dresser, given to all manner and colour of velours, suedes, and leisure suits, and that made him a character. He also had big plans for a state-of-the-art facility in the southern suburb of Richfield that would house the Crusaders and the Cavaliers.

After he was rejected by the NHL, Mileti called Davidson, and the WHA's president literally jumped into his Cadillac, raced to the airport in Los Angeles, threw his keys to a SkyCap, then took the next available flight to Cleveland. Davidson signed up Mileti that day, but the best part was his car was still in the parking lot when he returned to Los Angeles.

The new league was starting to gain momentum, but it was also entering a phase when franchises materialized, then disappeared between league meetings. In Boston, twenty-seven-year-old Howard Baldwin had just left the employ of the Philadelphia Flyers, where he'd worked as the team's ticket manager for three and a half years. He read about the WHA in the *Boston Globe*, contacted Murphy and Davidson, and the league's two power-brokers flew to Boston to meet with him and his partner, John Colburn. Baldwin was waiting on the Tarmac at Logan when the plane landed, and saw a short, stout man fall down the plane's stairs. That was Murphy.

Baldwin had set up an office in his hometown of Marion, Massachusetts. He didn't have any money, which meant he didn't have any furniture, but a family friend, Al Ford, was one of the biggest antique dealers in the state and he agreed to lend Baldwin some of his stuff for 1 per cent of the team.

"At least it looked like we had money," Baldwin says. "That office was the birthplace of the New England Whalers.

"They were suspicious about our age, but I think they were also intrigued," Baldwin continues. Murphy and Davidson "had been through it with the ABA, so what they said sounded believable. At least it was believable to a twenty-seven-year-old kid who had limited experience in these things."

Baldwin would miss the first round of WHA franchising, when teams were going for $25,000 a pop, and by the time the second opportunity rolled around a month later, he learned the price for a team had risen to $210,000. Undaunted, Baldwin had begun looking for a money man when a friend read about the efforts of Bob Schmertz, then a minority owner of the NBA Portland Trail Blazers, to bring a CFL team to New York. This marked Schmertz as a player in Baldwin's eyes and he made the call.

"We had the deal done in half an hour," Baldwin says. "He didn't know a thing about hockey but he was totally receptive to the idea. We hit it off from the beginning."

The Whalers would be announced as the WHA's newest franchise in late November 1971. A few days later, Baldwin was sitting in a coffee shop when he saw a column by influential Boston hockey writer Leo Monahan. The column said the two young New Englanders had two chances of making it with the new league: slim and none.

But "there's no question about it," Baldwin says. "The landscape was perfect. You couldn't do it today. You also have to remember that new leagues were working then. The AFL worked and the ABA was working."

In Toronto, meanwhile, Doug Michel had read about the WHA in a Toronto newspaper, phoned the NHL, of all places, for information, and eventually got Davidson's number from the *Toronto Star*. Michel was a hockey nut who'd sold popcorn at Maple Leaf Gardens as a kid and started up the Young Nationals minor-hockey program in Toronto. He also owned part of an electrical company.

The newspaper article reported that WHA franchises would cost a million. When Michel got hold of Davidson, he was told, "It's not really a million. It carries a lot of things with it. You don't really need that much cash." Michel would find out he

needed just $25,000 for the franchise, $10,000 for league operations, and a $100,000 bond in place by January 1, 1972. He then
headed to a series of meetings with Hamilton mayor Vic Copps,
who assured Michel a new rink was being built in Steeltown
and they were looking for an anchor tenant.

This is going to be easy, Michel thought.

Like Baldwin, Michel would miss the new league's first dead-
line. Unlike Baldwin, he didn't take the news of the newly
inflated franchise fee in stride. His partner, Jim McCreath, was
livid and wanted to quit. Michel would eventually negotiate new
terms and go it alone.

What followed was a living nightmare for a man who just
wanted to own a professional hockey team. Michel went back
to Hamilton, and Copps was now saying the city would donate
the land but Michel would have to build the rink. Good one,
Vic. He then went to Leafs owner Harold Ballard, who said he
was welcome to use Maple Leaf Gardens for $25,000 a game or
50 per cent of the gate after taxes plus a $500,000 bond.

Michel was now scrambling. He had to sell his half of his
electrical company for $105,000. His bank account was down to
$1,000, and he started living off his credit cards. He travelled to
Ottawa, where he talked with the Central Canada Exhibition
Association about playing in the new Civic Centre there. They
wanted $100,000 in cash as a guarantee, 15 per cent of any TV
revenue, plus rent.

Everyone, it seemed, was trying to screw Doug Michel and
no one wanted to kiss him.

Michel finally raised the $100,000. He borrowed $70,000
from the bank after his wife signed over their house to him, and
his father signed over his waterfront property. He also cashed in
a life-insurance policy and borrowed money from his former
partners in the electrical company to make up the difference.
When he made the payment, Michel had $3,000 left to operate
his team.

By this time, it was apparent to Michel he needed help. Someone in Ottawa told him about potential investors. "What do you know about these guys?" Michel asked Davidson. Davidson told him they were being investigated for their ties to organized crime.

Murphy eventually put Michel in touch with Nick Trbovich, a Buffalo businessman whose holdings included Munro Games, the manufacturers of the Bobby Hull table-top hockey game. (Students of Foreshadowing 101 take note.) Trbovich weighed well over three hundred pounds, and when Michel took him to breakfast to finalize their agreement he watched him inhale eight orders of bacon and eggs on one plate. The first question Michel asked of his new partner was "Do you have any ties to organized crime?" Michel wanted $400,000 for 66 per cent of the franchise. Trbovich gave him $200,000 for 80 per cent, and the Ottawa Nationals were born.

Doug Michel had a problem with an ulcer when he was a younger man. Six months after he decided he was going to own a hockey franchise, the ulcer was flaring up again. But he was a member of the WHA, and by the standards of new league his story wasn't that unusual. Paul Deneau, a wheeler-dealer from Dayton, Ohio, had lined up Lefty McFadden, who had run the Dayton IHL team, to operate his franchise. Soon Deneau became suspicious that McFadden was passing WHA information to the NHL and let him go. Someone gave Deneau the name of Bill Dineen, a former NHLer who'd played and coached in the minors forever. Dineen had been coaching the Denver Spurs in the Western Hockey League but was on his way to take over the Penticton junior team when Deneau called. Dineen flew into Dayton on New Year's Day, 1972, and the following morning was ushered to Deneau Towers – the biggest office building in Dayton, the old coach says without a trace of irony in his voice – where he was kept waiting for two hours. Deneau finally appeared, said, "Let's go to lunch," and at the restaurant started consuming double Scotches at an impressive clip while Dineen matched him with singles. After five or six drinks, the interview started.

*Deneau*: I see you can drink.

*Dineen*: I can drink.

*Deneau*: How are you with the women?

*Dineen*: I'm not in that business. I'm married.

*Deneau*: What are you, queer?

*Dineen*: Fuck you.

*Deneau* (after a pause): I like you.

Dineen would leave the next morning and make it as far as Chicago, where his flight was cancelled, which was just as well because Deneau called him back to Dayton. In the second meeting at Deneau Towers, the owner threw his American Express card at Dineen and said, "Go get me a hockey team."

The next order of business was finding a place to play. Dayton was getting a new arena, and one of McFadden's jobs had been to deliver the votes from city council to supply it with an ice-making plant. When Deneau whacked Lefty, however, city council stopped co-operating, which left the Dayton franchise, to be known as the Arrows, without a place to play. Gary Davidson assigned Jim Browitt from the WHA head office to help the Dayton boys find a new home. Deneau told Browitt to find the best rink in the U.S.A., and Browitt came back with Sam Houston Arena in Houston in the great state of Texas, a less-than-spectacular old barn that had been built in 1937.

Now Deneau's franchise had a place to play and a one-man hockey department who was armed with a credit card. The next thing they needed were hockey players, and in mid-February the WHA started that process when it held its inaugural player draft in Anaheim.

The WHA draft remains one of the signature events of the rebels' seven-year history. It was, by turns, brilliant, innovative, comedic, and farcical. It broke new ground in some areas and made the league a laughingstock in others. In all, just under 1,100 amateur, professional, and retired players were selected, including Minnesota governor Wendell Anderson and Soviet premier Alexei Kosygin. Bill Hunter opened the proceedings by declaring, according to Minnesota head coach and GM Glen Sonmor, "This is the greatest day in the history of the world." Sonmor then chose Henry Boucha from the American Olympic team with the first pick of the draft, thereby selecting, from the many hundreds of players for whom Hunter had made name cards, one player Hunter hadn't accounted for.

The whole ordeal took two days to complete. After seventy rounds, the teams arbitrarily decided to stop picking. In the late going – the very late going – the Arrows, who wouldn't officially move to Houston for a few weeks, and Los Angeles were the only teams still going at it. Dineen, who was running his team's entire draft by himself, looked over at the press table and saw that some of the scribes were starting to nod off. The Arrows' coach then leaned into the microphone and said, "Houston takes Phil Esposito," at which point some heads lifted on press row. For his next pick, he took Bobby Orr.

"The headlines the next day were 'DAYTON TAKES ORR AND ESPOSITO,'" Dineen says. "Deneau came up to me and said, 'Kid, we had a helluva draft.'"

Shortly after, Deneau flew some of his people down to Mexico for a fishing excursion. While waiting for their flight in Los Angeles, the new hockey man consumed a quart of Scotch, then looked out a window and saw an AeroMexico plane. Deneau thought about this for a moment. His team was moving to Houston, but the name "Arrows" meant nothing there. "Aeros," on the other hand, sounded like space travel, which sounded like Houston. Hockey fans in Houston can only be glad there wasn't a Virgin Airlines at the time.

Elsewhere around the draft, other notable events were taking place. Scotty Munro had hired Herb Pinder, who'd just graduated from law school after playing with Canada's national team, to help him select his team. Pinder's plan was to stock the Broncos with Europeans, specifically Eastern Europeans. This, remember, was before the Summit Series between Canada and the Soviet Union later that year, and the notion of drafting players from Russia was on par with drafting players from Mars. But with Munro cheering him on, Pinder calmly kept calling the names of Czech and Russian players, and the Broncos final draft list would include Valeri Kharlamov, Alexander Maltsev, and Vladimir Petrov. Eight months later, hockey fans in North America would become more familiar with those names.

"Scotty was at the table, saying, 'Get me another Chinaman. Get me another Chinaman,'" says Pinder. "The funny thing was, I met this guy at the world championship in Prague [later that spring], and he said we could get the players out. Everyone was laughing at us, but we were sincere. Everything we planned eventually happened."

The Broncos, alas, would never see the light of day. Bobby Brownridge, who was to provide the team's bankroll, was stricken with cancer, and Munro had no desire to fund the team himself. Herb Martin, the real-estate mogul in Miami, also dropped out after his dream of combining a rink with a shopping complex failed to materialize. Martin had succeeded in signing star goalie Bernie Parent away from the Toronto Maple Leafs, the WHA's first big signing coup, but when the end came he let a $10,000 cheque to the league bounce. Davidson would keep that cheque in his office as a souvenir, or a reminder, of the league's shaky beginnings.

Still, Davidson's and Murphy's experience with the ABA had taught them that attrition was part of the game in a new venture, and there was plenty of fresh blood out there in the startup phase. In Quebec City, a group had emerged led by Marius Fortier, which consisted of six men who'd owned and operated the successful Quebec Remparts junior team. When they approached the new league, they were told that notorious owner Charlie Finley had destroyed the hockey market in the Bay Area with the California Golden Seals and the WHA's franchise in San Francisco was therefore available. They were also told that the franchise was owned by Michael O'Hara, a former U.S. Olympic volleyball player and Don Regan's classmate at UCLA. As they explored the murky world of the WHA, however, the Quebecers learned the franchise, in fact, belonged to Davidson, and after going back and forth a couple of times, Fortier's group bought it for $210,000 the day before the league's player draft. After closing the deal in Anaheim they stayed up all night plotting their draft strategy while poring over the season-ending issue of *The Hockey News* and the *NHL Guide*. They would draft eighty-one players, including just about every francophone who played beyond bantam. The one player they didn't draft, J.C. Tremblay, was, of course, the one they signed.

The Quebecers were an able group who knew the game, but they had one problem. They didn't have any money. They made it as far as the player draft on $60,000 they'd received for selling their shares of the Remparts, but they were looking at a first-year budget of around $1 million and were having trouble attracting investors. At a crucial league meeting in the spring of 1972, Bill Hunter rose and said that he, personally, would guarantee Quebec's franchise fee, which was interesting, because he, personally, had less money than the Quebec group. For whatever reason, Hunter's pledge was good enough for the rest of the league, and in May Fortier recruited former Quebec premier Jean Lesage and powerful businessman Paul Racine to their group.

"Racine was the big guy," says Claude Larochelle, the former sports editor of *Le Soleil* in Quebec City. "He had the money. He had the influence. He had the prestige. He was the kind of guy we don't have in Quebec any more."

"Quebec was supposed to be a small city without much money," says Regan. "We were driving around in Paul's limo and he pointed to a ten-storey office building. He said, 'My brother and I bought that building.' I said, 'That's nice.' He said, 'Without a mortgage.' That changed my opinion of him."

With Quebec in place, the league's remaining franchises started to take shape. Neil Shayne's New York franchise had been purchased by a young lawyer from New Jersey named Dick Wood and a group of investors. At a bar meeting in Hershey, Pennsylvania, Wood ran into an Atlantic City lawyer of his acquaintance named Jim Cooper. Cooper asked Wood what he was up to. Wood told him he was going to Quebec City on WHA business. What's the WHA? This new hockey league, Wood said, I own a team in it. Cooper started thinking; it had been his lifelong ambition to own a team. He followed Wood up to Quebec City and, together with his money man, Bernie Brown, they bought the defunct Miami Screaming Eagles and even assumed Bernie Parent's massive five-year, $750,000 contract, which included a new boat and a new car for every year of the deal.

The WHA had its twelve franchises in place by late June of 1972. New York Raiders, Cleveland Crusaders, Philadelphia Blazers, Quebec Nordiques, Ottawa Nationals, and New England Whalers would form the Eastern Division. Winnipeg Jets, Alberta Oilers, Houston Aeros, Los Angeles Sharks, Minnesota Fighting Saints, and Chicago Cougars would form the Western Division. NHL players were also being signed. Los Angeles's Steve Sutherland was the first, and others would follow, but it wasn't the mass exodus the WHA had envisioned when they opened for business. It was almost as if the players were waiting for a sign, some confirmation, that the new league was legitimate and they'd make good on the crazy contracts they were offering.

In late June, they got their sign.

# CHAPTER 2

# "How'd you like to come play for me in Winnipeg?"

Beyond their exhaustive search for cold cash and warm bodies, the WHA really started when Ben Hatskin attended the 1971 Grey Cup in Vancouver accompanied by Bob Turner, a Winnipegger and former NHLer who'd played in Chicago in the early 1960s. In an interesting bit of timing, the Chicago Blackhawks were playing the Vancouver Canucks that weekend, and Turner was in the hotel lobby when the Blackhawks checked in. The old defenceman chatted amiably with a couple of his former teammates, then shook hands with Bobby Hull and drew him aside for a private conference.

"I've got a friend here I want you to meet," Turner told Hull. "He's got a suite in the hotel."

A few minutes later, Hull walked into the suite and was introduced to Hatskin, who, after some small talk, said, "How'd you like to come play for me in Winnipeg for $250,000 a year for as long as you want?"

Hull, who'd heard about this new league, thought for a minute, then answered, "That's very generous, but I've still got five months left on my contract with Chicago and I think I can get $250,000 from them."

"I thought that was the end of it," Hull now says.

Instead, it was the beginning of so many things for Hull, the Jets, and the new league.

Eight months after that meeting, Bobby Hull would become the WHA. He was its star, its face, its drawing card, and its roving goodwill ambassador. His presence encouraged a wave of NHLers to sign with the rebels and ensured the league would be more than a glorified version of the AHL. Hull didn't just give the league instant credibility; without him, it is doubtful the league would have survived its first year, and the NHL would have gone about its business of printing money and exploiting players.

The WHA could have signed a better hockey player to start up their league. Bobby Orr pops to mind. So does a young Guy Lafleur. But they couldn't have signed a better star to sell it.

"Bobby was perfect for us," says Dennis Murphy. "I've never seen a guy who was better at PR. He'd sign autographs for hours. He was always smiling. He had this charisma. He just looked like a star."

The Bobby Hull of 1971-72 was just starting the back nine of his hockey career, but he was still one of the three or four best players in the NHL and the Blackhawks' greatest star. He'd score fifty goals that season, his fifteenth in Chicago, and make the NHL's First All-Star Team for the tenth time. The previous season, the Hawks had played an epic Stanley Cup final with Montreal, which they lost in the seventh game.

But relations between the Golden Jet and the Blackhawks organization were beginning to strain. In the 1969-70 season, Hull staged a very public, very bitter holdout, in which he accused the Hawks – specifically Bill Wirtz, the son of team owner Arthur Wirtz – of reneging on contractual commitments. After a month-long standoff, which featured some fairly lively sniping between the player and the organization, Hull caved in, admitted he'd signed a valid four-year contract in 1968-69, and apologized to Wirtz, GM Tommy Ivan, and Hawks coach Billy Reay at a press conference. The presser was dubbed the "Surrender Press Conference" by the Chicago media. It was also the beginning of the end of Hull's career in Chicago.

"I can't say it had anything to do with my ultimate decision, but it didn't help," says Hull, who lost $17,000 during his holdout.

The next contract negotiation with the Blackhawks didn't go much better. Hull, whose deal with Chicago expired at the end of the 1971-72 season, was called to lunch with Arthur Wirtz, Ivan, and Reay early in the season. He thought a new offer was coming, but when they sat down the Hawks' brass simply asked him, "Are you happy here?" He answered, "Am I playing like I'm unhappy?" and the lunch ended with Hull in a confused state. Looking back, he now believes the Hawks had heard about the new league and were trying to find out where their star stood. They'd have a better idea in another eight months.

The WHA had determined that Ben Hatskin, who had the backing of the Simkins, one of Winnipeg's wealthiest families, would make the play for their future star. The next question was, which star would he go after? Gordie Howe, who'd just retired from the Detroit Red Wings, was considered, but Hull had all the intangibles the new league was looking for in its marquee player. He was a personality. He had charisma by the bucketful. The TV cameras loved him. The WHA's marketing man, Max Muhleman, was convinced Hull was the man, and Muhleman's opinion carried considerable weight in the Davidson-Regan-Murphy circle. Regan was given the Hull file and he and Hatskin plotted a strategy.

Together, they pulled off what was the biggest signing in the history of professional sport.

After Hatskin met Hull in Vancouver, Regan befriended Hull's agent and accountant, Harvey Wineberg, and the two men remain close to this day. Wineberg, in turn, impressed on his client that the upstart league was serious and he could virtually name his price.

"I wasn't going anywhere," Hull says. "I thought I had the Blackhawks emblem tattooed on my chest. Finally, Harvey said, 'Just give me a figure and we'll get on with our lives.' I blurted out a million dollars. In those days, a million dollars might as well have been a billion dollars. Nobody had ever heard of a million for a hockey player. I thought that was enough to scare them off. Had I known, I would have asked for twenty million. It was just a figure to get rid of them.

"A couple of days later, Harvey called. I asked him, 'What did they think about that?' He said, 'They asked me not to do anything with Chicago until I heard back from them.' I just said, 'Holy shit.'"

Far from being scared off by the million-dollar demand, Hatskin and Regan were actually encouraged by the news from Hull's camp. In April, Hatskin pitched the Hull plan to the rest of the league. He would cover his $250,000 salary, but the $1 million up front had to be a league-wide commitment, because the presence of Hull would benefit everyone in the WHA. In mid-May, Hatskin reported that Hull was interested in the WHA's offer. Hatskin began talking about it publicly because "even if you guys don't come up with the money, I'll get a million dollars' worth of publicity."

In June, Hatskin, Hull, and Regan holed up in a Denver hotel. After a day of meetings, Hatskin heard a commotion in the hall. He opened the door to his room just as Joanne Hull was yelling at her husband, "Why would you ever want to live in Winnipeg and play for that fat Jew?"

Hull, however, took a liking to Hatskin. "I had a good first impression of Ben," he says. "And generally I'm correct in my first impressions."

Finally, in late June, Davidson sent out a memo within the WHA announcing they had a deal with Hull. The Hawks, for their part, had finally gotten around to extending an offer to Hull, but they were too late.

"It was just a telephone conversation," Hull says, still incredulous three decades later at the sequence of events that took him from Chicago to Winnipeg. "There was nothing binding. I could have backed out any time I wanted. But I gave them my word and I felt I had to live up to it."

The matter of the signing bonus, meanwhile, turned into a typical WHA production. Nick Trbovich, who'd just bought into the Ottawa Nationals, balked at cutting a cheque for $100,000, and apparently he had company. According to the terms of the contract, the million bucks had to be in place twenty-four hours before Hull signed, but forty-eight hours before the deal was to be consummated, the money wasn't there. Regan now says Hatskin wired the missing funds at the eleventh hour, and he suspects it came from the Simkin family. Had Hatskin not wired the money, "that cheque would have bounced all over Winnipeg," says Regan. Howard Baldwin, for his part, says Hull's million-dollar signing bonus was covered by four teams, far from the league-wide investment that had been planned.

If Hull knew about the problems gathering his million, he didn't let on. The night before the signing, a party raged in a St. Paul hotel as Wineberg and Telly Mercury, Hatskin's lawyer, were working on contract revisions. At the same time, Regan was in Chicago fighting an injunction to prevent Hull from signing. The injunction had to be served personally to Hull, so Regan flew to Winnipeg, conferred with Wineberg, then collected Hull, rented a plane, and flew to Fargo, North Dakota, where the group reasoned they were safe from process servers. Hull signed on the runway.

The contract had to be signed in the U.S. for tax purposes, but it also had to be signed in Winnipeg for media purposes, so the group next headed to the Manitoba capital to put on a show. There, Hull signed the WHA portion of the deal with eleven different pens to represent the eleven other WHA teams, most of which hadn't contributed to his new wealth. Hull was then presented with a huge cardboard cheque for $1 million and, as he smiled for the cameras, Wineberg and Mercury walked over to a nearby bank and deposited the real cheque. Hull had told Wineberg to inform him if the cheque cleared. Half an hour later, while Hull was still working the room, he felt a tug on his jacket and turned to see his agent giving him a thumbs-up. Hull then signed the Winnipeg portion of the deal: five years at $250,000 as a player and five years at $100,000 for a front-office position. The total value of his new contract was $2.75 million.

The day ended with a press conference. Trbovich, who recognized a marketing opportunity when it was presented, had brought some of his Bobby Hull table-top hockey games with him, and while Bobby charmed the media, his sons Bobby Jr., Blake, and Brett played on the games emblazoned with their father's likeness. When the press conference broke up, the Hull family returned to their suite at the Viscount Gort hotel. Actually, the suite was a new feature at the hotel. Prior to the Hull signing, there were no luxury rooms at the Viscount Gort. Hatskin had wanted to make an impression on his new star, so, after some deliberation, he paid to have a wall knocked out between two rooms, *et voilà*, instant suite.

"I view Bobby Hull's signing in the same light as if he'd died, broken his leg, or retired," said Maple Leafs owner Harold Ballard. "We would have had to get along without him if any of those things had happened. He was a great player even though he's been going down the other side of the hill and only has two or three years left. In the WHA, he'll have another ten years."

Actually, he'd only play six full seasons. He did, however, score 303 goals in his WHA career.

Bobby, meanwhile, wasn't the only Hull to sign with the WHA that year. His brother Garry was retired and operating a farm in Millbrook, Ontario, when the Ottawa Nationals came calling. The Nats, to that point, hadn't signed a marquee player, and they attempted to pass off the middle Hull brother as a star. Looking back, they may have oversold him a tad.

"Garry is considered by many knowledgeable hockey people as the best 'Hull' of them all," the Nationals' press release read. "His brothers claim he is stronger than they are and given the chance he will be the best Hull to lace on skates."

Garry Hull was twenty-seven at the time. He never played a game with the Nationals.

All over the NHL, players watched the Hull deal unfold. When the Golden Jet signed with the Jets, it had the same effect as the storming of the Bastille. Hull was the thirty-fourth NHLer to sign with the new league. Over the next month alone, they'd sign twenty-five to thirty more.

Gerry Pinder, who'd been Hull's teammate in Chicago, led the California Golden Seals in scoring in 1971-72 and was offered a $500 raise to $28,500 by Seals owner Charlie Finley. Harvey Wineberg had also done some work for Pinder, and the right winger was aware of the status of Hull's negotiations. When he signed, Pinder accepted a two-year offer for $150,000, $50,000 up front, from the Cleveland Crusaders and Nick Mileti.

"We didn't want to do anything until Bobby signed," Pinder says. "We knew if he signed, others would come."

Paul Shmyr had also been Hull's teammate in Chicago and was another Wineberg client. In the late 1960s, Shmyr had been competing with Ray McKay for the sixth spot on the Blackhawks' defence and wanted a $2,000 raise. The Hawks sent Shmyr and McKay the same offer. McKay had signed right away. Shmyr didn't and spent two seasons in the minors before he was dealt to the California Golden Seals. After Hull signed, Mileti offered Shmyr a multi-year pact worth $50,000 annually, twice what he was getting with the Seals. When Shmyr made the All-Star Team in the first year, Mileti tore up that deal and gave him a new four-year contract. Mileti would also sign Boston goalie Gerry Cheevers to a seven-year, $1.4-million deal when the Bruins were offering him $80,000 a year.

In Buffalo, Al Hamilton knew Bill Hunter, his former junior coach in Edmonton, would come calling, and sure enough Hunter made the blueliner a five-year offer to play for the Oilers starting at $80,000 and increasing by $5,000 annually. The year before he'd been the Sabres only plus player and Punch Imlach had offered him a $2,000 raise.

"It was substantially more than I was making at the time, but I still wondered what the hell I had done," says Hamilton.

Seven years later, he was still playing in Edmonton. His number-3 jersey was retired by the Oilers and hangs in the rafters at Rexall Place.

Larry Pleau's story was typical of that first year. Pleau had been stacked up behind Jacques Lemaire, Peter Mahovlich, and Henri Richard on the Montreal Canadiens' depth chart at centre ice, and the Canadiens were projecting him as a career penalty killer. He asked Canadiens GM Sam Pollock for a trade and was told, "No. And there'll be no WHA, so you can forget that, too." A few days later, Pleau called Pollock back and said, "Mr. Pollock, I want you to know I'm going to sign with the New England Whalers."

Pollock's response? "Like I said the other day, there will never be a WHA."

The next thing Pollock knew, Pleau was gone.

Minor-leaguers celebrated a huge windfall with the new league. In place of the pittance they were making waiting for a shot in The Show, they were suddenly fielding offers for two and three times their minor-league salaries.

"It was fairly easy for us," says Bill Dineen, Aeros head coach and GM, who built his first-year team around minor-leaguers. "Most of those guys were making about $12,000 in the minors.

We offered guys $30,000. I didn't have to make a big sales pitch."

John Garrett's experience was similar to that of many others. Garrett, a goalie, was in the Chicago system behind Tony Esposito and Gary Smith and played the 1972–73 season in Dallas. Coach Billy Reay had told the twenty-one-year-old goalkeeper he might make the NHL by the time he was twenty-seven and offered him a two-year deal at $10,000 and $12,000 to play in the minors. The Minnesota Fighting Saints came along in Year 2 and offered Garrett $20,000 to sign and a two-year deal at $20,000 and $30,000.

"What was to decide?" says Garrett.

And the opportunities weren't just limited to the players. In Chicago, Hall of Fame defenceman Marcel Pronovost had been named the Cougars' head coach and went looking for an assistant. One day he asked Jacques Beauchamp, the distinguished columnist at Le Journal de Montreal, if he was aware of any bright, young up-and-comers. The newspaperman quickly offered the name of Jacques Demers, who was coaching a junior-B team in Montreal. Demers was also working for Coca-Cola at the time, and when the Cougars made him an offer, he asked the company for a sabbatical. Coca-Cola didn't give sabbaticals, he was told. He had to choose between security and hockey.

It wasn't a difficult choice.

"Are you kidding?" Demers says. "The Amphitheater [Chicago's home rink] was cramped, and it smelled, but honestly, who cared? I was making $6,500 at Coca-Cola and I was making $25,000 in Chicago and working in hockey. I was excited. The first time I ever took a plane was when I flew to Chicago."

Bill Friday, meanwhile, was third on the seniority list of NHL officials and had just finished his twelfth season when the WHA came along. Friday figured he might grind out three more years before the NHL retired him, and this was an era when referees worked off one-year contracts. Vern Buffey, whom the WHA had hired as their referee-in-chief, offered Friday a three-year deal at $50,000 a year. A natural showman, Friday would be the perfect referee for the new league.

"I wonder how he'll do," Toe Blake, the former Canadiens coach, observed acidly. "They don't have a TV contract."

"I went to [NHL referee-in-chief] Scotty Morrison and told him about the offer and he said, 'I'll talk to Mr. Campbell,'" Friday says. "They came back with a three-year offer for $26,000, $30,000, and $34,000, so there wasn't much choice for me. I was a little nervous, like everyone else. But in seven years I never missed a paycheque." He became the highest paid official in any sport in North America that season.

All told, some sixty NHL players would sign with the new league that year. The WHA, exacting revenge for losing Neil Shayne's Long Island franchise, signed seven of the New York Islanders' expansion picks. The Golden Seals lost ten players. Chicago, Boston, and Toronto were also hit hard. Those three teams would lead the NHL's anti-merger faction for the next seven years. The only team that responded to the WHA's challenge was the New York Rangers, who locked up their stars, including Brad Park, who'd sign a new deal with the Rangers for $250,000 annually. The average NHL salary jumped from $28,000 to $44,000 in the WHA's first year, and soared to $96,000 by Year 6.

The rest of the NHL, meanwhile, continued to sneer at the WHA even as they sought to crush them in the courts. In all, the NHL would file actions against the insurgents in fourteen different jurisdictions. Chicago filed against Hull and received an injunction. The Bruins took action against Cheevers and Derek Sanderson, who'd just signed a huge deal with the Philadelphia Blazers, and it was ruled the players wouldn't be free to join their new teams until October 1, the day their NHL contracts expired. The Bruins also sent the NHL rights to Johnny McKenzie, who'd signed with the Blazers, to Philadelphia, where the established league could fight the WHA on a new front. Another suit involved the New York Islanders and the many players they'd lost to the new league. Another was filed in Los Angeles.

The WHA, who had some lawyers of their own, fired right back. Hull counter-sued. In Boston, the WHA scored a huge victory when a judge refused to grant the Bruins an injunction against Cheevers and Sanderson. The rebels, in fact, would win in every jurisdiction except Chicago. Regan learned there wasn't much he could do about arguing the law in Chicago.

"I remember meeting the lawyers who were working on the case in Chicago, and there was an extra guy," Regan says. "I said, 'Who's that?' They said, 'He's the appeal lawyer. We're not going to win here. It's their judge.' Sure enough, it was the one place we couldn't win. I'd always heard about that stuff going on in Chicago, but I'd never experienced it."

Hull was sued off the ice by the Blackhawks, but on September 26 the WHA scored another significant victory in the courts when Hull's case was transferred to Philadelphia to be heard in conjunction with McKenzie's. The case was tried by Judge Leon Higginbotham.

NHL players to this day should celebrate Leon Higginbotham's birthday.

If the WHA had been allowed to hand-pick the judge who would determine its future, it couldn't have done better than Higginbotham. A native of Trenton, New Jersey, the good judge was appointed to the Federal Trade Commission by John F. Kennedy in 1962 and appointed district judge of eastern Pennsylvania by Lyndon Johnson in 1964. A man of colour, a teacher, scholar, and jurist, he became one of the most articulate and powerful voices on race relations and the civil-rights movement in America.

Two weeks before his death in 1998, Higginbotham also appeared before the House Judiciary Committee's hearing on Bill Clinton's impeachment and expressed the opinion that, in his view, Clinton's actions did not constitute an impeachable offence. A Republican member of the committee offered that "real Americans" felt otherwise.

"Sir, my father was a labourer and my mother was a domestic," answered Higginbotham. "I came up the hard way. Don't lecture me about the real America."

No, he wasn't exactly an establishment lackey.

Higginbotham heard arguments for a couple of days as the NHL sent in the imperial guard, the Washington-based law firm of Covington and Burling, to present its case. After the first day, Regan, who was just thirty-eight, looked over at his adversaries and saw Edward Bennett Williams, perhaps the most famous lawyer in the United States, sitting on the NHL's side. Williams was a close friend of Los Angeles Kings owner Jack Kent Cooke. He was also one of sixteen lawyers sitting at the NHL's table.

"I knew they were in trouble then," Regan says, still laughing at the memory.

"Our position was the NHL was trying to sue us out of business based on a position which wasn't legally valid and restricted trade in the U.S.," Regan continues. "Basically, we asked for an injunction against the NHL's lawsuits. They must have had fifteen guys there, but after the first day, my wife said, 'I thought they were supposed to be the best firm in the country.' They were arguing a position that didn't make any sense."

This was not lost on Higginbotham. The ruling was initially scheduled for October 11 to coincide with the start of hockey season, but it was delayed until the last week of October and again until November 8 as the judge sifted through 2,500 pages of testimony and briefs. When his judgment was finally released, it covered 124 pages.

It also sounded as if Regan had written it.

Among other things, Higginbotham ruled the NHL was "primarily a multi-state, bi-national business where the fundamental motive is the making of money." Then: "Despite the thousands of words uttered on this record by all parties about the glory of the sport of hockey and the grandeur of its super-stars, the basic factors here are not the sheer exhilaration from observing the speeding puck but rather the desire to maximize the available buck."

And Higginbotham was just warming up.

The NHL was "the result of a common agreement, mutual understanding and conspiracy by the NHL and its affiliate minor leagues to maintain a monopolistic position so strong that the NHL precludes effective competition by the entry of another major professional hockey league. . . .

"The record is devoid of any evidence implying, much less demonstrating, that the reserve clause has been retained as the result of serious, good-faith collective bargaining. . . .

"Injunctions against players who have signed with the WHA team prohibiting them from playing for their WHA teams would signal the death of the World Hockey Association."

Higginbotham's ruling, in short, was an utter and complete victory for the new league. He ruled the NHL was a monopoly. He ruled it restricted free trade. He didn't rule on the reserve clause, per se, but he ruled there was no legal basis for the NHL's injunctions against the WHA and left little doubt how a subsequent hearing on the reserve clause would be judged. In essence, he granted an injunction against any further litigation based on the reserve clause. The judgment was rushed to Chicago, where the order restraining Hull from playing was lifted. That night he suited up in an uneventful 3-2 loss against Quebec in front of 10,126 fans at Le Colisée. On December 22, Hull made his return to Chicago, playing in front of a near-sellout crowd of 8,856 at the Amphitheater. During the game he got into a fight with former teammate Reggie Fleming, and signed autographs while he was in the penalty box.

"You have to have the facts on your side," says Regan, "but we had a lot of things going for us. Nobody could have won that case for them, especially against a tough, independent-minded judge who knew a little about being an underdog. I would have fallen over backwards if we had lost. But I didn't realize the victory would be that complete. It was all we could have asked for."

Still, it was not without cost to Hull. In mid-July, coach Harry Sinden released the names of the thirty-five players invited to play for Team Canada in the upcoming Summit Series with the Soviet Union, and Hull's name was not among them. Canadians who didn't have an opinion about the war in Vietnam immediately rose as one and protested the NHL's pettiness. John Munro, the minister of health and welfare, who was also responsible for sports, was swamped with letters. There was pressure on Prime Minister Pierre Trudeau, most notably from former prime minister John Diefenbaker, to exert his influence on Hull's behalf. Even Maple Leafs owner Harold Ballard, whose feelings toward the WHA weren't exactly kindly, said Hull should play for Canada.

"I don't give a damn if Hull signed with a team in China," Ballard said. "He's a Canadian and he should be on the Canadian team."

In a rare display of spinelessness, Hockey Canada at a special meeting voted down Hull's participation 9-2 with two abstentions. By extension, J.C. Tremblay, Cheevers, and Sanderson, all of whom were likely candidates had they stayed in the NHL, were also prohibited from taking part in the Summit Series. The NHL had argued before the courts that Hull couldn't play with the Jets because he was NHL property. They were now arguing Hull couldn't play for Team Canada because he was WHA property. Hockey Canada, for its part, while denying Hull, a Canadian citizen, the right to play for his country, granted a special waiver to Stan Mikita, who was born in Czechoslovakia but raised in Canada, to play for Team Canada. It was not one of Hockey Canada's prouder moments.

Hull, meanwhile, had tried to keep in shape while his case dragged on. He stopped drinking beer in July and swears that caused him to lose weight. His body was also used to starting training camp in September and playing in October, but the period of forced inactivity seemed to disorient him.

Or maybe it was the beer.

"To tell you the truth, I was kind of fucked up," he says. "I wasn't doing much of anything and I was getting these pains in my stomach. Then Judge Higginbotham's ruling came and I was so relieved. I could finally join my team and have a cold one."

The Quebec Nordiques had managed to steal J.C. Tremblay away from the Montreal Canadiens in the summer of 1972, but the Nords' biggest problem as the hockey season approached wasn't signing players. It was signing a coach. The organization approached former NHLer Phil Goyette about the job and was rejected. Attempts to land Orval Tessier, a good young coach in the Quebec junior league, were also unsuccessful. Maurice Filion, the Nords' chief scout, finally told general manager Marius Fortier that the team was having problems getting commitments from players because it didn't have a coach. Fortier considered things for a minute, then said, "I'll get you a coach. Give me Rocket Richard's phone number."

Richard, of course, was the greatest francophone star of them all. He starred with the Montreal Canadiens from 1942 to 1960 and scored 545 goals in his career, the highest total in NHL history to that point. He was also a figure who transcended the game. Richard was one of the first stars of the new Quebec, a fiery, passionate performer who rose to prominence as the province was forging a new identity. "I have the impression that Maurice Richard was one of the original men responsible for giving a special meaning to Québécois," said Claude Charron, the former minister for youth, sport, and recreation in Quebec. On the ice, he meant everything to the people of his province.

But off the ice, he was a quiet, private man who enjoyed hunting and fishing and solitude. He had neither the personality nor the desire to become a coach. All too late that would become obvious to the Nordiques.

Fortier drove out to the Richards' home in Montreal, met with the great man, and was immediately told the Rocket would rather move to Toronto and drive the Zamboni at Maple Leaf Gardens than coach the Nordiques in Quebec City. His son had played in the famous peewee tournament there a few years back and he'd been booed.

"I'd never be accepted by the people there," he told Fortier. "It's crazy. It doesn't interest me even a bit."

But the idea interested his wife, Lucille. During the course of a private conversation, Mme. Richard confided to Fortier that she missed life in the spotlight. When she was at the Forum, she felt like a queen. She told Fortier, "I'm going on holidays with my husband for ten days. This thing will get done."

While Lucille was working on the Rocket, Fortier organized a Maurice Richard night at a Quebec City Carnivales' minor-league baseball game. A crowd of six thousand people turned out and greeted Richard with a three-minute standing ovation. The fifty-one-year-old legend was moved to tears. Six weeks later, he signed on as the Nordiques' first coach for $40,000 and a $4,000 signing bonus.

Richard was contractually obligated to take a tour group over to the Soviet Union for the Summit Series and missed most of the Nordiques' training camp. When he returned for a pre-season game against Philadelphia on October 3, it was immediately obvious something was wrong. He stood woodenly behind the bench and kept referring to the roster he'd written down on a sheet of paper.

In the locker room, things were even worse.

"He'd go around the room and he'd say, 'Bobby Guindon?' and Bobby would have to put up his hand," says Richard Brodeur, the Nordiques goalie that season. "Then he'd say, 'Pierre Guite?' And Pierre Guite would put up his hand. Then he'd say, 'You two are playing together.' It was awful.

"He was put in a tough spot, but he was smart enough to know it wasn't going to work. It's funny. I did some autograph shows with him later, and I said, 'You used to coach me.' He said, 'I didn't coach you. I was just there.'"

And not for long. The Nordiques opened their season on the road in Cleveland. Before they boarded their flight, Fortier gave Richard a list of the Crusaders' players. The Rocket looked at him sadly and said, "What's the use? I read the names and they don't mean anything to me." The Nordiques put down in Toronto, and while they waited for their flight to Cleveland, Richard stared outside at other planes landing and taking off, then called Fortier over and said, "You know, Marius, I'm going to miss hunting season for the first time in twelve years."

After the Nords' opener, a 2-0 loss to the Crusaders, Richard and Fortier drove from Montreal to Quebec City together, and the Nordiques' coach told his boss he couldn't go on.

"I'm depressed," he said. "I'm not sleeping. I'm not eating. I'm going to die behind the bench. Find yourself another coach, and you'd better hurry."

The Nords beat the Alberta Oilers 6-0 the next night in their home opener before a sellout crowd at Le Colisée. J.C. Tremblay changed the lines and Richard excused himself to vomit in the Nordiques' dressing room three times.

The next day, Fortier went to pick up Richard for lunch and the Rocket had already packed up his apartment. After lunch, Richard jumped in his car and headed back to Montreal. Fortier, who talked Maurice Filion into taking over as coach, noticed the colour had returned to the Rocket's cheeks.

Two weeks later, the Nordiques sent Richard his first pay-cheque and he sent it back, telling Fortier, "No sir. I didn't do any work. I don't want any money."

His journey with the WHA had come to an end.

For so many others, it was just beginning.

# CHAPTER 3

# "You'll rue the day you got all this money."

W hile they didn't earn any style points along the way to their first season, the WHA had already scored some significant victories. They beat the NHL in court and signed Hull and a second tier of name players. Some sixty NHLers jumped to the rebel league in Year 1. They had franchises in New York, Chicago, and Los Angeles, as well as owners in nine other markets who, if they weren't going to live and die with Murphy and Davidson, were at least reasonably committed to the cause. Bill Hunter was in Edmonton, Ben Hatskin was in Winnipeg, the group in Quebec had the Nordiques up and running, and Doug Michel had survived the new league's mysterious business practices and put a team in Ottawa. That gave them a solid base in Canada. Elsewhere, they'd lined up the dynamic and sharply dressed Nick Mileti to operate the Crusaders in Cleveland, a new rink was under construction in St. Paul, Paul Deneau's credit card was still functioning in Houston, and Howard Baldwin had things under control with the New England Whalers. That left the

Philadelphia Blazers, nee Miami Screaming Eagles, but their aggressive ownership tandem of Jim Cooper and Bernie Brown had signed the biggest names of any team.

Davidson looked at his creation and saw that it was good. At least, it was better than the ABA's beginning, and in some respects his confidence was justified. In most others, well, the WHA never allowed you to get too comfortable, and by the end of that first season the Blazers would be on the move after a calamitous campaign in which they paid their biggest star $1 million not to play.

"Right from the start we've been ahead of schedule," Davidson said midway through Year 1. "We're three to five years ahead of where the ABA and the AFL were at this point in their history."

But Davidson, like the Philadelphia Blazers, would be gone by the end of that season.

Derek Sanderson had been raised in the Boston Bruins system from adolescence and signed his first contract when he was nineteen. Hap Emms, the Bruins' general manager, told him, "I'm going to take care of you, kid. You've got the look of an eagle." He then signed him to a three-year deal worth $39,500, which made Sanderson feel like the richest man in the world.

"Here I was, nineteen, and I was making more than my dad made working at Kimberly-Clark in Niagara Falls," the Turk says.

His attitude toward money would subsequently change. Come to think of it, his attitude to most everything would subsequently change. Just five years after he won the Calder Trophy as the NHL's rookie of the year, Sanderson would be caught in a vortex of powerful forces that reshaped the business of professional sports if not modern popular culture. Long before the concept of crossover appeal was introduced, Sanderson was perhaps the first hockey player to become famous for being famous. He embodied the new hedonism that swept North America. He was young, free-spirited, and outspoken. He led a

certain lifestyle that seemed to involve a lot of fun and a lot of
women. In the new media, athletes were becoming stars, and
Sanderson had star appeal. The problem was, in the hockey
world he was never a star. He was a spectacularly solid two–way
centreman, maybe the NHL's best penalty killer in the late 1960s
and early 1970s, but never a player who'd score 50 goals or get
100 points.

Still, the WHA didn't see that. What they saw was a virile
young stud with the hair and the moustache whose circle of
friends included Joe Namath and Ken Harrelson and who dated
Joey Heatherton, and they said, "There's our guy." Soon
enough, Sanderson started to believe he was the big star people
said he was and not the checking centre from Niagara Falls who
just wanted to play with the Bruins. And that's when his world
started to fall apart.

"That's why I got in the investment business," says an older
and wiser Sanderson. "I never paid attention to that stuff when
I was playing. I learned the hard way. Your ass can only sit in one
car at a time. Your head can only sleep on one pillow.

"I'll never forget what [Bruins owner] Weston Adams said to
me when he heard about the offer. He said, 'You'll rue the day
you got all this money.' I said, 'I don't really want to go.' But no
one thinks they're going to be sixty-five."

Sanderson is now pushing sixty. He makes his living looking
after other people's money. The irony of that is not lost on him.

In securing the services of Bobby Hull, the WHA signed a
superstar of substance to their new league, a player who could
dazzle the media and the fans with his 1,000-kilowatt smile,
then dazzle them with his game. They thought they were
getting a similar player in Sanderson, which proves they weren't
paying attention.

The Turk was a key performer on two Bruins Stanley Cup
teams, but he was hardly the team's star. His best season was

1970-71, when he totalled 29 goals and 63 points to go along with 130 penalty minutes – a half-season's work for Phil Esposito. He was essentially Boston's third-line centre, and with veteran winger Eddie Westfall he formed the league's top penalty-killing unit. Had he stayed on track, he likely would have built a career similar to Bob Gainey's in Montreal or Esa Tikkanen's in Edmonton: a vital support player on a legitimately great team. But this new league came along in 1972-73 and they needed stars.

About the time the WHA was getting underway, Sanderson had his own TV show in Boston and was part-owner of four nightclubs: Bachelors III, where his partners included Namath; Daisy Buchanan's; Scott's; and Zelda's. Never mind that Sanderson thought *The Great Gatsby* referred to a Detroit Red Wings defenceman named Bill. He was a man about town, and the town, along with scores of young women, loved him.

"Business was terrific," says Sanderson. "I went to my four places every night. Namath gave me a Lincoln, $30,000, and the power of the pen. That was a serious fucking mistake. 'I'll take care of this. I'll buy a round for everybody.' I bought the world a drink."

Life was equally good with the Bruins, who won Stanley Cups in 1970 and 1972 with a team built around Orr and Esposito and seemed poised to win many more. But in the summer of 1972, cracks were starting to appear in the team's foundation. First, Westfall was lost in the expansion draft to the New York Islanders. Then Johnny McKenzie, Sanderson's roommate on the road, signed a deal with the WHA's Philadelphia Blazers to become their player-coach. The new league would also sign away Bruins goalie Gerry Cheevers, maybe the best money goalie in hockey at the time, and defenceman Ted Green. The Bruins haven't won a Stanley Cup since 1972.

Sanderson, for his part, had already been through one contract beef with Adams by the time his deal expired at the end of the 1971-72 season. After he won the Calder, he had approached the Bruins' owner about a new deal, but he may as well have approached him about a new rocket ship. "You made a bad deal," Sanderson was told. "Talk to me when it's up." The Turk then huddled with Harrelson, the Red Sox slugger. Harrelson lined him up with agent Bob Woolf, who got him a new one-year deal for $25,000.

When his contract expired, and with the WHA creating a new market for players, Sanderson reasoned he was in line for a big payday with the Bruins. By playing his cards right, he might be able to squeeze eighty grand a year out of old man Adams, then he could go back to the business of winning Stanley Cups and living the life. About that time, McKenzie told the Turk the Blazers were interested in him and he should at least listen to what they had to say. Sanderson listened. He still can't believe what happened next.

"I'm at Daisy's, and I've got six or seven beers in me," he says. "I'm supposed to meet them at 4:00 p.m. I go into Bob's office and Jim Cooper's there. They offer me $2.3 million. I'm fucking stunned. I didn't know what to do."

So he said nothing in reply, and Cooper told him he'd go to $2.6 million – a $300,000 raise in fifteen seconds for not opening his mouth. Not bad.

And it would get better.

"I said, 'There's not a lot of security in you guys,'" Sanderson continues. "'The first time I heard of you, you were the Miami Screaming Eagles. Now you're the Philadelphia Blazers. How do I know you're going to stick around?'"

It was another shrewd business ploy.

"Cooper said, 'We won't move the team without your permission.' Then I didn't have to play a road game because I was afraid to fly. Then they couldn't trade players without my permission. They couldn't send them to the minors without my permission. I had to be on the power play. He said, 'With the money you'll make, you'll never be off the ice.' So there it was.

I negotiated the best deal in the history of sport and I didn't say anything."

He also learned a valuable lesson.

"What I learned is you can win any negotiation if you don't want to do it," Sanderson says. "I didn't want to go. I was making more than I ever dreamed of, I was playing with Bobby Orr, and I had two Cups. Life was perfect. Then this guy comes along and gives me $2.6 million."

The final deal is generally reported as a ten-year contract worth $2.6 million and change. Sanderson requested five banking days to ponder the Blazers' staggering offer and called Adams, hoping the Bruins' owner would talk him out of becoming a millionaire at age twenty-five. Adams's first response concerned the WHA. "Rogues and thieves," he said. "I've got all this handmade china and they're just picking off the pieces they want." Then he looked at the proposal, looked at Sanderson, and said, "Derek, as your friend, I've got to tell you to take this. It's security forever. Make sure you get this in the hands of a money manager today."

Sanderson eventually extracted an $80,000 offer from the Bruins and went back to the Blazers, who weren't easily discouraged. They offered his father, Harold, a five-year scouting contract at $50,000 a year, and Harold only had to travel between Niagara Falls and St. Catharines. At a crucial meeting with the Bruins, Sanderson stipulated he didn't want team lawyer Charlie Mulcahy present, and when Mulcahy walked into the room, Sanderson left and signed with the Blazers.

He was rich.

He would soon be miserable.

Like any self-respecting young millionaire in the 1970s, Sanderson's first order of business with his new-found wealth was to go out and buy a Rolls-Royce convertible. He walked into a dealership in Philadelphia wearing jeans and was promptly ignored by the staff. When a salesman finally deigned to help him, it was a snooty Brit, and as Sanderson tells it, the ensuing exchange sounds like a comedy sketch.

"He looks at me like I'm a dirtbag. I said, 'How do you buy one of these things?' He said, 'Sir, you order a Rolls by the phone.' I said, 'Why do you have a showroom, then?' I said, 'How much is this?' He said, '$68,000.' It was burgundy and sand. He said, 'Sir, this is a Silver Shadow. If you purchase it, you'll probably be sitting in the dark.'

"So now I'm going to get this guy. I walked around it and I literally started kicking the tires. I asked him about the mileage. He said, 'Does the phrase "penny-wise, pound-foolish" mean anything to you?' That's it. I said, 'Get the owner.' I'm thinking, I'm going to buy this fucking thing today, drive it through the windows and you're not getting a cent. I phoned the bank, the money was there, and I got my Rolls."

Some years later, when things had gone bad for Sanderson, he still owned a hobby farm and some horses on Lake Erie. After he was forced to sell his pickup trucks, he used the Rolls to take hay out to his horses.

"That Rolls is the only thing he ever took care of," says McKenzie.

Life with the Blazers, meanwhile, was equally unsettled. Harry Sinden, Sanderson's former GM with the Bruins, wanted him for the Summit Series with the Soviets, but the NHL and Alan Eagleson had already frozen out WHA players. The Turk also recalls a pre-season game in Sherbrooke, Quebec, where Bernie Parent, the Blazers goalie, counted fifty-two people in the stands during the warmup. Parent said to Sanderson, "Derek, there are fifty-two people here. I'm not risking my life for fifty-two people." Parent retired to the Blazers' dressing room, where he stayed. As it turned out, Blazers winger Claude St. Saveur was from Sherbrooke and the crowd was almost all his friends and relatives.

McKenzie, who was supposed to whip the Blazers into shape,

broke his arm in the pre-season and missed a month and a half. Parent would break his ankle in mid-November and miss a month. McKenzie would also be replaced by Phil Watson as the team's coach within the first month of the regular season, but he knew early on he wasn't cut out to be a coach in the new league.

"We're at our camp in Roanoke, Virginia, and I've got to make a speech," McKenzie says. "I said we don't have a lot of rules here. We're in by 11:00. We wear jackets to restaurants. And if you get any girls after 11:00, you have to send them down to the coach. Big joke, right? The first night, there's a knock on the door and it's two guys with these two girls. 'We're finished with them, coach.'

"I expected everyone to play like the Bruins, where you worked like a bastard," McKenzie continues. "I was skating around, trying to get myself in shape, and I look over at these guys hanging off the boards and shooting pucks. Derek hated it there, and it showed. He showed up to camp thirty pounds overweight. Nobody knew him. In Boston, he couldn't walk down the street. He was a big star."

But in Philadelphia, Sanderson was the lead clown in a circus. On opening night, the Blazers were set to meet the New England Whalers, and their first home game might even have been played if someone at the Philadelphia Civic Center had known how to make ice. According to Sanderson, there was no cement floor at the Blazers' home rink; the pipes were simply covered with sawdust, which made for a thin, brittle playing surface. It wasn't good for hockey, and it wasn't any better for Zambonis. Before the game, the Zamboni crashed through the ice, and try as he might, the driver couldn't get it out. Referee Bill Friday was summoned to the accident scene and he offered the Blazers a choice.

"[Jim] Cooper came up to me and said, 'What do we do?'" Friday says. "I said we can either put pylons around the Zamboni and play the game or we can cancel it."

Sanderson had been watching the comedy unfold from the Blazers' bench. Also in attendance was Philadelphia mayor Frank Rizzo. It was decided the modest crowd, who'd all been given orange pucks as a souvenir of the Blazers' first game, would be told of the cancellation from the ice. The responsibility quickly fell to Sanderson to break the news.

"Rizzo was beside me, and he's got the mike," Sanderson says. "He said, 'Here, Derek, take the mike. You learn in politics when things go bad, you get out.' And he jumped into the penalty box and down a hallway and he was gone. So now I've got the mike, and I say, 'On behalf on the team, I want to apologize –' and, *pow*, the first puck hit the glass. So I kind of move, and it's *pow, pow, pow*. Now I'm blocking them. I get the fuck out of there and I head down the hallway and I can still hear the pucks bouncing everywhere."

"All I can say is, it's a good thing it wasn't a sellout," says Friday.

Sanderson had driven his Rolls to the game, and when he came out there was a huge dent in the body. "You didn't see a lot of Rollses in that neighbourhood," says André Lacroix, the Turk's teammate with the Blazers.

In the ensuing weeks, things didn't get much better for Sanderson in his strange new home. Under McKenzie, the team roared off to an 0-7 start, and the media coverage was almost as hilarious as the Blazers themselves. "SANDERSON READY TO START PAYING BIG WHA MONEY BACK," read a headline in *The Hockey News*. The story said, "One thing's for sure. Sanderson's multi-million dollar contract isn't going to change his life, he insists." But the next week, Sanderson was bitching to the press. "I'm a marked man in this league. Every time I turn around someone is hanging off me."

In the Blazers' seventh game, Sanderson had actually scored a couple of goals against his old pal Cheevers, when he jumped out of the penalty box, went after a loose puck, and landed on a piece of debris on the ice. He was helped off with a reported severe lower-back sprain. He would play one more game with the Blazers and was never remotely close to being the same player after that injury.

"I slipped a disc and I could feel it right away," he says. "It was like puke pain. I've never had pain like that. They wanted to operate on me right away, but they couldn't guarantee I'd ever play again. So they gave me this little physiotherapist who was about a foot shorter than a parking meter, and he and I became good friends."

Actually, Sanderson made other friends as a member of the Blazers. After one of his workout sessions with the vertically challenged therapist, he walked to his Rolls outside the Civic Center and found some kids hanging around. The kids tried to sell him some goalie pads they said they'd just found. Really. Sanderson, who was a little rough around the edges himself, took an immediate liking to the delinquents and they became his crew.

"He'd drive them around in his Rolls," says McKenzie. "We called them the Dead End Kids. We'd be out practising, and they'd be going through our stuff in the locker room. He had no friends. Those were his friends. They were nice kids, but they were crooks."

Things didn't get any better for the Blazers with Sanderson out of the lineup. After seventeen games they were 3-14, Phil Watson had replaced McKenzie as coach, and their crowds were pathetic. They drew 790 fans for a win over the New York Raiders. Cooper quit around mid-season, selling his interests to Brown. Brown immediately started to look for ways to save money and couldn't help but notice he had a $2.6-million hockey player who wasn't playing. The Blazers' owner offered his injured star $1 million in the way of a buyout, which Sanderson gleefully accepted. He had played eight games with the Blazers, recording three goals and three assists.

"They wanted me out of there," Sanderson says. "McKenzie was down. Parent was down. Phil was telling me, 'Look in the mirror. How can you take all that money and not play?'"

The Blazers, miraculously, would rally from their miserable start and actually make the playoffs, with Lacroix (50-74-124) and Danny Lawson (61-45-106) enjoying huge years and Parent playing sixty-three games in goal. Parent, however, would walk off the team in the middle of their playoff series with Cleveland after the Blazers missed some manner of payment. The next year he won the Stanley Cup with the Philadelphia Flyers.

The Blazers were swept in their series with the Crusaders and, over the summer, they were sold to Jimmy Pattison, who moved the team to Vancouver. Sanderson returned to Boston the next year and played two seasons with the Bruins before he started wandering around the NHL, playing with five teams over his last five seasons, his career disappearing in a cloud of drugs and alcohol.

Sanderson claims he went through $4 million in those lost years, and he can't begin to account for any of it. He was in and out of rehab. His weight ballooned to 230 pounds. Eight years after he signed his enormous contract with the Blazers, he was a drunk and virtually homeless.

The light finally went on for Sanderson in 1980 after some of his old Bruins teammates came to his aid and he found sobriety through Alcoholics Anonymous. He began speaking about addiction at Boston-area schools. He became the Bruins' colour commentator, then found his way into the money-management game. He's been sober for twenty-four years.

Some time ago, Sanderson sat down with some money people he worked with and calculated his Blazers contract in contemporary dollars. The figure they came up with was $15.7 million.

"I never really understood what I got," the Turk says.

The WHA had to have a franchise in New York. The Big Apple was the media capital of North America, and if the league was to succeed – and make everyone wealthy beyond their wildest dreams – they had to have a presence there. Dick Wood was equally determined that he would be the operator.

Wood was a successful young lawyer and a sports fanatic in 1972 when Neil Shayne, the area's original franchise-holder, let his option expire, largely because Shayne had wanted his team on Long Island. Wood, then thirty-two, read about this development during his lengthy commute to his office in Trenton and, in time, the idea took root in his active imagination. He dreamed of owning a team in New York. He visualized himself owning a team in New York. Soon he was meeting with Rangers owner Bill Jennings and negotiating a deal to rent Madison Square Garden.

Wood would get fleeced in that particular deal, but he would also leave the WHA just one year later as the only owner to make money in the rebel league. This alone should qualify him for a lifetime achievement award in the world of business.

"It worked out well for us because our plan had been to get the team up and running, then sell," says Wood, now retired in Florida. "We did that. We met our goal. I saw the potential in the league, but I knew you had to have a lot of staying power."

Wood wasn't keen on overstaying his welcome in the WHA. Nor were the Raiders/Golden Blades/Knights.

In its remarkable two-year history, the New York franchise would be known by three different names, owned by five different groups, and managed by three different men. The original GM, Marvin Milkes, was a former baseball executive. He also managed the team in its last incarnation in Cherry Hill, New Jersey, where it played in likely the worst facility in the history of major-league professional sports. At one point defenceman Jean Gauthier jumped from the team to Rochester of the minor-league American Hockey League. At another, the aforementioned André Lacroix, who played with the Golden Blades/Knights in Year 2, was sent a $20,000 bonus payment by the Philadelphia Blazers. The team intercepted the cheque, then told Lacroix the money had been used to write a fight song for the franchise.

"That must have been some song," Lacroix says.

But Wood, at least, saw potential in the franchise.

Shayne, as we've seen, was aced out of Long Island by the NHL, but Wood believed he could run a successful operation out of Madison Square Garden. His meetings with Jennings didn't discourage him from that position. Then again, there wasn't exactly full disclosure in Wood's meetings with the Garden's people.

"There were costs at the Garden they didn't tell us about," he now says tersely.

The rent at the Garden was more than reasonable. Wood paid just $1,700 for a Sunday-afternoon date, about $3,500 on average, and if that were all he had to worry about, the Raiders would have thrived. The problem was a series of union contracts that guaranteed certain staffing quotas in the areas of concessions and maintenance. The rent might have been $1,700 on Sundays, but when you added in the costs of all those support workers, the actual price for staging a game was close to $20,000.

"It was okay if you were drawing 18,200 like the Rangers," says Wood. "But we were averaging about 4,500, and it was killing us. We went to the union and asked for a break. We were told, 'We have to have a full staff every night in case there's a sellout.'"

As if. The Raiders' roster lacked the name power to excite the market, and they would average just under six thousand fans per game. Ron Ward, who earned the unlikely nickname "Magic," led the Raiders with 118 points in Year 1, but Ward would also play for seven WHA teams in five years. The Raiders' Alton White became the second African Canadian to play major professional hockey, and there were former NHLers Bobby Sheehan, Norm Ferguson, and Wayne Rivers, but no one to sell the team.

At the end of the first year, Wood unloaded the Raiders to an investment group, turning a tidy profit in the process. The new owners renamed the team the Golden Blades, hired Jerry DeLise to manage its affairs, and promptly missed a payroll early in the season. They attempted to market Lacroix, their one star, and set up a lunch meeting with a magazine. Lacroix arrived at the appointed hour and saw a gentleman sitting with two flashy women, who, it turned out, were *Penthouse* centrefold models. The man then told Lacroix he represented a magazine called *Viva* and they wanted the Golden Blades centre to pose naked for it. Lacroix came from a strict Catholic family of fourteen kids, had a brother in the priesthood, and his wife was pregnant at the time.

"I said, 'I think you better try Derek,'" Lacroix says.

In December, and with the Blades threatening to go belly up, the league took over the team, named it the Jersey Knights, and moved it to Cherry Hill, New Jersey, the former home of the Eastern Hockey League's Jersey Devils and the only rink in North America that featured moguls on its ice surface. Milkes was recalled to run the team and, in January, the league sold it to some guy named Joe Schwartz.

No, his name really was Joe Schwartz. The new owner would then move the team to San Diego for Year 3, which, fittingly, was about as far away from New York as they could get. The next year Lacroix would become just the fourth player in major-league hockey history to record 100 assists in a season, but he would ultimately set another milestone. In his seven seasons in the WHA, Lacroix played for six teams and was never traded. In each case, the team either folded or moved.

"I made money in the WHA I never would have made," says Lacroix. "And I can tell you, I saw things in the WHA I never would have seen anywhere else."

New England and Winnipeg would take command of their respective divisions and win the first-year pennants comfortably, but the real story of Year 1 – the real hockey story at least – was the somewhat riveting playoff battle in both the East and West.

The Blazers, as mentioned, rallied from their early adventure with Sanderson and finished third in their side, but the more noteworthy comeback belonged to the Ottawa Nationals. The Nats, who had barely scraped a team together, opened the season on October 11 at home against Alberta in the first-ever WHA game and were drilled 7-4 by the Oilers on national television. Doug Michel, their nervous leader, had sold just 400 season tickets, and twenty-four hours before opening night they were looking at an embarrassingly small crowd. The Nationals' crack marketing department then got on the phone to the city's minor-hockey associations and offered free tickets to every kid accompanied by an adult. As a result, that first game featured two thousand paid ticket-holders and three thousand screaming kids who spent the evening running around the Civic Centre.

Things didn't get much better. In an early-season game against Chicago, the Nationals drew 1,539 fans; the next night a crowd of 9,742 showed up to watch the junior 67s beat the London Knights. By early February they were twelve games under .500 and Michel's ulcer was starting to act up again. He approached Bill Ballard – who was running Maple Leaf Gardens because his father, Harold, was detained at Millhaven Penitentiary on a tax-evasion charge – about finishing the Nats' schedule in Toronto. And that's when the Nationals caught fire behind a goalie who believed he'd been an adviser to an Egyptian pharaoh in one of his past lives.

Somehow, it seems to fit.

The issue with Gilles Gratton was never talent. The issue was whether the mothership from Pluto would call him home during a game. Gratton, who earned the not-inaccurate nickname "Grattoonie the Loonie," not only believed he'd been reincarnated several times but could recite his past lives in chronological order. In addition to the gig with the pharaoh, he'd been a priest in a Mayan temple and a landowner in seventeenth-century Spain. When he was with the New York Rangers, he begged out of a start because he had sore ribs, the result of a spear wound he'd suffered three hundred years earlier.

"It's not a belief," Gratton said. "It's my experience. I can remember my past lives, that's all there is to it. I could talk about it for hours. You have some programs on *Star Trek* that are very close to my experiences. It's like I'm in two places at one time."

You have to admit, that's a handy skill to have when you're a goalie. But Gratton's alternative world view extended beyond the question of his past lives. He studied the astrological charts of his opponents, and if he saw too many signs he didn't like, he wouldn't play. He skated around Maple Leaf Gardens naked. He quit one game after two periods and headed back to the team's hotel because he felt he'd faced enough shots. When the action around his net became too stressful, he'd whisper, "*Poisson mort, poisson mort* [Dead fish, dead fish]" to his defencemen and he'd pretend to pass out.

But when the spirits moved him he could play goal. That season, Gratton took over from veteran Les Binkley as the Nats' number-one goalie and carried the team down the stretch. Over the final twenty-two games, they went 15-7 and beat out Quebec for the final playoff spot in the East. Just as the WHA seemed to be catching on in Ottawa, however, Michel's landlords, the Central Canada Exhibition Association, threw a final curve at the Nats' president. They demanded a $100,000 bond for the second year of the Nationals' lease in March of the first season and Michel simply threw up his hands. He went back to Toronto and negotiated a deal with Bill Ballard that Nick Trbovich closed with a call to Millhaven and Harold. The Nats then beat the Whalers in one of the games in Toronto before they were knocked out in five games. That summer, John F. Bassett would buy the team from Trbovich for $1.8 million and Doug Michel, who'd sold his business, cashed in his life savings, and lived off his credit card, all so he could own a WHA franchise, was out of the hockey business.

Gratton was last found in France, where he was working as a photographer. He told a reporter he'd seen his life four hundred years in the future and advises that our planet in the twenty-fourth century is a much happier place to live.

In the West, meanwhile, the Alberta Oilers and Minnesota Fighting Saints were racing down the stretch for the final playoff spot. The Saints had started the season with Glen Sonmor as their head coach and GM, but midway through the season Sonmor moved into the manager's office permanently and handed the coaching reins to his assistant, Harry Neale, late of the Hamilton Junior Red Wings.

"Glen became so busy trying to steal players from the NHL that I became the coach," is how Neale explains his promotion.

The Oilers, for their part, started the season slowly under coach Ray Kinasewich and late in the season went on an eight-game losing streak. In what would become a recurring pattern with the Oilers, Bill Hunter then stepped behind the bench to rally his troops.

Hunter, who believed he was a leader of men and a coaching savant, would pull this stunt three times in the four years he was the Oilers' GM. He did it to Kinasewich. He did it to the next coach, Brian Shaw. He did it to the one after that, Clare Drake. That first year, Kinasewich remained the "official coach" and ran the practices. But for games, he moved up to the press box and Hunter would step behind the bench.

"Bill was a promoter and a salesman, and he always seemed to fire the coach halfway through the season," says Al Hamilton, an original Oiler who played all seven WHA seasons with the club. "I don't know if he ever made a difference, but in his mind he did."

"He was an old-school coach who believed in a very simple game and lots of emotion," says Ken Brown, the Oilers' backup goalie in Year 1. "I don't know why, but before one game we're in the dressing room going, 'We're the Oilers and we know it, clap your hands.' Bill watches this and goes, 'Goddamn it, boys, I love it.' Then we won the game, and we had to do it for the rest of the season. He said, 'Mr. Brown, you're in charge of enthusiasm,' and if we didn't do it loudly enough, he'd make us do it over. That made me real popular with the guys."

Hunter also loved to give speeches. In addition to his other talents, he considered himself a master motivator. Before one game in Houston, he sensed the Oilers were in need of one of his pep talks. True, he wasn't with the team, but that wasn't a problem, because Hunter had a speakerphone brought into the room where the Oilers were having their pre-game meal and began orating. As Hunter droned on, a couple of the Oilers mooned the speaker. A couple more thumbed their noses at it. Still more simply got up and left. By the time Hunter was finished, the room was virtually empty.

Hunter's larger success that season was, as usual, off the ice, where he helped finagle the Edmonton city council into putting $15 million toward Northlands Coliseum. The Oilers played their first two seasons in the wheezing old Edmonton Gardens, which had been condemned as a fire hazard in the mid-1960s before it was renovated. In November of Year 3, they moved into Northlands, the first modern, major-league facility to be built in western Canada. Today, as Rexall Place, it remains the rink in which the Oilers play.

"It was a spectacular thing," says Brown. "In the second year, [Hunter] took us over to the site, and they'd just started working on it. He said, 'This is it, boys. This is where you're going to be.' The first night, people got to the rink at 5:00 and just walked around with their mouths open. I was one of them. I was in awe of the place."

When Hunter took over for Kinasewich, the Oilers were a couple of games under .500. He improved them modestly to the .500 mark before the final game of the season, when they met the Fighting Saints in the Saints' new home, the St. Paul Civic Center, with the fourth and final playoff spot on the line. A win for the Oilers would give both teams a 38-37-3 record, but Alberta, in Hunter's mind at least, would go on to win the tie-breaker and therefore secure the playoff spot because of their superior record over the Saints in head-to-head games.

As luck would have it, the Oilers beat the Fighting Saints 5-3 and Hunter immediately congratulated himself on his masterstroke.

There was just one problem. In the event of a tie for the final playoff spot, according to WHA bylaws, there would be a one-game playoff to determine who would advance.

"We thought that was the rule, too," says Neale. "We start going home. We found out the next day that wasn't the rule. The rule was there would be a sudden-death playoff. Now we've got a furor on our hands. One of my jobs was to go to the airport and intercept guys on their way home."

"It was 10:30 and guys were fully intent on doing some serious partying," Brown says of the Oilers' post-victory euphoria. "All of sudden Bill walks into our dressing room and says, 'Boys, we've got a problem.'"

Actually, they had another problem. Where would they play the game? The WHA wanted the game in St. Paul, where the Fighting Saints were drawing well, but Hunter howled for a neutral site. The game was ultimately set for Calgary, which was a neat trick, because Calgary, technically, didn't have a franchise in the WHA.

"The neutral site was Calgary," says Neale. "Really neutral. Hunter was just livid we had to play them, and we won, which didn't make him any happier."

It would get worse for Hunter. In the run-up to Year 1, the Oilers' boss had continually reminded Davidson and Dennis Murphy that they knew nothing about hockey and they should leave all decisions relevant to the game to someone who did know – namely him. At the end of the 1972-73 season, however, Murphy's Los Angeles Sharks finished in third place in the West with a 37-35-6 mark, two spots ahead of the Oilers. At the league meetings in La Costa that year, Murphy made up a huge poster of the Western Division standings, then had his coach, Terry Slater, parade the poster around the room. After a couple of circuits, Slater stopped, Murphy rose, and, in his best courtroom voice said, "I rest my case."

Despite the Saints' win over the Oilers, they were dispatched in five games by the Jets, who then swept Houston to reach the final. They met the New England Whalers, and if there was a success story in the WHA's first season, it was in Boston, where Baldwin, the president who was younger than most of his players, and Jack Kelley, the coach who'd cut him at Boston College, built the league's best team with Bob Schmertz's money.

Unlike so many of their competitors, the Whalers of Year 1 hadn't signed a name NHL star and didn't skew their payroll with two or three monster contracts. They did, however, have depth and balance, and they could come at you several different ways. The goaltending was ably handled by Al Smith, whom Baldwin signed from Detroit. The blueline featured four legitimate NHLers in Ted Green, Jim Dorey, Brad Selwood, and Ricky Ley. Up front, Terry Caffery and Tom Webster both recorded 100-point seasons, Larry Pleau, a Massachusetts kid and the organization's first player, scored 39 goals, and Tim Sheehy, who'd played at Boston College, chipped in 33. They even had a quality stick boy in Jack Kelley's son David, who'd play hockey at Princeton. David Kelley, alas, never made it in the game and decided to give television a try. He went on to produce the hit shows *Chicago Hope, Ally McBeal*, and *The Practice*, and he's now married to Michelle Pfeiffer, the poor slob.

"Jack was a great coach and he was an important figure in New England," says Baldwin. "He gave us instant credibility, and we drafted smart. We took pros with a New England background and college players when no one was taking college players."

Baldwin's blueprint, in fact, would have been flawless except for one small detail. The Whalers didn't have their own rink, and they were never going to be successful in Boston competing against the Bruins in the Bruins' own building.

In Year 1 of the WHA, the Boston Garden was the home to the Bruins, the AHL's Braves, and the WHA's Whalers. Things got so tight in Beantown, the Whalers had to schedule games at the Boston Arena, the old downtown mausoleum where Babe Ruth had scrimmaged with the Arena A.C. team when he pitched for the Red Sox in the late 1910s. The Boston Arena, built in 1910, is the oldest rink in the United States, and Baldwin's father had played college hockey there in the 1930s. When Howard told his dad the Whalers would be playing games at his old rink, Baldwin senior said, "I hope it's better than when I played there."

"You have to remember, the Bruins were at the peak of their power, and the Braves were doing well," says Baldwin. "But we were young and naive enough to think we could make it work. The Bruins did everything they could to kill us, and I probably would have done the same in their situation. We had Saturday- and Sunday-afternoon dates, and they weren't bad compared to the Mondays. There was just too much hockey in Boston that year."

Still, the Whalers would lead the WHA in attendance in Year 1 with an average crowd of (yikes) 6,981. For the playoffs, they averaged just under 9,000 fans per game, which, again, was the highest total in the league by far. In the first round, they took out the Nationals in five games before ousting Cheevers and the Crusaders in five games in the Eastern final.

The first league-championship series was a one-sided affair in which the Whalers took a 3-1 series lead with game five set for Boston. Prior to Year 1, Dennis Murphy had sold the naming rights for the WHA's championship trophy to the Avco financial group, but while Baldwin attended to details before game five of the final, it occurred to him he hadn't actually seen a trophy.

"Everyone's going, 'Where's the Cup? We don't have a Cup,'" Baldwin says. "I sent my PR guy out, and he came back with this huge trophy he bought from a sporting-goods store. I think it cost $1.99, but it looked good on television. It kind of looked like the U.S. Open tennis trophy."

It would come in handy when the Whalers thumped the Jets 9-6 to win the first-ever championship. Pleau scored three goals in the deciding game. Webster added a pair. And the Whalers hoisted the hardware, ending the WHA's first-ever season. By the end of the next season, they'd be playing at Eddie Shore's old rink in Springfield, waiting for their new home in Hartford, Connecticut, to be completed.

"We thought we really had something to build on, but it was exactly the opposite," says Baldwin. "It was like hockey had peaked in Boston, and by mid-November [of their second year], I realized our goose was cooked. They were putting up a new building in Hartford, I had a meeting with the CEO of Aetna [the life-insurance company], and we closed the deal in a day."

But they didn't leave Boston quietly.

Baldwin still owed the Bruins rent money when the Whalers were packing up to leave for Springfield at the end of Year 2, and he wasn't in a hurry to pay it. The Whalers had their truck outside their locker room and were loading their gear when Bruins owner Weston Adams had the Garden's Zamboni block the truck's exit. Baldwin was at home sick when he got a frantic call from the Whalers' equipment manager.

"I just said, Look, they're going to have to move it sooner or later," Baldwin says.

Good call, Howard. The Zamboni eventually had to be moved because it was also blocking the Corvette belonging to Weston Adams, Jr., and when the Zamboni moved to let the owner's son out, the Whalers effected their escape with their equipment.

"It wasn't that we didn't have the money," says Baldwin. "We just wanted to stick it up the Bruins' ass. We paid them back eventually."

In addition to the Whalers' move, Baldwin would be occupied by other ventures in the 1973-74 season. After Year 1, Davidson left to start up his life's calling, the World Football League, and brought a lot of his WHA buddies in on the ground floor. Baldwin was given the Portland franchise, Nick Mileti was given the Chicago franchise and flipped it for half a million bucks. John Bassett was given a franchise for Toronto, which was blocked by the minister of health, Marc Lalonde, and Bassett took the team to Memphis, where he signed Larry Csonka, Jim Kiick, and Paul Warfield away from the Miami Dolphins. In one of the stranger developments, Benny Hatskin of Winnipeg was offered a franchise in Hawaii, but passed.

Davidson poured himself into the WFL and, to this day, maintains it was better organized and better funded than either the ABA or the WHA. His timing, however, left a little to be desired. The new league kicked off with interest rates at record highs and the economy in tatters. President Nixon had resigned. There were oil embargoes. New leagues depend on new owners to keep them alive, and in the mid-1970s, there just weren't that many venture capitalists available to the world of sport.

"I'd played football and the WFL was my dream," Davidson says. "It's funny. We did so many things right and we had a real opportunity, but we were killed by things beyond our control."

It's also funny that, of the three leagues he was instrumental in starting, Davidson made the biggest impact with a league in the game he knew the least about. He was there at the WHA's startup. He played a role in attracting investors, and he, more than Murphy or Hunter or any of the pioneers, was the league's face in its embryonic stages. He also sold his franchise in San Francisco as fast as humanly possible and he was out the door by the league's second season.

As the men of the WHA would attest, Davidson is not an easy figure to sum up; on some levels a fly-by-nighter, on others a visionary. But it's impossible to overestimate his effect on the world of modern professional sports. Davidson recognized the established pro leagues were a monopoly. He recognized the players were treated as chattels. He recognized the business of pro sports was out of step with fundamental legal principles. In the end, he helped unleash the forces that would liberate the game from a handful of capitalists, and everyone who draws a paycheque in professional sports today should be aware of his contribution. True, if you add up their collective time in operation, his leagues didn't live as long as a good dog, but Davidson is also right there with Pete Rozelle, Mark McCormack, Marvin Miller, and Roone Arledge as a seminal figure in the development of the business of modern sports.

"Honestly, I probably created as much work for players, lawyers, and agents as anyone in the last thirty years, but I don't think about my legacy or what it means," says Davidson, now sixty-nine and still putting deals together in southern California. "There are a lot easier ways to make money than starting up a league. We made more money off real-estate deals and practising law than starting up leagues. But there's an excitement about sports that's hard to deny. The NHL tried to litigate us out of business, and it always seemed like we were facing an intriguing challenge.

"We had a lot of fun."

# CHAPTER 4

## "It brought the love of the game back to me."

While so many of his colleagues had delusions of grandeur, Bill Dineen was realistic about life in the new league. Dineen, who'd played and coached all over the minors before Paul Deneau hired him to run the Houston Aeros, eschewed the big-name signings and built his team around an assortment of fringe NHLers and top minor-leaguers with whom he was familiar. He grabbed Ted Taylor, Murray Hall, John Schella, and Poul Popiel from the Vancouver Canucks organization. Gord Labossiere was signed from the Minnesota North Stars and led the Aeros in scoring their first year with 96 points. Andre Hinse, Frank Hughes, and Larry Lund came out of Phoenix in the old Western Hockey League. The goaltending was ably handled by Don McLeod and Wayne Rutledge. Under Dineen's guidance, this motley assortment finished second in the Western Division and won their first playoff round before they were swept by the Winnipeg Jets in the division final.

"I'm very frugal with my own money, but I'm *extremely* frugal with other people's money," Dineen says. "That made me unusual in that original group.

"Without a doubt my background helped. I knew the minors and I decided to go after the borderline guys who were close to playing in the NHL. Everyone else was taking all these NHL guys, and I knew you were only going to get a couple of them. The newspapers said we had the worst draft of all the teams, but we finished second in the West that year and we had a pretty good nucleus."

They had everything, it seemed, except star power – and you can say this for Dineen, when he addressed that problem, he didn't fool around.

Dineen had played with Gordie Howe in Detroit in the early 1950s, and it was Howe who helped hang the nickname "Foxy" on the old hockey man. After one season, Dineen proudly reported to his teammates that he'd negotiated a $500 raise with Jack Adams, the notoriously tight-fisted Red Wings GM. Howe had to tell Dineen the league's minimum wage had gone up exactly that amount that year.

Over the years the two men kept up a friendship, and by the early 1970s Dineen knew Howe was desperately unhappy in his meaningless job in the Red Wings front office. The Aeros coach and GM was also aware that Howe's two boys, Mark and Marty, were emerging as elite-level prospects, a bit of inside knowledge shared with, oh, every hockey man in North America. Marty, a rangy defenceman with a mean streak, had gone to the Toronto Marlboros as a seventeen-year-old in 1971-72, and Mark, a glittering all-round talent, followed a year later. Together, they led the Marlies to the 1973 Memorial Cup where, under the proud gaze of Gordie and their mother, Colleen, they pummelled the Quebec Remparts 9-1 in the championship game.

"Colleen and I were sitting in the stands, and Mark took a penalty in the first period, and Quebec scored," Gordie says. "This French-Canadian gentleman started laughing at me. Then Mark went out and scored five goals. I didn't say anything to the guy. I didn't have to."

The game's grand old man exaggerates his son's accomplishments, but only by a bit. Mark, in fact, recorded two goals and three assists in the final game and was named the tournament's MVP. Dineen and his assistant coach, Doug Harvey, were also in the crowd, and the Aeros' brain trust, such as it was, made their way down to the Marlies' locker room to congratulate the Howe boys. The first people they ran into were Gordie and Colleen. They would meet again in the Howes' summer home in Traverse City, Michigan, in a couple of weeks, and together they would write one of the most remarkable stories in the history of professional sports.

Gordie Howe now says the idea of playing with his boys occurred to him long before he ran into Dineen at the Memorial Cup. In the latter years of his career, he'd bring Mark and Marty out to practise with the Red Wings, and Mark's talent, in particular, was self-evident. A number of the Wings used to pester Howe to bring his middle son out, and both boys were around the team as long as anyone could remember. Gordie would also drive them to and from their games and tell them, "You guys keep it up, and one day we'll be teammates."

Ha-ha. Good one, Gordie.

In February of 1971, Marty returned to Detroit from the Marlies to take part in a charity game between the Junior Red Wings, Mark's club at the time, and the NHL's Red Wings. Marty suited up with the big Wings, Gordie played with Mark on the Junior Red Wings, and after the game Howe senior told a TV reporter: "It would be great if I could play with my two sons."

"I think that planted the seed for him," says Mark.

But it was Dineen who made certain that seed would germinate.

At the Memorial Cup, Dineen approached Colleen Howe and struck up a conversation, saying it was a shame that a kid with Mark's ability had to go back to junior. Colleen agreed and said Mark should be playing in the pros. Dineen moved on to congratulate Gordie, talked briefly with Mark and Marty, then collected Harvey, the Montreal Canadiens Hall of Famer, and started scheming.

The WHA draft was set for Toronto five days after the Memorial Cup final, and on the train to the Big Smoke, Dineen posed a question to Harvey. The Howe kids were making sixty bucks a week with the Marlies. That was against NCAA and international rules. So what was to stop them from taking them in their pro draft? The question, of course, was purely rhetorical, because even if there had been a snag to signing the Howes, the WHA would have found some way to circumvent it. As it was, Dineen and Harvey decided there on the train that the Aeros would draft the two boys, and, once that was done, landing the old man would be a piece of cake.

"I knew how Gordie felt about it," Dineen says. "I saw the look in his eyes around his two boys. I knew there was no way they were coming to Houston without him."

A half-hour before the draft, Dineen called the Howes to let them know of the Aeros' intentions, and after the Houston coach and GM's lengthy conversation with Colleen, Gordie asked his former teammate, "What would you think of a third Howe?" Number 9 has since told the story that he then heard two sounds: the phone hitting the floor, followed shortly by Dineen. Dineen, for his part, says simply, "I knew it was coming," which was more than the WHA could say.

At the pro draft, Dineen stood and said, "With their first pick, Houston takes Mark Howe," and an uproar immediately ensued. Later in the draft, Dineen stood up again and said,

"Houston takes Marty Howe," at which point Bobby Hull bellowed, "Why don't you take Colleen, too?"

Mark, meanwhile, had gone out with his Marlies teammates after their big win and celebrated a little too enthusiastically. He missed the subsequent victory parade and was still a little green around the gills when his parents called.

"I was feeling under the weather, really under the weather, and I got a call from my mom and dad telling me about this new league," Mark says. "I didn't know anything about it. I just said, 'Fine.' We'd been drafted but I didn't read too much into it. Maybe I should have been paying attention."

And maybe it didn't matter what the youngest Howe thought. Some ten days after the draft – and after NHL president Clarence Campbell had called Gordie, urging him to stop Mark from signing with the rebels – Dineen, Harvey, and Aeros president Jim Smith convened in Traverse City, Michigan, with Gordie, Colleen, and their representative, Gerry Patterson. They eventually agreed on a package worth $2.2 million: Gordie would receive $1 million over four years and Mark and Marty $600,000 each over the same term. Marty, who'd spent two full seasons with the Marlies, was eager to sign. Mark, however, balked until his father sat him down and offered some kindly advice.

"Dad was great," Mark says. "He told me the best way to improve was to play against better players. He said that would make the learning process quicker. Then he said, 'If you don't sign it, I'll break your arms and sign it for you.' He had a way of being convincing."

Funny story. Here's another one. In his last year with the Red Wings, Gordie Howe, arguably the greatest player who ever lived, made $100,000. His two sons each surpassed that with their first contracts.

"Things were tough at the end in Detroit, and I wasn't happy working there," Gordie says. "I remember in one of my last years we got Bobby Baun from Oakland. Bobby took me out to lunch and told me, 'I've got something to tell you, and it might bother you.' I said, 'What's your problem Bobby?' And he told me he was making twice as much as I was. That hurt. I can tell you, that hurt.

"Playing with the kids was like a tonic for me. I remember meeting with Colleen and Gerry Patterson and the Houston people in Traverse City, and I was prouder than hell, because the kids were getting more money than I ever made and now I had a chance to play with them."

The Howe signings would also be one of Doug Harvey's last acts with the Aeros, and, by extension, one of the last acts of his brilliant, tormented career. He is, indisputably, one of the two or three best defencemen to play the game, and by all accounts a brilliant hockey mind and a generous soul whose life was undone by alcohol. In the early 1960s, he was banished from the Canadiens family due in large part to his role in the fledgling NHL players' union. He then played three seasons in New York, where it seemed he was being groomed for the general manager's chair. But Harvey wanted to keep on playing and instead spent the next four years in the minors, where, among other things, he played with Dineen for a season in Quebec City.

Midway through his first season in Houston, the Aeros coach offered Harvey a job in his one-man hockey department as his assistant and the franchise's chief scout. Dineen now says Harvey immediately went on the wagon and stayed dry for almost a full year before he fell hard, and he was released at the end of the 1973-74 season. He died in 1989 after a lengthy battle with cirrhosis of the liver.

"Everyone wanted to put him on the right path, but there was nothing to be done," Rocket Richard said at the time of Harvey's death.

Those words resonate with sincerity, because despite his addiction Harvey was a much-loved figure in the hockey world.

Dineen says Harvey kept the peace between the French and English factions on the old Canadiens teams, and he was one of the few players who could get away with needling the Rocket. Red Fisher, the venerable *Montreal Gazette* hockey writer, has a number of Harvey stories, but delights in telling of a summer's day when the great defenceman picked him up in his car and took him to the Laurentians, where they spent the day painting cottages at a camp for kids. Gordie tells of Harvey taking Marty under his wing and teaching him more in half an hour than he'd learned from all his other coaches combined.

"He was one of the biggest-hearted guys I've ever met in my life," says Dineen. "He also had an unparalleled knowledge of the game. He was a genius in disguise."

The Howes arrived in Houston amid much fanfare. A banner hung from a skyscraper saying, "WELCOME TO HOWESTON." The media came out to watch the forty-five-year-old living legend and his two teenage sons. Everyone agreed the Aeros had plotted an exciting new course.

And the Howes were wondering just what the hell they'd gotten themselves into.

Mark, in particular, suffered under the strain of his sudden notoriety as the saviour of the Houston franchise. In his early teens, he'd suffered from migraine headaches, and he was still susceptible to them. The Aeros also started working out in the late summer when the temperature in Houston routinely hit the high nineties Fahrenheit, and humidity was just as bad. In the first day of practice, Mark lost eight pounds, which, coupled with the stress of his situation, produced the Anvil Chorus in his head. It also started a vicious cycle that took him a week to break.

"Those were the days when they didn't let you drink water during practice," Mark says. "So I'd get overheated, and with everything else going on the migraines would kick in. Then they gave me salt pills for the dehydration and that gave me diarrhea, which made me more dehydrated and made the migraines worse.

"Finally, Dad and Bill took me aside and said, 'Look, kid, relax. You've got the team made. Just go out and play.' That helped a lot."

Howe *père*, meanwhile, wasn't doing much better after two years away from the game. While with the Red Wings, Gordie referred to his front-office position as his mushroom job, because he was kept in the dark and every once in a while someone would open the door and throw some shit on him. As bad as that was, though, it was still better than the prospect of coming out of retirement and making a fool of himself.

In the Aeros' first week of practice, Howe almost killed himself a couple of times. He had no wind. He had no legs. His timing was brutal. Each day he'd go to practice and each night he'd return home and wonder if his game would ever come back. Three days into camp he went to Colleen and said, "Oh, god, I think I've made a mistake."

"Dad struggled," says Mark. "He was pretty red in the face, and we were kind of worried."

"There were," says Marty, "some very interesting shades of purple that first week."

Gordie had a sit-down with Dineen and told the coach of his fears. The Aeros were about to start two-a-days, and Dineen told Howe he could join the team for just one of the sessions. Howe pondered this, then said, no, he'd always been a team player. Either he was in or he was out.

"I figured the two-a-days would either kill me or make me," Howe says. "And the minute we started them it was like I'd never been off the ice."

"We were all concerned after that first week, but he came out one day and it was like somebody hit him with a wand," says Dineen. "Doug was on the ice with me, and I said, 'Look at the old man!' After that, everything was fine."

After his dreadful start, it seemed someone had held a seance and summoned back the Gordie Howe of ten years before. His kids, of course, were all over the old man.

"They asked me if I was feeling better," Gordie says, "and I said, 'Yeah, I feel like a million dollars! Why?' They said, 'We noticed there was some pink in the ashen colour, and we didn't hear you puffing all day.'"

They were astounded at what they witnessed. In the Aeros' first exhibition game, after he was presented with his Aeros jersey, which read "GORIDE HOWE," Gordie scored twenty-one seconds after the opening faceoff and never looked back. Later in the pre-season, he flattened New England's John French, then told reporters, "Ah, I'm just a tired old man." He started the season modestly with 18 points after the first fifteen games, but two months later he was fourth in the league in scoring, and by the end of February led all scorers with 84 points in fifty-nine games. He would finish the year with 31 goals and 100 points in seventy games and was named the league's MVP as the Aeros waltzed to the Avco Cup.

"He was, hands down, the best player in the league in the first year and one of the three or four best in the second," says Mark. "To do the things he could do at his age was just amazing, and I got to watch it every day. It would have been a thrill to have him as part of our team anyway, but when it was your dad, it was just that much more special."

"He just owned people," says Marty.

The boys had obviously followed their father's career in Detroit, but it was one thing to watch him through the worshipful eyes of a child and another thing to watch him as a teammate. From their front-row seat with the Aeros, they witnessed one of the greatest comebacks in sports history. Howe senior says he was better his first two seasons in Houston than he'd been his last five with the Red Wings. His sons don't disagree. He was a different player.

"It brought the love of the game back to me," Gordie says. "It gave me a chance to play with my boys. I couldn't have asked for anything more. People say I made this great comeback and everything. Well, it's amazing what you can do when you're happy."

Gordie had suffered from arthritis in his wrist during his last couple of years with the Wings, and the condition had weakened his once-fearsome shot. Undeterred, he became Mark's set-up man and the guy who did most of the dirty work in the corners and on the forecheck. Mark would score 38 goals that season and was named the league's rookie of the year, and he now says he's never played with a better linemate. Still, the chemistry between father and son didn't come immediately.

"The first two weeks he passed the puck real soft to me," Mark says. "They were beautiful passes, flat and right on the tape. But it took so long to get there, the defenceman was arriving the same time as the puck, and I got hammered a few times. I finally said, 'Look, Dad, you've got to pass the puck harder or you're going to get me killed.' It was hard saying that to my dad, but I'd put up with it for two weeks and I had to say something."

Gordie still laughs at the memory of that confrontation.

"I was just leading him a little," he says. "Maybe I was leading him too much. Finally he said, 'Dad, can you put that son-of-a-bitch in there quicker.' It's funny. I always told him the puck was like a piece of cowshit during fly season. The softer it was, the more flies were attracted to it. I had to take my own advice."

But he seemed to catch on. It took Mark and his dad, who played with centre Jim Sherrit, a few weeks to get comfortable, but once they figured out each other's style, they tore the league up. On the forecheck, Mark would flush the play to Gordie's side of the rink and head to the net. Gordie would then extricate the puck from the corner and find Mark in the slot.

"I've never seen a better guy in the corner," Mark says. "It didn't matter if it was one guy or two. He used to tell me, 'Go

in and do your thing, then get your ass in front of the net.' I'd
get there and this blind pass would come right out on my stick."

"He was just so strong," says Marty. "If he went into a corner
with one guy, he was going to get the puck. With two guys, he
was probably going to get the puck, and with three guys he still
had a fifty-fifty shot. You'd stand back and watch him, because
the elbows would be flying and the stick would be going and he
could hit you just as easily as one of them."

Gordie might have lost some things to age, but he still had
hockey sense in spades, and when all else failed he was still the
meanest player in the WHA. His two boys will go on about their
dad and his many talents, but both Mark and Marty say the
thing that stood out most about him was his appetite for
destruction. He recorded just 46 penalty minutes that season
but, apparently, he didn't waste them. Word also got out around
the league that if you messed with either of the boys, you had
to answer to the old man, and that was not a pleasant prospect.

"He was the nicest person off the ice you'd ever meet," says
Mark. "On the ice, he was the meanest SOB I've ever seen. He
was fine as long as you left him alone, but if he got mad, watch
out. And he'd hurt you. He'd knock every tooth out of your
head. He doesn't like hearing that, but that's the way he was."

"He had his rules, and if you went along with them, everything was fine," says Marty. "If you didn't, there was trouble."

Just ask Roger Cote, a minor-league defenceman who caught
on with Edmonton during the Howes' first year in Houston.
During the course of a line brawl with the Aeros, Cote, who
played with a toothpick hanging out of his mouth, became
tangled up with Marty and ended up on top of the young blueliner. Mark was standing near the pile when he saw the Oilers'
Jim Harrison trying to hold Gordie back. He heard Gordie say,
"That's enough, let him up." Cote looked up and offered the
usual profane hockey response.

Mark will never forget what he saw next.

"All of a sudden Dad reached over Cote's shoulder, buried two fingers in his nostrils, and tried to rip his nose off his face. It was one thing to think of doing that. It was another to actually do it."

Marty says, "All I remember is Cote saying, 'Okay, I'm up. I'm up.'"

History does not record what happened to Cote's toothpick.

That season, and all the seasons the Howes were together, would play out like a bizarre combination of *Father Knows Best* and *Reservoir Dogs*. Gordie didn't fight in the WHA, but as Mark points out, his stick was still effective. His philosophy of the game is best captured by the counsel he used to give the Philadelphia Flyers' Tim Kerr when Mark played in Philly. The senior Howe advised Kerr, a giant but mild-mannered sniper, to pick out three games a year that were broadcast on national television and go medieval on some poor schmuck. That way, he'd score ten more goals a season.

"That's the way he saw the game," Mark says, before adding, "I think Dad would have a hard time playing the game today, because he'd be suspended a lot."

But juxtaposed against that vicious streak was a tender side that was made apparent many times in their years in Houston. Howe's relationship with his boys was formed long before they started playing together. In the summer, Gordie would tour Canada doing promotional work for the Eaton's company, and Mark and Marty would often travel with him. They played golf together. They fished together. At times it seemed Gordie had two buddies who just happened to be thirty years younger. On the ice, things were just as easy.

"It was just an extension of our relationship," says Mark. "For the most part he left us alone and let us learn from our mistakes. The odd time he'd say, 'Here's a piece of advice. Do what you want with it.' But he never forced anything on us."

"He was easy to play with," Gordie says of Mark. "I wish all my wingers would have listened to me like Mark. Whatever I said, he took as gospel."

If things were any different with Marty, it didn't show in the way the father and son interacted. Marty's first love was football, and he didn't concentrate on hockey until he went to the Marlies. He played a different position than his father and his brother, and he wasn't blessed with Mark's natural talent. But he also carved out an under-appreciated twelve-year pro career and scored 17 goals and totalled 45 points in Year 5 with the Aeros.

"I was always the tall, uncoordinated kid you put on defence," Marty says. "Mark always had the skills and he was a big scorer. Hockey wasn't even my number-one sport.

"Everyone says it's the coaches who teach you the game, but it's the players you play with and against. You learn by observing, and you learn through competition. We were lucky, because we had the best guy to watch and it was our dad."

And they watched over their dad closely. The boys and Colleen suggested to Gordie that wearing a helmet might not be a bad idea. Gordie would rather have worn a tutu, but during one practice he took a tumble and cracked his head into the boards.

"Whatever you do, don't tell your mother I hit my head on the boards," he instructed his sons as he gathered himself. "Just call her and tell her something else."

"Mom, Dad hit his head on the ice," Mark immediately reported to Colleen.

Gordie's tolerance for pain is well documented, and Mark swears his father spent the night before their first game in Houston in the hospital with back spasms, then got out of bed and played the game.

"He was the toughest man I've ever seen," Mark says, and then adds, "On the ice he was Gordie until he got hurt. Then he was Dad."

The Howes would solidify the franchise in Houston and in many respects the entire league. Bill Dineen credits Bobby Hull with getting the WHA off the ground, but in the next breath says, "I don't think the players or the fans felt we were a real league until we got the Howes." That was certainly reflected in the Aeros' attendance. In Year 1, playing out of Sam Houston, they averaged 4,616 fans per game. The figure jumped to an average of 6,811 in Year 2 with the Howes on board. The team's success also gave the city of Houston the impetus to build the Summit for the NBA Rockets and the Aeros. In Year 4, their first full year in their new home, the Aeros drew just over 9,000 fans per game.

They also remained very much the creation of Dineen. Gordie and Mark were the team's offensive stars, but the Aeros' coach and GM surrounded them with an able supporting cast. John Schella and Poul Popiel formed the number-one defensive pairing and they were a nasty bit of business. The second line consisted of Larry Lund, Frank Hughes, who had a couple of forty-goal seasons with the Aeros, and Andre Hinse, whom Dineen calls the best player never to suit up in the NHL. After Harvey lost his way, Dineen did much of the scouting and took Gordie along on a few trips. He then hired as his scout Barry Fraser, who would also work with Cincinnati before Glen Sather hired him for the Oilers. Fraser was the Oilers' head scout in their ridiculously successful drafts of the early 1980s.

Dineen, meanwhile, augmented the team's core with a series of savvy signings. He secured Ron Grahame to play goal, and Grahame was twice voted the WHA's best. He added youngsters Rich Preston, Morris Lukowich, Terry Ruskowski, Scott Campbell, and under-age power forward John Tonelli. When the Aeros ran into injuries on their blueline, Dineen moved Mark Howe to the back end: he would later become a Norris Trophy–calibre defenceman in the NHL. Under Dineen, there wasn't a better-run organization than the Aeros in the WHA. In his six seasons in Houston, the Aeros won two Avco Cups, four division pennants, made the league final on another occasion, and finished with a cumulative record of 285-170-19. Had Dineen the resources to maintain his team, there would likely be an NHL franchise in Houston today.

"I respect Billy as much as any coach I've ever had," says Mark. "He's one of the best hockey men I've ever been associated with. When we lost, you'd feel bad because you let him down, and I can't think of too many coaches I can say that about. Without a doubt, he was the guy who built the franchise and held it together."

But the Aeros could never find an owner who was interested in supporting the franchise over the long haul. Midway through the second season, Paul Deneau, the party hound, sold the team, and after a while it was sold to a local group. By Year 5, that group was running out of money. The Howes were always paid on time, but other players had their paydays deferred, which caused predictable tension. Colleen, who was listed by the Aeros as a consultant in marketing, public relations, and special events, began speaking publicly about the franchise's financial problems. "It doesn't appear Gordie, Mark, and Marty will be in Houston next year," she said, before adding, "Our problem isn't with Bill Dineen. It's with ownership."

"I wish they'd leave or just shut up about it," an unidentified Aero was quoted as saying.

"Nobody said anything to us, but I'm sure guys thought that if we left, it would affect their jobs," says Mark Howe. "It was a tough situation. They were running out of money and they couldn't pay us any more."

Still, the Aeros appeared to be hanging on for the merger with the NHL, and prior to Year 6 Dineen was convinced his team would go as part of an expanded proposal, the work of Whalers president Howard Baldwin and Stingers owner Bill DeWitt, Jr. That plan, however, would be voted down by the small but virulent anti-WHA faction on the established league's board of governors, and with that vote the life was sucked out of the Aeros.

In short order, the owners contacted Howard Baldwin and said they could no longer afford the Howes. After the Red Wings made overtures about signing the Howes, and after serious negotiations broke down with the Boston Bruins, Baldwin then negotiated a deal with Colleen, making her the first female agent in the game's history, and hockey's first family moved to Hartford. The Aeros, for their part, missed a payroll early in Year 6 and were sold to another local group for $50,000. The new owners posted $130,000 to cover the payroll and immediately made brave noises about hanging around for the merger. They lasted until the end of the year, but when another merger effort imploded, the Aeros folded. The ownership group would sell thirteen player contracts to the Winnipeg Jets for half a million dollars, including Ruskowski, Preston, Lukowich, and Campbell, and those players would help Winnipeg win the final Avco Cup. Dineen was offered the head coach and GM's job in Cincinnati but ended up in Hartford when Gordie asked him to coach the Whalers. "I felt I owed him something," says Dineen, who was fired the next season but stayed in the organization as a scout and personnel director.

"It was tough," Dineen says of the Aeros' collapse. "I built that team up from nothing and I put a lot into it."

But they had themselves a time in Houston. The franchise that started with Paul Deneau's credit card would bring major-league hockey to Texas, but more importantly it provided the stage for the Howes and reconnected Gordie with the game he loved. Thirty years later, the story is a hockey legend. Gordie played with his sons for seven seasons, finally retiring when he was fifty-two. They won championships together. They fought together. They survived the WHA together. They even made it back to the NHL together. The dad and his two boys.

While we're contemplating their careers, here's another thought about the Howes. How the hell is Mark not in the Hockey Hall of Fame?

Mark and Gordie figured in literally hundreds of goals during their WHA careers, and in the league's final year they'd play in an All-Star Game with a young centreman named Wayne Gretzky. But Mark has no trouble identifying the goal he remembers best while playing with his father. In the 1975-76 league semifinal, the Aeros held a 1-0 lead over New England late in the third period of game seven with the faceoff deep in the Aeros' end. The Whalers were preparing to pull their goalie for an extra attacker, and their defence was split a little wider than usual to accommodate the extra man. Gordie took a look at the hole, looked at Mark, then prepared for the faceoff. When the puck was dropped, Gordie won the faceoff and poked the puck toward the hole, where Mark was headed at full speed. Mark gathered it in and scored on a breakaway.

The Whalers won the game 2-0.

"It was all done without a word," Mark says.

Between a father and a son, some things don't have to be said.

# CHAPTER 5

# "We had every idiot who ever played."

Glen Sonmor's original intentions with the Minnesota Fighting Saints were purely noble. In their first year, the Saints largely comprised former collegians and NHLers with a Minnesota connection who favoured a speed-and-skill game. The Saints of 1972-73 included former Minnesota high-school legend Mike Antonovich and former University of Minnesota Golden Gopher stars Keith Christiansen and Gary Gambucci. Former North Star Wayne Connelly led the team in scoring, and Ted Hampson, another ex-Star, was the captain. A story in *The Hockey News* suggested the team should change its nickname from the Fighting Saints to the Skating Saints. A year later, no such suggestion was being made.

Sonmor was pleased with the direction he'd chosen for the fledgling franchise, but a year-end fan survey after the first season made it apparent that he'd grossly misread the St. Paul market. As he would discover, fans in the Twin Cities weren't interested in seeing former high-school stars and Golden Gophers; they'd followed those players their whole careers. The prevailing sentiment was, if the Saints really wanted to grab the city's attention, they would have to go out and sign some Canadian players. To Sonmor, who earned a reputation as a fearsome fighter when he played minor pro in St. Paul, that meant one thing. And it wasn't to add more fancy pants.

"We were conscious of what sold in our market," he says.

"One of Glen's great quotes was, 'If we don't stop this fighting, we're going to have to build bigger rinks,'" says Harry Neale, the Saints' coach. "In St. Paul, the fans loved a scrap. As the league grew, most teams had that dimension. You had to have it. Of course, maybe we overdid it."

Maybe. In Year 2, Sonmor added Gordie "Machine Gun" Gallant, then signed minor-league tough guy Bill Goldthorpe for their playoff series against Houston. Goldthorpe would play just three post-season games with the Saints before he was sold to Baltimore, but he would achieve a level of renown that far exceeded his meagre talents. In Year 3, they added Jack "The Big Bopper" Carlson, Ron Busniuk, and Curt Brackenbury. In Year 4, Carlson's brothers, Jeff and Steve, joined the Saints, along with twenty-year-old St. Paul native Paul Holmgren. That team, if properly equipped, had a legitimate shot at over-running France.

"Everybody wanted to be the Philadelphia Flyers [a.k.a. the Broad Street Bullies] in those days, and Glen might have come the closest," says Saints goalie John Garrett. "In my first camp we had every idiot who ever played. It was scary."

But the seeds for the Fighting Saints were sown while they still largely comprised collegians and other nice-mannered boys. Prior to their Year 2 season, Sonmor staged a series of free-agents' camps throughout Minnesota. The old coach now says the camps were held mainly as a public-relations gesture, but at the first open tryout three brothers arrived from Virginia, Minnesota, who would put the Fighting in the Saints' nickname. In time, the Carlson brothers, who were immortalized on

The WHA Founders Club: from left, Scotty Munro, Bill Hunter, Ben Hatskin, and Gary Davidson. The picture was taken in October 1971, shortly before Munro folded the Calgary franchise. Hunter's Edmonton team and Hatskin's Winnipeg team would survive to the NHL merger. (© *Bruce Bennett Studios*)

Bobby Hull and his wife, Joanne, pose with the million-dollar bonus Hull received from the WHA for signing with the Winnipeg Jets. Forty-eight hours before the ceremony, the new league didn't have the money in place for the record contract. (© *Bruce Bennett Studios*)

In the first years especially, Hull worked tirelessly to promote the WHA. Here he signs autographs in the concourse of the Winnipeg Arena. (© *Bruce Bennett Studios*)

Harry Neale, looking sharp in his seventies' duds, took over from Glen Sonmor as the Minnesota Fighting Saints' head coach in Year 1. Neale would coach in the WHA for six years before graduating to the NHL and, ultimately, the broadcast booth. (*Larry Sexton/Hockey Hall of Fame*)

Jack Carlson, the most accomplished of the three hockey-playing brothers from Virginia, Minnesota, was called up to the Fighting Saints midway through Year 3, losing his chance to appear in the movie *Slap Shot* in the process. (*Minnesota Fighting Saints*)

The three Carlson brothers as they appeared with the Minnesota Fighting Saints before they could afford contact lenses. Steve (21) was likely the most skilled of the three brothers. Jack (20) and Jeff (22) were both heavyweight tough. (*Minnesota Fighting Saints*)

Jack Carlson in his familiar role with the Fighting Saints. Sonmor said, with the exception of John Ferguson, Carlson was the best fighter he ever saw. (© *Bruce Bennett Studios*)

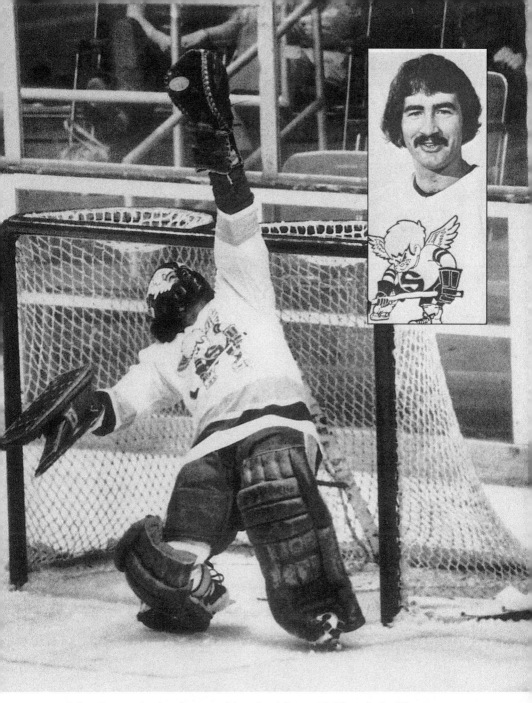

John Garrett (main photo and inset), nicknamed Cheech for his resemblance to comic Cheech Marin, played goal for four WHA teams in six seasons. Note the Plexiglas boards behind Garrett's net at the St. Paul Civic Centre. (© *Bruce Bennett Studios*, inset *Minnesota Fighting Saints*)

The Fighting Saints' Mike Walton fends off the Jets' Joe Zanussi as he charges after a loose puck. Walton led the WHA in scoring his first year in the league. Joe Daley is the Jets' goalie. (© *Bruce Bennett Studios*)

Walton checks Cleveland's Gerry Pinder at the '73-74 WHA All-Star game in St. Paul. Bobby Hull looks on in the background. The game drew over 13,000 fans and Walton scored three goals in a losing cause. (© *Bruce Bennett Studios*)

Bill Goldthorpe's career with the Fighting Saints consisted of three playoff games against the Houston Aeros, but the minor-league tough guy made a lasting impression in his brief WHA career. (*Minnesota Fighting Saints*)

Derek Sanderson in the uniform of the Boston Braves, farm team of the Bruins. He had signed a $2.6 million deal with the Philadelphia Blazers and lasted all of eight games. (© *Bruce Bennett Studios*)

celluloid as the Hanson brothers in the epic film *Slap Shot*, would become as famous as the game's greatest stars. But in 1973, little was known of them beyond their hometown.

"We knew a little about Jack but nothing about the other two," said Sonmor. "That changed in a hurry. The two best fighters I've ever seen in hockey were John Ferguson and Jack Carlson. Honestly, we should have sent them to Johnstown [the Jets, the Saints' affiliate in the North American Hockey League] the first year and brought them up in Year 2."

That, however, would have had a devastating effect on two of the brothers' film careers.

"We saw them at that first camp and they just terrorized everyone," said Neale. "So we brought them to another camp and we figured they couldn't do it again but they terrorized that camp too. Then we brought them to our main camp and it was the same story. About then we started to think we had something."

Oh, they had something all right. At the Saints camp that preceded Year 2, Neale hit on the bright idea of staging an intrasquad game between the rookies and the veterans in Mankato, Minnesota. During the contest, Mike "Shaky" Walton, whom the Saints had signed away from Boston that off-season for huge dough, became involved with Steve Carlson when big brother Jack arrived on the scene.

"Jack comes and says, 'Shaky, let him go,'" Garrett recalls. "Mike looks at him and goes, 'Fuck you.' Jack goes *wham*, and breaks his nose. They beat us like 10-1."

Neale now says that game was an incredible bonding experience for his team. On the way back to the Twin Cities, the Saints got roaring drunk and stumbled off the bus arm in arm. At the end of training camp, Jack, Steve, and Jeff were sent to play senior hockey in Marquette, Michigan.

The Saints, meanwhile, plugged on with Walton as their star, their drawing card, and the perfect man to lead the lunatics who made up their team. One of the few Alan Eagleson clients to sign with the WHA, Walton used to work with Bobby Orr at a hockey school in Orillia, Ontario, that Sonmor and Neale frequented regularly. The Saints would eventually make a half-hearted attempt to sign Orr, but prior to the 1973–74 season they pried Walton loose from the Boston Bruins with a three-year deal worth $450,000.

Walton's nickname, "Shaky," remains one of the most appropriate monikers in hockey history. On the ice, he was an explosive offensive player who seemed to be moving a million different directions at once. Like most WHAers, he also had a huge slapshot, and even if he didn't apply himself on a consistent basis, he showed up enough nights to lead the league in scoring his first year with 57 goals and 60 assists. Off the ice, meanwhile, the Shaky handle was equally apt. Walton, who'd been groomed as the next great star of the Toronto Maple Leafs in the late 1960s, had a well-developed sense of self-esteem. Throw in a predilection for bizarre behaviour, and it ensured things were seldom dull around the Saints.

"He was one of the game's great natural talents but a psychiatrist's dream," says Garrett. "Eagleson used to say Punch Imlach drove him nuts in Toronto. He was nuts long before Punch got a hold of him."

"He was a talented guy," says Neale. "I had a soft spot in my heart for Walton even though he made it hard to coach the team. You had to give him the credit card, but then you had to lay the law down to someone else. The players were actually very good about it. Pretty well everyone knew that if we wanted to get the best out of Shaky, he had to get preferential treatment. He lived about three blocks from me, and once a month I'd call and say, 'I'm picking you up, Shaky,' and we'd have a little chat. I'd tell him, 'You've got to come close to toeing the line.' He wouldn't give a shit some nights, but the nights he did, watch out, because he could do it all."

It was those other nights, however, that secured the Walton legend. During a game in Edmonton, Walton, who lived for breakaways, was in the process of breaking in alone on the Edmonton net when teammate Gordie Gallant took a penalty behind the play. Walton immediately began screaming at Gallant and followed him to the penalty box, berating him every step of the way. That was his first mistake.

His second was still to be around when Gallant got out of the box. After serving his sentence, Gallant made a beeline to the Saints' bench and without breaking stride jumped at Walton and began to throw punches.

"The referee came over and said, 'Harry, I've got to give you a misconduct,'" says Neale. "I said, 'As far as I know, it's not a penalty when two guys on the same team fight.' He said, 'You might be right there.'"

Then there was this tale from Winnipeg. Walton had enjoyed a big night against the Jets and an even bigger night after the game. The next morning, the Saints were bused to practice at the St. James Civic Centre, which held a swimming pool adjacent to the rink. Walton arrived still glowing, and after the workout he decided to provide his teammates with some laughs. He skated off the ice, opened the door to the pool, and in full equipment jumped in the shallow end as his teammates roared. Walton began splashing around the pool and they roared some more. Then the splashing became more frantic and the laughter stopped. His equipment had become waterlogged and Walton was going down.

Coughing and spitting, he was fished out of the pool by his teammates. But that was only the beginning of his problems. This, remember, was Winnipeg in the dead of winter, and the Saints had arrived in their hockey gear. Walton had to make his way back to the team bus in his drenched equipment. By the time he took his seat, he resembled a Captain High Liner frozen fish stick. When his teeth stopped chattering thirty minutes

later, he called for Saints trainer Don Niederkorn and instructed,
"Nieder, this stuff better be dry by tomorrow or you're not
getting a cent from me at the end of the year."

In Year 2, then, the journey began with Walton, the flaky
star, a few holdovers from Sonmor's team in Year 1, and Murder
Incorporated. The Saints would finish second in the Western
Division in Year 2 behind Houston with 90 points. After
dusting off Edmonton in the first round of the playoffs, they
met the mighty Aeros in a Western final that was memorable
for (a) the huge crowds in St. Paul, and (b) the WHA debut of
Bill Goldthorpe.

Sonmor, for reasons that are still unclear, felt he needed
another tough guy at the end of the season and asked his father-
in-law, John Mitchell, GM of the Johnstown Jets, if he'd recom-
mend anyone. Goldthorpe, the real-life inspiration for *Slap Shot*'s
Ogie Oglethorpe, had accumulated a hard-earned 287 penalty
minutes in just fifty-four games with Syracuse of the North
American Hockey League and drew an unqualified endorsement
from Mitchell. Say this for the man, he knew his goons.

Goldthorpe was just twenty when he joined the Fighting
Saints that spring, but his reputation had long since been established in hockey circles. He'd played his junior in Thunder Bay,
Ontario, and was arrested in his hometown of Homepayne one
summer for his part in a fight. During hockey season, he was
allowed to serve his sentence in Thunder Bay, which meant, for
practices and games, he was released on a day pass.

"He was already a legend at that point," says Dave Hanson,
who played junior against Goldthorpe. "There were stories he
was assigned a police escort to the games. I kind of hit it off with
Goldie, if anyone could say they were friends with him. But I
never got too comfortable with him. He was kind of like a
Doberman. You never knew when he'd turn on you."

That much seems true about Goldthorpe, who worked as a
gravedigger one summer. Paul Stewart, the former WHA player

and NHL referee who started his career as a tough guy in the NAHL, was playing in Binghamton one year when Goldthorpe arrived on the team.

"We're at the team Christmas party," remembers Stewart, "and he comes up to me and says, 'I'm the tough guy here,' and sucker-punches me. I get up, we go outside and fight, and he bites me. I had to go to the hospital for tetanus shots."

The long-time Vancouver Canucks scout Ron Delorme roomed with Goldthorpe in Denver and says it was like rooming with Kato, Inspector Clouseau's combative manservant in the old *Pink Panther* movies. "He always wanted to wrestle. It didn't matter where or when. He'd jump out from behind a door or a closet and I'd have to wrestle him."

And he wasn't particular about who he wrestled. Jack McCartan, a native of St. Paul and the hero of the U.S.'s gold-medal win at the 1960 Winter Olympics, was winding his career down as the Fighting Saints' backup goalie and assistant coach when Goldthorpe was assigned as his roommate. One Saturday morning he awoke and found Goldthorpe already watching cartoons. After an hour, McCartan, who was in his late thirties at the time, asked if he could find some other programming.

"I tell you what, McCartney [sic]," Goldthorpe answered. "I'll wrestle you, and the winner gets to pick the show."

The biggest problem with any attempt to recount Goldthorpe's remarkable career, however, is separating fact from fiction. When he was released from Baltimore, for example, a story went around that he'd hung Blades star Gary Veneruzzo over a hotel balcony for insulting him at a team function. Neale says no; after the Saints sold Goldthorpe to Baltimore, he got a call from Blades coach Johnny Wilson that went something like this. "Who the fuck did you send us? He just put a bear hug on Veneruzzo and broke two of his ribs."

Goldthorpe, for his part, says the incident followed a team outing in which a brawl had taken place in a Baltimore restaurant and some bent-nose types had followed him back to his hotel. Goldthorpe tried to enlist the aid of Veneruzzo, his offer was declined, and, naturally, a fight broke out that Goldthorpe did not lose.

"Because of *Slap Shot*, everyone wants to tell a story about me doing something crazy," Goldthorpe now says. "If I dropped a beer by accident, the story would come out I threw it against a wall. I did a lot of things, but not as many as people think. I guess now that I'm older the stories are funny."

You might say. Just prior to the playoffs, Sonmor went to pick up Goldthorpe, the new addition to his arsenal, at the Twin Cities' airport and couldn't believe what he saw. Given Goldthorpe's reputation, the Saints' GM was expecting a monster. Instead, he saw a wiry little guy in a muscle shirt – maybe five-foot-ten, maybe 170 pounds – and possessed of a magnificent blonde afro.

"I thought, Who the hell is that?" Sonmor says.

He would know soon enough.

In addition to everything else, Goldthorpe was a workout fanatic and a practitioner of martial arts. Before practices with the Saints, he would walk into the dressing room while the other players were putting their gear on, pull out a set of nun-chaks, and perform a Bruce Lee routine in the centre of the room. Then he would put the nunchaks away and without a word begin to get dressed for practice.

During games, Goldthorpe also liked to work out between periods. While still in full equipment, he'd do clean-and-jerks with 225-pound weights.

"People think he didn't exist," says Garrett. "Oh, he was real all right. I mean, it was scary. People watch *Slap Shot* and they go, 'That never happened.' But it happened."

Goldthorpe would dress in three games in the 1973-74 playoffs, picking up 25 penalty minutes and getting tossed in game four of the Houston series. Sonmor recalls Goldthorpe kept up a running dialogue with Houston's Gordie Howe. He never did confront Howe physically, but at one point advised, "You can't play forever, old man, and when you retire, I'm going to get your kids."

On another occasion, Goldthorpe started in on Howe from the bench. "I'm going to fucking kill you," he screamed. "I'm going to cut your head off." Howe then lowered his Clint Eastwood stare at the Saints' bench, at which point the mild-mannered Keith Christiansen, who was sitting beside Goldthorpe, exclaimed, "It wasn't me, Gordie! It wasn't me!"

On still another occasion, Goldthorpe was sent to serve a major for Walton, who'd been kicked out of the game for his part in a scrap with Aeros defenceman John Schella. Neale was peeved that Schella had gotten his star ejected and instructed Goldthorpe that if the blueliner was on the ice when his penalty was up, he was to draw him into a fight. Five minutes later an enormous ruckus broke out, with Goldthorpe and Schella, who knew each other from Thunder Bay, swapping knuckles. At the end of the fight, referee Bill Friday gave Goldthorpe an extra two minutes.

"For what?" screamed Neale.

"Harry, he left his stick and gloves in the penalty box when he went after Schella," Friday said.

The Saints actually took a 2-1 lead against Houston in a series that would mark the high point of their franchise. Game three in St. Paul drew 16,412 fans, and game four drew 17,211. Neale recalls the turning point of the series came in game four when the Civic Center's organist played "The Old Grey Mare" as Howe skated on the ice.

"About ten minutes later, he didn't look like an old grey mare," Neale says. "Gordie had scored a goal, and our guys had these cuts and bruises they couldn't explain. We didn't win another game the rest of the series."

The Houston Aeros would close out the Saints in game six in Minnesota. Before the game, Walton had made arrangements with one of the Civic Center's workers to leave his car parked on the ramp behind the Zamboni, because, as Neale says, "Shaky couldn't park where everyone else parked." After the traditional handshakes, Walton skated off the ice, out the Zamboni gate, and into his car. His teammates found him drinking at the bar half an hour later, still in his equipment.

If the WHA were ever going to take hold in the Twin Cities, it would have been with those playoffs, but the Saints would never again draw the same kinds of crowds in St. Paul. The team continued to be an interesting mix of thugs and real players. They also had success on the ice. But they never captured the full attention of their market and could not attract much more than eight or nine thousand fans to their splendid new rink.

Still, they tried. Midway through the following season, Year 3, Jack Carlson, who'd been promoted to Johnstown, the Saints' minor-league affiliate in the North American Hockey League, was starting to draw considerable attention for his unique combination of production (27 goals in fifty games) and destruction (248 penalty minutes). With Carlson's notoriety growing, Neale was dispatched by Sonmor to scout a game in Utica.

"We were playing in Cleveland and we had a couple of days off," Neale recalls. "Sonmor said, 'Why don't you go down to Utica and see Johnstown play?' So I head over there, and I see these three guys wearing black safety glasses and terrorizing the other team and the fans. They won the game, and two of the three of them end up in the stands fighting with fans at the end of the game. They got arrested and I had to go post $200 for their bail. [Former Maple Leaf] Brian Conacher was the coach in Utica, and he was so pissed off. He wanted them to stay in jail."

Carlson, who, with his long blond hair, bore an uncanny resemblance to tennis star Steffi Graf, joined the Saints midway through the season and made an immediate impact. Literally. In his third appearance with the Saints he helped ignite a bench-clearing brawl with Phoenix when he duked it out with the

Roadrunners' John Hughes. The next week, a fan in Cleveland dumped a beer on Neale's head, and Carlson led the Saints' charge into the stands.

Before Jack Carlson was promoted to the Saints, his teammates on the Johnstown Jets included his two brothers, Jeff and Steve, Dave "Killer" Hanson, former Bowdoin college star Ned Dowd, and goalie Louis Levasseur. The Jets' general manager was Sonmor's father-in-law, John Mitchell. Early that season, Dowd's sister Nancy arrived in Johnstown and spent some time around the team. There, she was introduced to an ensemble who would inspire the characters in *Slap Shot*, which, as every cinephile knows, is the greatest movie ever made.

Nancy Dowd was a screenwriter who later won an Oscar for *Coming Home*, starring Jane Fonda, Jon Voight, and Bruce Dern. Hanson can't remember how long she was around in the 1974–75 season, but she stayed in Johnstown long enough to capture the essence of minor-league life and the bizarre world of the Jets.

Mitchell would become McGrath, the Charlestown Chiefs general manager, played in the movie by the brilliant Strother Martin. Ned Dowd became Ned Braden, played by Michael Ontkean, and in one of those moments of verisimilitude that distinguishes the classic movies, Dowd himself played Ogie Oglethorpe. Levasseur, the goalie, inspired the creation of Chiefs keeper Denis Lemieux. And the Carlson brothers and Hanson became the Hanson brothers, right down to the black safety glasses and the slotcars.

"We were kind of aware what was going on, but we weren't overly concerned about it," said Hanson. "Nancy Dowd was more like a fly on the wall. She came out drinking with us a couple of times and just watched us do our thing. But I can tell you that movie is more real life than fiction."

The Jets, in fact, provided Dowd with all the material she'd need for her script. The Carlsons really did wear the black safety glasses, because they couldn't afford contacts, and really did race slotcars in their spare time. Ned Dowd really was a collegian trying to make it in a brutally tough league. Levasseur really was something of a flake. At one Jets team party, he outfitted himself in the host's fishing gear, put a bar of soap in a fishbowl, and spent two hours trying to hook it with a lure.

A few months after Nancy Dowd left Johnstown, Hanson was preparing for his pre-game nap when his doorbell rang.

"There was this guy there, standing on the step, who said he was Paul Newman," Hanson recalls. "I go, 'Right.' Then I looked, and it really was Paul Newman. He said, 'I've got some guys here. Do you mind if we look at your place?' I said, 'Fine, but I'm going back to bed. I've got a game tonight.' Then he said, 'One other thing. Do you have any beer in the fridge? We'd like to watch the [auto] races.' I said, 'Help yourself.' That's how we met. It was about then I started to think there might be a movie after all."

*Slap Shot* started filming in the spring of 1975, when the eldest Carlson was toiling for the Fighting Saints. The producers' original intention was to use actors to play the roles in Nancy Dowd's script, and in addition to Newman, they considered casting Nick Nolte, Peter Strauss, and Donny Most of *Happy Days* fame. Of course, Nolte, Strauss, and Most could barely stand on skates, problematic for a hockey movie. According to Hanson, Nancy Dowd asked the producers to go back to Johnstown and give some of the Jets themselves a shot. And thus the Hanson brothers were born.

"If you were going to go by history, it should have been Jack, Jeff, and myself playing the Hansons, or Jack, Jeff, and Steve playing the Hansons and me playing Killer Carlson [another character in the movie]," says Hanson. "Steve was more of a skill player, but Jack epitomized the Hanson brothers. He was one of the toughest fighters in the game. He could take a punch and, believe me, he could throw. It was bad luck he got called up, but good luck for me."

Jeff and Steve Carlson and Dave Hanson played the three brothers who ran roughshod over the Charlestown Chiefs' opposition and were blindly devoted to player-coach Reg Dunlop, played by Newman. Over the years, the characters have become iconic figures in the game. The Carlsons and Hanson also made a tidy living touring and making personal appearances as the brothers for Anheuser-Busch before they scaled back their schedule. They still appear as the brothers in the oldtimers' circuit to this day.

"We were travelling more than when we were playing," says Hanson. "The thing was just so popular, and it took on a life of its own. I still can't believe it when I think about it.

"We had no idea what we were getting into. We were nineteen and twenty, in our second year of pro. To us, when the season ended, you went home, played softball, and drank beer. Then they started filming, and to be honest it got boring. It was like a job. We'd sit around all day. At one point, Jeff, Steve, and I said we've had enough and we all took off. Then they got a hold of Steve and said, 'Get those guys back here or we'll sue.' We came back and finished, but we still had no idea what we were getting into."

But they started to enjoy life on the set. Newman, who would drink a beer, took a liking to the three hockey players and regularly entertained them. The great actor loved Coors beer, but it wasn't available in Johnstown, so he had a hundred cases shipped to the movie set. Newman also accompanied the two Carlsons and Hanson to their favourite haunts in Johnstown and would stay until he was recognized. Once his cover was blown, he'd quietly leave.

Jeff Carlson dated Newman's daughter Susan, who appears in the movie as the pharmacist who dates Denis Lemieux. Again, art imitates life.

"We had no idea what we were doing," Hanson said. "We just knew the food and the beer was free. And they were paying us to goof around with Paul Newman. Who wouldn't love that?"

The summer the movie wrapped up, Hanson got married and invited Newman to the ceremony. There was a conflict in Newman's schedule, but he telegrammed Hanson and invited him to call when he was in California. A couple of months later the Carlsons and Hanson had to travel to Hollywood for voice-overs for the movie and Newman threw them a party at his mansion.

"He was just a real solid, regular guy," says Hanson.

Following their epic encounter with Houston in Year 2, the Saints met the New England Whalers in the first round of the Year 3 playoffs in an equally memorable series. The two teams split the first two games in New England, but Neale says the series turned in the Saints' game-two overtime loss when he put out a line of Jack Carlson, Bill Butters, and his latest hellion, Curt Brackenbury. Brackenbury, according to Bill Friday, used to wrap his hands in foil – à la the Hansons in *Slap Shot* – then wrap them in tape. Whenever Friday asked him about this practice, Brackenbury would tell him, "They're so sore, Billy. I don't even know if I can play." The Saints' George Morrison eventually ratted out Brackenbury, and the WHA put in a rule, later adopted by the NHL, that called for a match penalty if a player had tape or foil or brass knuckles or anything similar on his hands during a game.

"They really should have called it the Brackenbury rule," Friday says.

When Neale started the three sluggers, famously named the BBC Line, in game two, he achieved predictable results. New England coach Jack Kelley started a line centred by Larry Pleau, and "the puck wasn't this far out of the referee's hand when our three guys jumped their three guys," says Neale. "Larry Pleau still stops me once a year and says, 'The BBC Line? You prick!'"

Pleau, now general manager of the St. Louis Blues, still has a tape of Whalers play-by-play man Bob Neumeier calling the fight, which lasted twenty minutes and went from bench to bench. At one point, the Whalers' Nick Fotiu, a former Golden Gloves champ and one of the most feared fighters in the WHA, grabbed Saints defenceman Rick Smith's jersey and started squeezing. Smith passed out. "We thought he was dead," says Garrett.

Following the melee, the two teams shared a charter back to Minnesota – the WHA rules stated that the losing team had to board first – and the Saints would win three of the next four games before they were ousted by Quebec in the next round. Neale, however, will always remember the series with the Whalers for reasons other than his team's victory.

Heading into the first two games of the series in Hartford, the Saints' coach, who wasn't exactly a stern taskmaster, imposed a midnight curfew on his team for one of the few times that season.

"I said to the players, 'These are the playoffs. We've got to get off to a good start.' All that bullshit. I did it about five times a year, just to send a message, and this time I called the rooms. Mike McMahon was rooming with Gordie Gallant, and he answered the phone. 'Where's Gordie?' 'Harry, he's not here.' 'Well, he knows the drill. Tell him he's fined $100 and I'll see him tomorrow.'"

About an hour later, Neale was fast asleep in a room he shared with Jack McCartan when McMahon called to tell him Gallant had returned and he wasn't happy with Neale's ruling. A minute later, Gallant started pounding on the door. Neale thought about the situation, reasoned he'd always gotten along with Gallant, and opened the door.

Bad decision.

"I open the door and, *whack*, he knocks me back in the room," Neale says. "I don't know how, but I ended up in the hallway in my underwear, and the door got locked behind me. I hear Jack in the room, 'Get in here! Get in here!' and all this banging and crashing. Then everybody came out of their rooms and filled up the corridor. Finally it stopped. Gordie walked by me and headed to his room."

The next day, Neale and Sonmor met and reluctantly agreed Gallant had to be released. Gallant told the press that the confrontation had been building all season, fuelled, in large part, by Neale's habit of indulging his stars.

"He gives the superstars preferential treatment, then takes it out on the little guys," Gallant said, which suggests not all the Saints understood Neale's handling of Walton.

"I've seen Gordie Gallant since and he apologized," says Neale. "We laugh about it. I tell him, 'For a tough guy, you couldn't even knock out a fat coach with a sucker punch.'"

In the summer of 1975, the Saints received considerable publicity for their largely fictional attempts to land Bobby Orr. A story in *The Hockey News* breathlessly reported that the Saints were preparing an offer that included a $1-million signing bonus and "three or four times Bobby Hull's salary." Sonmor was quoted as saying the Saints had a fifty-fifty shot at signing Orr. As late as September, a *Hockey News* headline read, "WHA WANTS ORR – BUT WILL THEY PAY?"

The stories, of course, were planted by Alan Eagleson in a clumsy attempt to drive up the superstar's price with Boston. Orr would play just ten games with the Bruins that season before he was shipped to Chicago. But at least one person found the Saints' story believable.

"My contract was up and my wife was pregnant," says John Garrett. "We heard rumours that the owners were in trouble, but they were negotiating with Bobby Orr for all this money.

How could they be in trouble? I went to Eagleson and asked him, 'Should I buy a house?' He says, 'Sure, this thing is solid.' So I signed this contract and bought a house. I should have known better, because it was too good to be true."

"Too good to be true" is a good description of that last, fateful season of the Fighting Saints. In the off-season they signed Johnny McKenzie, late of the Vancouver Blazers, and Dave Keon, who, like so many former Leafs stars, had fled Harold Ballard's zoo in Toronto.

Neale still regards Keon as the greatest all-round player ever to wear the Maple Leaf, and that season did little to change his opinion of the brilliant centreman. "I knew Dave, I knew he was pissed off at the Leafs, and I knew his contract was up," says Neale. "I said to Sonmor, 'We should try to get him.' He was the best forechecker I've ever seen. Ricky Ley tells this story of when he was playing with Hartford. Keon was forechecking, and Ley had this talent for pivoting. As he came out of his spin, Keon was in his face and he started to laugh, 'You thought that was going to work?'"

Unfortunately Keon and McKenzie joined a team that was strong everywhere but at the bank. Sonmor now says the ownership group was underfunded and had neither the inclination nor the resources to cover the team's losses. The Saints continued to draw eight to nine thousand fans per game, but it wasn't enough to sustain the franchise, and that soon became apparent to the players.

"By December it was obvious something was wrong," Garrett says. "Keon and McKenzie would start showing up late for practice. They'd go and cash their cheques, and I mean they'd get cash for their cheques. Of course, there was only enough money to cover a couple of them, so by the time we got to the bank, forget it."

"I have the softest spot in my heart for that team, because we had guys who could have gone to the NHL or any other team in the WHA, but they stuck it out," says Neale. "We played six weeks without getting paid and got paid once in eight weeks. The only time we lost was on the first and the fifteenth, when we didn't get paid, and guys got depressed. I used to tell Sonmor, 'We have to give them meal money. I can get them to play as long as they have meal money.'"

A look at the Saints' final season bears this out. On December 31, the Saints' payroll wasn't met, and on their next payday, January 15, they lost to San Diego, then to Phoenix the next night. From January 25 to 31, they went on a four-game winning streak before dropping four straight beginning on February 1. Another three-game winning streak followed, from February 10 to 12 (yes, they played three games in three nights), and on February 14 they lost to Phoenix. The Saints played their final game on February 25, a 2-1 loss to San Diego, but those final two months are one of the most remarkable chapters in the WHA's remarkable history.

Wayne Belisle, who led the Saints' ownership group, at one point offered the players limited partnerships in the franchise. "They can become investors and part owners with little personal risk," the Saints' president said. Predictably, none of the players took him up on his offer. The Saints were also told a group from Chicago was going to buy the team. Then the Teamsters were going to buy the team. Then it was a group from Alaska who ran an oil pipeline. They may as well have told the players Aristotle Onassis was going to step up and buy the team, because the Saints kept playing and no one was paying. Walton's teammates believed that his contract had been paid in full by January 1, but other than that everyone was in the same boat.

"When we were folding, we'd have a meeting every day," says Garrett. "Are we going to keep on playing? Do we go on strike? We had a bunch of home games, and they wanted the gates. We weren't going to get paid unless they got those gates. So we kept on playing.

"We were playing unbelievable at the time. We couldn't lose, because the guys were so loose they didn't care. Guys were turning pop machines upside down and shaking the change out. They'd steal everything they could out of the dressing rooms. When I look back at that stuff, I still don't believe it."

Neither can Neale, who had to use his considerable powers of imagination to keep the team motivated. In early January, the Saints were in Cincinnati when Neale got the bright idea that his team wouldn't take the warmup.

"I told them, 'We're just going out there for the opening faceoff and we'll kill them,'" says Neale. "They look at me and go, 'What a great idea!' The next thing you know, they're knocking on the door for us to come out for the warmup. I tell them, 'I can't get these guys to warm up. They haven't been paid. They're pissed off.' Then the DeWitts [the Stingers' owners] come to the door. They said, 'You've got to come out. This is one of our biggest crowds of the season.'

"Then Bill Friday tries to get us to come out. Finally, we go out, and within the first minute Cincy scores on the first shot. I remember on the bench telling our guys, 'This is only going to be funny if we win.'"

The Saints, of course, won the game 7-4.

Later on, the Saints were preparing for a lengthy road trip and Neale didn't have the all-important meal money to pass around to the players. Knowing this might be the final straw, he made a hurried call to Belisle. Belisle, who had ownership in a couple of bars around the Twin Cities, said he'd see what he could do, and as the team was boarding its flight he came sprinting toward the gate with a big brown paper bag in his hands.

"He'd gone around to all these bars and stuffed fives and tens and twenties in the bag," Neale says. "He just passed us the bag and said, 'There, that should be enough.' So Glen and I got on the plane, flipped our tray down, and started counting out piles of twenties. All the time there's this lady looking over her seat at us.

"About five minutes later, the captain comes back and asks, 'Could you tell me what you gentlemen are doing?' We told him we were the Minnesota Fighting Saints and we were going on a road trip, and the guy breaks out laughing. He said that lady in front of us thought we'd just robbed a bank."

By the end of February, however, there'd be no more laughter for the Saints. Henry Boucha, the team's first draft pick, had already decamped for the NHL with former Bruins defenceman Rick Smith. In late February, Belisle sold the team to a Minnesota group for a buck, but the new owners backed out when they were informed they had to come up with over half a million dollars in missed payroll alone.

After the February 25 game in San Diego, the players voted to withhold their services for a game in Cincinnati three days later. Members of the Stingers arrived at the Riverfront Coliseum expecting to play the Saints and couldn't understand why the Houston Aeros were in the building.

"It's over," Belisle said.

Well, yes and no. The next year, Nick Mileti moved the Cleveland Crusaders into St. Paul and resurrected the Saints. That team, alas, ceased operations in mid-January. Louis Levasseur, the goalie who inspired the Denis Lemieux character in *Slap Shot*, was the Saints' goalie that season and played out of his head. Sadly, the Saints had folded by the time Levasseur was named to the All-Star Team, but he still paid his own way to the All-Star Game and was named the Eastern Conference's player of the game.

"It was like a horror movie," Garrett says. "You had the Minnesota Folding Saints. Then you had Return of the Minnesota Folding Saints."

Neale, meanwhile, would catch on as the coach in New England and take many of his former players when the Saints II died in its sleep.

"That was one of the best ways to improve your team in the WHA," he said. "You waited until someone folded then you'd grab their players. We got Keon, Jack and Steve Carlson, Johnny McKenzie, and Mike Antonovich that way."

Garrett, for his part, was placed in one of the WHA's many dispersal drafts and picked up by Toronto. The next year, the Toros moved to Birmingham and the All-Star goalie had to renegotiate his dream contract.

He sold his house in St. Paul later that year and, of course, took a loss. Garrett also had a $20,000 bonus in his contract for thirty wins. When the Saints folded, he had twenty-eight.

# CHAPTER 6

# "You just saw things in the WHA you never saw anywhere else."

He probably didn't think it would be an issue when he joined the WHA, but in addition to his many other personality quirks Mike Walton was deathly afraid of spiders, cockroaches, and anything else that crawled and had six or more legs. Sadly, this phobia qualified as something of an occupational hazard for Shaky, because the new league, in the early years at least, played in places that did not discourage the presence of insects.

The Sam Houston Arena, for instance, built in 1937 and famous for its Friday-night wrestling cards, was fairly typical of the first generation of WHA rinks. Owner Paul Deneau invested enough money to bring it up to code and even installed Plexiglas in place of the chicken wire that was still in use in many of the old rinks. "I thought it was okay," says Dineen.

Still, no one was mistaking it for Madison Square Garden.

"We used to have cockroach contests in the dressing room," says John Garrett. "We'd be putting our equipment on, and a cockroach always got in your skates or your sweater. If you got a really big one, you'd hang it from a skate lace in the middle of the dressing room. Then the other guys would try to get a bigger one. There was no money involved. We just did it for the honour."

Which was funny to everyone except Walton. During one road trip, the Saints played in Houston before taking off immediately for Baltimore. The accepted WHA procedure after a game in Houston was to shake your equipment vigorously to dislodge any unwanted guests, who could, if left unattended, multiply and eat your brain. Walton, sadly, forgot this safety precaution, which caused some excitement when he took his skates out of his bag in Baltimore.

"I was in the coaches' room and I heard this horrible scream coming from the dressing room," says Harry Neale. "I thought, Oh my god, someone's cut their hand off. Then I see this cockroach coming out of our dressing room and I figured out what had happened.

"I think the cockroach made the rest of the road trip with us and he didn't ask for a per diem so we kept him around."

The pioneers of the new league would experience many such indignities in the WHA's seven-year existence. While they were grateful for the opportunity, to say nothing of the paycheques, NHL veterans who'd lived the life in The Show would often look at their surroundings and ask the great existential question, "Just what the hell am I doing here?"

Some of them never received a satisfactory answer. But the journeymen and minor-leaguers endured the league's more unusual aspects with patience and humour, because they knew the WHA was infinitely superior to the alternative.

"I wasn't like Keon, McKenzie, or Walton," says Dave Hanson. "I had nothing to compare it to. I just thought this was the way things were, and it was a great adventure. We had a lot of fun."

One of the WHA's biggest sources of amusement was its buildings. In time, the rebels could boast a series of new arenas that were years ahead of the NHL's and foreshadowed the great steel-and-glass mausoleums of today. There was the new St. Paul Civic Center. The Oilers moved into Northlands Coliseum midway through Year 3. The Indianapolis Racers played in the magnificent new Market Square Arena. Nick Mileti would build a new facility for the Cleveland Crusaders in Richfield that, at the time, was the most luxurious in hockey. Cincinnati and New England would also move into new buildings. But over the first couple of years, the league was jammed into a collection of dusty old pre-war rinks that, while not without their own charms, fell somewhat short of big-league.

"You just saw things in the WHA you never saw anywhere else," says Paul Shmyr.

And Shmyr knows whereof he speaks. The defenceman played in all seven years of the WHA, his first four in Cleveland as the Crusaders' captain. In his first two seasons, the Crusaders played out of the old Cleveland Arena in an area of town that was scarier than *Nightmare on Elm Street*. Five Crusaders had their cars stolen out of the parking lot at the Arena, and two of them, Wayne Muloin and Tom Edur, lost new Thunderbirds on the same night. Steve Thomas, the Crusaders' trainer, was mugged three times one winter. A would-be thief demanded Thomas's watch. "They got that last week," Thomas answered.

"It was a war zone," says Shmyr. "You didn't take your helmet off going from your car to the rink for practice."

"If you didn't get mugged during that first year, they didn't think that much of you," says Gerry Cheevers, the Crusaders' goalie.

Inside, it wasn't much better. Like a number of the old WHA rinks, the Cleveland Arena featured chicken wire instead of Plexiglas. As every WHA player knew, chicken wire had two distinct disadvantages: (1) You could pour beer through it, and (2) it produced some very strange bounces.

"There were two standard lines when you were getting beer

dumped on you," Shmyr says. "The first one was, 'If you're going to pour beer on me at least hit me in the mouth.' The second one was, 'Hey, that isn't my brand.'"

But the wire also gave the Crusaders a clear home-ice advantage. Neale says when you played there only a couple of times a year, fundamentals such as dump-ins and hard-arounds became a complete mystery to the visiting team. The savvy Cheevers, meanwhile, became a master at reading dump-ins off the mesh.

"It was like watching Yastrzemski play the Green Monster at Fenway," Garrett says of Cheevers.

"There wasn't much to it," Cheevers shrugs. "When the puck hit the screen, it would just drop."

At the other end of the ice, the Crusaders' Gary Jarrett was equally adept at reading the caroms and ricochets in the offensive zone. Jarrett recorded 40 goals and 79 points in the Crusaders' first year and 31 goals and 70 points in Year 2. However, when the Crusaders moved to their splendid new home in Richfield, and away from the chicken wire, Jarrett's totals fell to 41, then 33 points, and he retired after Year 4.

Jarrett, mind you, was probably the only player sad to see the Crusaders move in Year 3 into their new $20-million palace in the Cleveland suburbs. Widely described as the finest indoor facility in North America, the Coliseum had a seating capacity of just under twenty thousand, private boxes, a Jumbotron, and a fancy-schmancy restaurant long before those amenities were the industry norms.

"It was the nicest rink by far in all of hockey, and it compares to anything they've built today," says Shmyr.

There were, however, a few problems. The roads into the Coliseum, for starters, were unable to handle the traffic it created. Opening night featured a Frank Sinatra concert and a massive traffic jam in which ticket holders, dressed in tuxes and formal gowns, simply abandoned their cars on the highway miles away and hiked to the Coliseum in their evening wear.

The Crusaders' first game was scheduled the next night, but it had to be postponed because the new rink's ice plant malfunctioned.

"It took us two days to open," says Neale, then with the Fighting Saints. "We came out for the warmup and the ice wasn't ready. We went back to our dressing room. They said, 'It's fixed.' We came back out and it wasn't fixed. We tried warming up three times before they finally cancelled the game."

But the biggest problem with the Coliseum, and the problem that ultimately sank the Crusaders, was its location. Mileti, who'd been feuding with Cleveland city council, built his Taj Mahal in the suburb of Richfield, forty-five minutes from Cleveland, convinced the city would eventually grow that way. But, as Shmyr so eloquently puts it, "It was in the middle of nowhere. And it still is."

The Gund family would eventually sell the Coliseum in 1999 to the Trust for Public Land for $7.45 million, and the site is now a park. The Crusaders, for their part, managed to draw the same seven to eight thousand who had gone to the old Cleveland Arena, but they looked lost in their cavernous new home. Mileti sold the team before the start of Year 4. By the end of that year, the Crusaders were missing payrolls, Cheevers obtained his release and returned to Boston, and Shmyr and his teammates wore black arm bands to protest ownership's attempt to buy the NHL's Kansas City Scouts.

The Crusaders, who'd started so promisingly in their hovel of a rink, folded after the season ended.

The Cleveland Arena, mind you, was just one of the quirky old barns you could visit in the WHA. Houston we've heard about. The L.A. Sports Arena was a dark, dingy cave. Varsity Arena in Toronto wasn't much better. The Oilers played their first couple of seasons in the Edmonton Garden, which featured a three-tiered players' bench. When players came off the ice they would climb up to the third tier, then move their way down to the lower rungs as their next shift approached. In theory that worked fine, but if someone lost their place or coaches were trying to match lines on the fly, "all hell could break loose," says Neale, who adds, "The other beauty of Edmonton was you could watch the game from the best seat in the house if you were benched."

Then there was the Chicago Amphitheater. The Cougars, who were counting on a new building, spent their first three seasons playing in the decrepit nine-thousand-seat bandbox located in the less-than-picturesque south side of Chicago hard against the stockyards. Fans of irony should note Bobby Hull used to show his prize cattle near the Amphitheater when he played with the Blackhawks.

"Chicago could have handled two teams, but the new rink [in the suburb of Rosemount] came in late," says Cougars goalie Dave Dryden, who assumed ownership of the Cougars with teammates Pat Stapleton and Ralph Backstrom when the Kaisers, the original owners, pulled out of the team. "The Amphitheater wasn't built for hockey. I'm not sure what it was built for."

But it was not without its quaint charms. The visitors' radio booth, for example, hung right over the net at one end, which encouraged a certain alertness among the league's play-by-play men.

"You had to be sharp or you'd catch a slapshot on the melon," said Bob Neumeier, then the Whalers' play-by-play man. "I felt that helped me get in the game."

The ice surface at the Amphitheater was also suspended over the floor of the building, which, when skated upon, created an eerie, hollow sound.

"I remember being the first guy on the ice for practice," says Mark Howe. "I stepped on the ice and it made this cracking sound like you hear on a lake. The place was empty, and it just echoed around the whole building. It was the neatest sound. Every time we went to Chicago, I tried to get on the ice first so I could hear it again."

"It was weird," says Garrett. "But if you listened closely, it helped you read the play, because you could tell who was coming with speed and where he was coming from."

Reading the play in Chicago was important, because you couldn't see it. Dryden reports that goalies had trouble picking up the puck because the Amphitheater was so dark. One year, in an attempt to spruce up the joint, player-coach Pat Stapleton had the home team's locker room painted bright white. "That only made things worse," says Dryden. "You'd sit in this bright dressing room, your pupils would open wide, then you'd go out to this dark rink and you had trouble seeing. After a while our dressing room went back to normal and we made the visitors' room bright. That was our home-ice advantage."

But the feature the men of the WHA remember most about the Amphitheater is the gentle fragrance that wafted into the building from the neighbouring stockyards and abattoirs. Jacques Demers, the Cougars' assistant coach, says simply, "That smell was not pleasant."

Says Neumeier, "There was this smell that came from the stockyards you couldn't miss. It just hung over the rink like a cloud."

"The smell was awful," agrees Garrett, "but the worst part about playing in Chicago was getting out of that neighbour-hood after the game. We used to turn the lights off on the bus just to make sure nobody would shoot at us."

Still, as bad as the Amphitheater was, it was Buckingham Palace compared to the rink in Cherry Hill, New Jersey, home of the fabled Jersey Knights. The Knights were the bastard offspring of the New York Raiders/Golden Blades, who were forced out of New York after one and a half regrettable seasons at Madison Square Garden. The Blades missed their first payroll of the season in Year 2 and would become insolvent. Midway through the season, the league assumed control of the franchise and moved it to Cherry Hill and the four-thousand-seat former home of the Eastern Hockey League's Jersey Devils.

They could have picked a better place.

The rink at Cherry Hill was almost Gothic in appearance and possessed of more oddities than the British royal family. There were no showers in the visitors' dressing room, which meant players would dress at the nearby Holiday Inn, bus to games, play, then return to the hotel and clomp through the lobby in full equipment. More than one wedding reception was interrupted by a sweaty, bloody WHA team making its way back to their rooms. Then again, it must have made for some interesting pictures in the wedding album. There's Uncle Bernie. And that's cousin Warren from Yonkers. And, look, there's Ted McCaskill from the Los Angeles Sharks!

"You'd see Gordie Howe or Bobby Hull coming off a school bus with his skates around his neck like a kid," says André Lacroix, who toiled for the Golden Blades/Knights that season. "It was embarrassing."

Nor was Cherry Hill a place for the squeamish. During Edmonton's only trip to New Jersey, Oilers defenceman Bob Wall had to avail himself of the facilities. Wall emerged from the restroom just as the toilets backed up, spewing raw sewage into the tiny visitors' locker room and sending his teammates running and screaming into the hall.

But perhaps the most endearing trait about Cherry Hill was the ice, which resembled a mountain-bike trail more than a playing surface for the world's fastest game. In speaking to WHA veterans, it's hard to determine precisely how the ice was shaped at Cherry Hill. It's safe to say, however, it wasn't flat.

"There was this hill at centre ice," reports Lacroix. "You could actually get a lot of momentum off it. It was like coming off a turn on a ski hill."

Shmyr, for his part, says you could stand at one end of the rink, shoot the puck along the ice, watch it disappear into a depression, then take flight as it reappeared.

"The goalies used to say if you slap it along the ice at the red line, it will be just under the bar when it got to the net," says Neale.

"There was a crown in the middle," says Garrett. "A pass that was going along the ice would jump five feet in the air all of a sudden. You really had to keep your head up when you were going through the neutral zone."

In San Diego, finally, the Mariners played out of the Sports Arena, a relatively new facility that served its purpose in the old Western Hockey League but didn't compare to the new buildings going up around the WHA.

Then again, there was just something about the Mariners from the start that didn't seem to fit in with the rest of the league. Before they ever played a game in San Diego, city officials were threatening to bar the Mariners from the Sports Arena. Their objection, according to an article in *The Hockey News*, was "the alleged underworld associations of team owner Joe Schwartz."

Schwartz would sell the team to Ray Kroc of McDonald's fame, and Kroc's son-in-law, Ballard Smith, was installed as the team's general manager. Shmyr landed in San Diego for a season after the Crusaders folded and says Kroc offered him a McDonald's franchise as part of his new six-year deal.

"I thought, What the hell do I want with a burger joint?" says Shmyr. "I had no idea what they were worth. I just wanted the money."

Kroc and Smith started complaining about conditions at the Sports Arena from the minute they took over. Kroc said the washrooms were "despicable." He threatened to move the team to Seattle if the city didn't clean the rink up.

Smith, for his part, wasn't exactly embraced by the rebel league's hockey men. After a particularly vicious game with the Fighting Saints II, the Mariners' GM protested about the violence in the game. This drew the following response from Saints head coach Glen Sonmor: "That Smith knows nothing about hockey. The first week they taught him what a puck is. The second week they taught him what a goon is. They're obviously going too fast for him."

There was even something peculiar about the groupies in San Diego. One of the most famous in WHA annals was a gal known as San Diego Bev, who had a very high opinion of goalies. San Diego Bev would do just about anything for a goalie as long as he was wearing a piece of equipment specific to his trade when the action started. As a result, when visiting teams hit San Diego, WHA goalkeepers would tell the team's equipment manager they needed to take their blocker or mask back to the hotel to work on, then sneak it out for a rendezvous with San Diego Bev.

Funny how goalie porn never caught on.

At the end of Year 5, the Mariners folded.

"We had the best five thousand fans in hockey," said Smith. "I just wish we had five thousand more."

"I will pay for pleasure," said Kroc. "But I didn't get a lot of pleasure out of hockey."

Before the Mariners left town, however, the old chicken wire at the Sports Arena was replaced by Plexiglas. We don't know if that had any effect on the team. We do know it came one year too late for a fan named Jim Crush.

Late in Year 3, the Fighting Saints were playing in San Diego when Crush started in on Walton.

"This guy was on Walton the whole game," says Neale. "In San Diego, you could stand in one end and get your face right up to the chicken wire. All of a sudden Walton was knocked into the screen and this guy is still on him. So Shaky butt-ends him in the forehead and the guy goes down like he's shot. You could almost see the square from his stick. The guy charged him with assault."

Walton stood trial that summer and Neale testified on his star's behalf. Criminal charges were ultimately dismissed.

"We convinced the judge this guy was not a normal fan," Neale says.

Makes sense. It wasn't a normal league.


Bill Hunter loved everything about the WHA. He loved owning a team. He loved coaching one. He loved the players. He loved the competition, and he certainly loved the notoriety that accompanied his position. The one thing about the new league, however, that Hunter hated was the price of hotel rooms in New York, and he would do anything within his power to avoid paying for them.

During one road trip in Year 1, Hunter's Alberta Oilers were in Cleveland and scheduled to play in New York the next night. Rather than fly out of Cleveland immediately after the game, Hunter reasoned he could have the team leave the next morning, bus to Madison Square Garden, play the game, then bus to the airport and fly to their next destination. That way he wouldn't have to pay the usurious hotel rates in the Big Apple. That, at least, was the plan.

"Of course, it's snowing, so the flight's delayed," says Ken Brown, the Oilers' backup goalie that season. "Guys are trying to get their pre-game naps in at the airport in Cleveland. We finally get out of there, and we arrive at Madison Square an hour late. Now the problem is, the equipment hasn't arrived. We're sitting around in the nude or in our underwear and nobody's eaten.

"That's when Bill gets this idea. He calls over John Fisher, gives him twenty dollars and says, 'John, go get some chocolate bars for the boys . . .'" Brown pauses for full effect before delivering the punchline in Hunter's distinctive voice. "'And John, make sure they're big ones.'

"We played the game and we even made our flight, so Bill didn't have to pay New York hotel prices. That made him happy."

If, as we've seen, many of the destinations in the WHA weren't exactly in the *Michelin Guide*, then the process of getting there was often equally trying. The new league, for starters, didn't have the travel budget of the NHL. The locations of the league's member cities – your Edmontons, your Quebecs, your Clevelands – also made flight connections an interesting challenge. Finally, as with most other aspects of life in the new league, there was just something about travel that took on a uniquely WHA flavour.

John Garrett, for example, remembers a twenty-one-game road trip with the Fighting Saints that started in San Diego and Phoenix, went to Edmonton and Calgary, *then* took the team to the East Coast.

"How do you pack for a trip like that?" Garrett asks rhetorically. "You had to take four suitcases. And it would take two stops to get from San Diego to Edmonton. During that trip we got in the air, then they found the cargo door wasn't closed, so they had to go back. That was life in the WHA."

Paul Shmyr describes a road trip with the Mariners in which their flight out of Quebec City was snowed in. They had to take a train to Montreal, then walk a mile in the snow to a bus station where they caught an iron lung out of town. Dennis Sobchuk tells of a charter flight from Cincinnati to Calgary on Wright Airlines – Wrong Airlines as it was known to the Stingers – that stopped three times for fuel. André Lacroix recalls his adventures with the New York Raiders/Golden Blades/Jersey Knights, who were always one step ahead of their creditors: "We'd be on the road, and buses wouldn't show up because they hadn't been paid, or we had to change hotels because they skipped out on the bill," says Lacroix. "We had to sit in the back of the plane on these special tickets with no food service. It was brutal."

The Oilers, meanwhile, sprang for their own plane, a twin-prop job that, according to Brown, might have been the plane Lindbergh used to cross the Atlantic.

"You could fly to Europe faster on a normal plane than you could fly to Winnipeg in that thing," Brown says. "We had to stop twice for refuelling on the way to Quebec."

Still, there were some perks associated with travel in the WHA. The new league had franchises in markets like San Diego, Phoenix, and Houston long before the NHL ever thought about moving into the smaller Sun Belt cities. Trips into Phoenix, for example, would provide a welcome break from the harsher climates in Winnipeg and Edmonton. But they could also work against the visiting team.

When he played for Edmonton, Hall of Fame goalie Jacques Plante once spent a pleasant afternoon by the pool in Phoenix, caught a sunburn on his face, and didn't play that night because he couldn't get his mask over his reddened visage. Sobchuk tells of when he was a member of the Roadrunners and the Indianapolis Racers came in, spent three days soaking up the rays in Phoenix, then showed up for the game looking like lobsters.

"For the first period, all we did was get the puck in deep and hit them," says Sobchuk. "You could almost hear their skin crackling. By the end of the period they were just cringing. By the third period, they didn't want to get hit any more. We beat them 12-2."

The Sun Belt cities also presented temptations that could lead a man astray. Literally. The Stingers departed for San Diego with twenty-two players on one trip and came back with sixteen. Two of their members were arrested for fighting in the hotel bar. Another got lost in Tijuana. Another got lost, period. Two more were hurt. Sobchuk, who was in his early twenties at the time, was dispatched to the San Diego jail at midnight to bail out his teammates.

"I've been in better places," he says.

San Diego was also reasonably close to Las Vegas, which created a huge problem for the Calgary Cowboys one year. The team played San Diego twice in a five-day span and between games organized a field trip to Sin City. Their plane stayed in San Diego, but the pilot, much to his discredit, didn't refuel while the team was in Vegas.

After playing the second game, the Cowboys boarded their plane around midnight for the flight home, only to be informed, "Folks, we've got a problem. We don't have enough gas to get back to Calgary."

There was, however, one aviation gas station open that night, and Cowboys coach Joe Crozier ordered his team to go through their pockets. Apparently, Las Vegas hadn't been kind to the players; they could only raise a hundred bucks. Faced with the prospect of spending the night on the Tarmac, Eric Bishop, the Cowboys' late play-by-play man, pulled out his wife's Texaco card and asked aloud, "I wonder if this will work?" The plane taxied over to the pumps, filled up, Bishop offered his wife's credit card, and soon the Cowboys were on their way.

"We only used that card two or three times a year," said Bishop. "I often thought about the shock the guy got at the Texaco office when he went through our purchases – $10, $12, $10, and $1,500."

Bishop, meanwhile, played a starring role in another unforgettable WHA tale from the road. There was no press box in Indianapolis, which meant Bishop and his colour man, George Bilych, had to broadcast from a table perched in the middle of the stands. Their broadcasting equipment, such as it was, was powered through a little box plugged into an outlet in the seats.

You can probably guess where this is going. Racers fans, predictably, threatened to kick the plug loose a couple of times during the game, and each time it happened Bishop became increasingly agitated. One fan finally succeeded in dislodging the plug and Bishop snapped. He whipped off his headset, cut loose with a string of profanity that would have made Redd Foxx blush, then plugged his unit back in.

About five minutes later, he got a call from Calgary asking if he was aware he'd been on the air the whole time. The unit, apparently, came with backup batteries in case of an emergency. Bishop, according to Bilych, thought his career was over, but when he got back to Calgary he met with the station manager and they laughed about the whole thing.

Rod Phillips, the Oilers' play-by-play man, was involved in an incident on the road that wasn't quite as funny. Frank Beaton – whose original nickname, "Never," was amended to "Seldom" midway through his career – played for three WHA teams and recorded 614 penalty minutes in 153 games. Beaton, apparently, had a fearsome temper, and while playing in Cincinnati in Year 4 he punched out a service-station attendant. The story goes that the attendant spilled gasoline on Beaton's prized Corvette, the two men argued, and the attendant grabbed a tire iron, which proved, as former Stingers captain Rick Dudley notes, "he didn't know who he was dealing with, because Frankie could fight."

The next year, the Oilers were checking into their hotel in Cincinnati when two plainclothes policemen approached Phillips and attempted to serve him with a warrant.

"You're Frank Beaton," one of the cops said.

"No I'm not," Phillips protested.

"Yes you are," he said, and left Phillips with the warrant in his hand.

The Oilers broadcaster left the warrant at the hotel's front desk and informed Beaton he was a wanted man. The next night, the Oilers noticed the same two cops at the game, and Beaton was alerted. With about ten minutes left in the third period, the fugitive winger slid off the players' bench and, crawling on his hands and knees, made it to the Oilers' dressing room. He then had the Oilers' trainers zip him into an equipment bag and toss the bag on the truck. The truck left Cincinnati. A few miles out of town, it pulled over and Beaton jumped out. The Oilers' team bus picked him up a few minutes later.

Alas, the long arm of the law would catch up to Beaton the following season while he was playing in Birmingham. This time, Cincinnati's finest left nothing to chance. During the first period, a bunch of cops appeared by the Bulls' bench. Taking note of this development, Beaton skated off the ice with the Stingers and took refuge in their stick room. The cops, meanwhile, entered the Bulls' dressing room with their billy clubs drawn and started to check IDs. They finally found Beaton in the Stingers' stick room, allowed him to shower, then took him out in handcuffs.

Later that night, Dudley took some food down to Beaton in the jailhouse while Stingers head coach Jacques Demers bailed him out.

"I did everything I could to get the police to let him finish the game," Demers said at the time. "But they said he'd slipped away before."

"It was a joke," spat Bulls head coach Glen Sonmor. "The police completely disrupted our concentration."

Okay, one more WHA story from the road. By Year 3, Ron Ryan had succeeded Jack Kelley as coach of the Whalers, and the pressure was getting to him. Shortly after his team landed in Toronto for a game against the Toros, Ryan collapsed at the airport in the throes of an anxiety attack. As the Whalers gathered around their fallen coach, Wayne Carleton threw off Ryan's shoes and began rubbing his feet. The coach eventually came around and the Whalers boarded their bus.

While they were headed toward their hotel, Larry Pleau asked Carleton about his ministrations.

"He said, 'I've got some horses, and that's what they do on the farm when the horse has a problem,'" Pleau says, still cracking up at the memory.

Bobby Hull loved the curved stick, and he did more than any other player to popularize its use. When he was playing in Chicago, the NHL used to measure his blade before games to make sure it conformed to the league's one-and-a-quarter-inch limit. André Lacroix, who played with Hull on the Blackhawks, reports that the door wouldn't be fully closed after the officials left before Hull had his blowtorch out, turning his stick into a semicircle.

It should come as no surprise, therefore, that one of Hull's preconditions for joining the WHA was to maximize the legal limit for his curve. At first, Hull, whose shot was once clocked at 118 miles per hour, pressed for no limitation. When league officials said, "Come on, Bobby, we've got to have something," he settled on an inch and a half.

"Considering I didn't want anything, I thought that was reasonable," says Hull. "It was still a pretty good hook."

"Bobby had to have the unlimited curve and that was fine for him," says WHA referee Bill Friday. "But I used to say the difference between the National Hockey League and our league was they could hit the net. They should have given those seats away in the end blues, because the fans were taking their lives in their hands."

As much as the movie *Slap Shot* defined a certain part of life in the WHA, the slapshot itself also became an indelible aspect of the league's culture. With the big curves and the even bigger windups, a generation of players eschewed the game's more refined skills – the backhand, the backhand pass, taking a pass on the backhand, anything, come to think of it, to do with the backhand – and let fly with the high hard one. As a result, the WHA produced some of the most unlikely fifty-goal scorers – Wayne Rivers? Tommy Simpson? – in hockey history.

"When I was growing up, I never took a slapshot, because if you broke your stick, you couldn't afford another one," says André Lacroix. "It wasn't the best training for the WHA."

Lacroix centred a line with Rivers and Dick Sentes in San Diego, the year Rivers, a little-known journeyman, scored 54 for the Mariners. In truth, Rivers's productivity that season had more to do with Lacroix's sublime passing skills than with his obscenely curved stick. But the hook didn't hurt, either.

"I've never seen a curve like that," says Lacroix. "It was like a shovel. And he didn't take the big slapper. He had a good snap shot, but the curve was so big the goalies never knew where the puck was going."

Neither did the players. Tommy Simpson – known to the fans as Shotgun, known to his teammates as Shotglass – was a rotund bon vivant who had a cannon for a shot.

"Tommy Simpson used to send them into the upper deck all the time," says Friday. "He had no idea where they were going. I told him, 'Tommy, if they ever put a goal in the twentieth row, you'll score fifty.'"

Despite playing at 220 pounds, about forty pounds over his ideal weight, Simpson actually scored 52 with Toronto in Year 3, a feat at which Friday still marvels. And Simpson wasn't the only journeyman who mastered the curved stick. John Garrett, who played goal with four WHA teams, rattles off names like Bobby Whitlock, Mike Ford, and Gary MacGregor when asked who could make the puck dance with the big hooks. They were further aided by the many compact playing surfaces around the WHA – shooters' rinks, in the game's parlance.

"They were never goal scorers before or after the WHA, but they could make it dip and dive on request with the curved stick," says Garrett. "It was amazing."

Garrett recalls watching J.C. Tremblay working on his shot with the banana blade. To the goalie's utter astonishment, the Nordiques' defenceman would practise cutting across the puck with his stick on an outside-in path, the way a golfer tries to hit a slice. Tremblay was trapping the puck on his stick's heel, then releasing it from the toe after it had travelled along the curve. The resulting knuckleball would have made Hoyt Wilhelm proud.

However, not everyone connected with the WHA was thrilled about the fascination with the slapshot. Dennis Sobchuk, who had a pretty good slapper with the Stingers, said the backhand goal virtually disappeared from the WHA because of curved sticks.

"Guys would have to turn their bodies completely around to get in on their forehand," Sobchuk says. "No wonder we were always slapping it."

Coaches noticed this as well, and a couple of them tried to crack down on the slappers in practice. In Edmonton, Oilers coach Brian Shaw banned slapshots after goalie Jack Norris took five off his head in a two-week span. "He lost his confidence and as a result started playing poorly," Shaw said, before adding, "We've missed goals because guys are taking slapshots from fifteen feet."

In Minnesota, meanwhile, Harry Neale threatened a $500 fine for anyone who hit the goalie in the head with a slapshot.

"He didn't enforce it all the time," says Garrett, "but if someone was being a real asshole about it, you'd tell Harry. Five hundred bucks was a lot of money in those days."

Coaches, moreover, weren't the only WHAers who grew testy about slapshots. The league's goalies also had something to say about it. Sobchuk recalls sending a tracer past Indianapolis goalie Andy Brown's ear late in the third period of a one-sided win for Phoenix. That Sobchuk was still firing away in a game that had been decided was bad enough. But Brown was also the last goalie in the WHA, or the NHL for that matter, to play without a mask.

"I was still skating in, and Andy was coming out after me with his stick over his head," says Sobchuk. "He would have killed me, but someone intercepted him."

Sobchuk also nailed Houston goalie Ron Grahame in the coconut before the puck bounced into the net. "Bill Friday disallowed the goal," says Sobchuk. "He ruled Ronnie was out cold before the puck entered the net, so it didn't count. I don't know how he figured that, but only Bill would make a ruling like that." Sobchuk then pauses before adding, "You know, I got my payback. My son was a goalie."

Life was equally perilous for forwards and defencemen in the WHA. Garrett notes there weren't a lot of great shot-blocking defencemen in the league. Sobchuk talks about trying to check the Winnipeg Jets line of Bobby Hull with Anders Hedberg and Ulf Nilsson.

"They'd do all these criss-crosses and drop passes, and the puck would just be sitting there between the dots while you took your man to the net," says Sobchuk. "Then you'd look up and see Bobby going a hundred miles an hour with his stick over his head. You'd just close your eyes and you wouldn't open them until you heard the puck hit the glass or the crowd react to the goal. It was one of the scariest sights you could imagine."

And one of the strangest were the blue pucks, which were supposed to be one of the league's great innovations. Friday now says the blue pucks were only used in pre-season games, but Garrett says he saw them in the regular season. He and other goalies also saw those pucks do things never seen before or since.

"The blue pucks didn't freeze properly because of the blue dye," says Garrett. "They became oblong over the course of a game. You couldn't believe the way some guys could shoot that thing. It was all over the place."

"We had the blue puck our first game, and every time it hit the boards it would lose its shape because of the rubber," says Crusaders goalie Gerry Cheevers. "It was like playing with a tennis ball after a while. It just bounced all over the place."

As for Hull, he is unapologetic about the havoc his curved stick raised in the WHA.

"It was never a problem if you knew what you were doing," he says. "Goalies are always whining about something. In my day it was the curved stick. Now it's all the padding they wear. Shit, I could play goal with that armour they've got on now."

You just wonder what kind of hook he'd have in his stick.

# CHAPTER 7

# "It was too much, too soon."

G ary Davidson and Don Regan didn't know a lot about hockey, but they did understand the law was their ally in their war with the NHL. They looked at the option clause in the standard player's contract and knew it was unenforceable. They looked at the NHL's business practices and knew they were restrictive and monopolistic. Looking back, it seems like Law 101, but in the early 1970s these concepts were revolutionary.

"The system in place was grossly unfair," says Davidson. "Any lawyer could have seen that. It's funny. When you challenge the existing order, the defence is basically, 'Well, that's the way we've always done things.' But that doesn't make it right."

It was the same story with junior players. In 1972, the NHL and the Canadian Amateur Hockey Association – the governing body of the Canadian major junior leagues – enjoyed a cozy arrangement that existed despite its blatant illegality. Agents, in many cases, were chosen for the players by their junior teams. The draft-eligibility age was set at twenty, which meant the NHL was selecting seasoned, physically mature players who could make an immediate contribution to their teams. The CAHA, for its part, was able to keep its stars for several years, whether they wanted to stay or not, and a player like Denis Potvin would spend five full seasons with the Ottawa 67s. As was often the case in that era, the needs of the NHL teams were satisfied, the needs of the junior teams were satisfied, but the rights of the players were violated to an almost illogical extent.

To Davidson, Regan, and the WHA's founding fathers, however, the agreement represented an opportunity, a supply line to a generation of exciting young stars. The notion that eighteen-year-olds are free to earn a living doesn't seem all that remarkable today, but during the time of the WHA it stood the hockey world on its ear. The CAHA threatened government intervention. The hockey establishment, which included the media, predicted all manner of dire consequences. Even the WHA was conflicted on the issue. But in the end, the under-agers provided the rebel league with some of its biggest stars and ultimately ensured that the merger with the NHL would take place. Its effect on the young men involved is still a matter of some debate, but its impact on the league is not.

"You look at the young kids who played in our league and there were some great players," says Gilles Léger, the long-time coach and general manager in Toronto and Birmingham. "Most of them went on to have great careers, and they brought a sense of excitement to the WHA. They were also the reason why the merger got pushed through. The NHL wanted our players. It was that simple."

Then why did it seem so complicated at the time?

"The NHL basically sat around, lit up their cigars, and decided among themselves they weren't going to draft anyone until they were twenty," says Regan, the WHA's legal counsel. "It was clearly for the benefit of the NHL. But just because a group agrees to something among themselves doesn't make it legal.

There was no legal basis for what they were doing. Any lawyer could have seen that."

Now that idea seems like common sense. At the time, it was Armageddon. As far back as 1972, a full year before the Aeros signed an under-age Mark Howe, the CAHA was already making brave noises about taking the WHA to court to defend its indefensible position. "If they start any of that nonsense, they better be ready for a fight," said Joe Kryczka, the CAHA's president. The following September, NHL president Clarence Campbell said his league would formulate a plan that would, "as rapidly as possible, provide solutions to the problem." The WHA even got in the act, working out peace accords with the CAHA even as they continued to sign under-agers. At one point, league president Ben Hatskin fined Whalers president Howard Baldwin $100,000 for signing eighteen-year-old defenceman Gordie Roberts. "What are you going to do, kick me out of the league?" Baldwin responded, and the fine, of course, was never paid. Birmingham Bulls owner John Bassett was supposedly suspended for six months for signing under-agers. He never left his office in Birmingham.

The game's larger problem, in fact, revolved around policing the agents who represented the kids, and one of the most infamous cases of agent fraud in the history of sport was a direct result of the game's inability to govern itself.

Richard Sorkin, a relative of original New York Raiders owner Neil Shayne, was introduced to the business of sports representation by agent Marty Blackman. At his peak he was one of the most powerful agents in professional sports, and he built his practice around hockey players. He was also a compulsive gambler who was convicted of seven counts of grand-theft larceny. It's estimated he skimmed $1.2 million out of a fund set up with his clients' money.

Sorkin, a slick, smooth-talking former sportswriter, was very much a product of the times. In 1972, the Western Canada

Hockey League added a clause to its standard player's contract that gave its teams "the exclusive right to appoint a mutually agreed upon person to be the sole representative and negotiator for the player." The clause was designed to protect the teenagers from the shysters, but it opened the door for Sorkin, one of the agents who was approved by the WCHL. His clients would include Western Leaguers Lanny McDonald, Tom Lysiak, Ron Greschner, Bob Nystrom, and Lorne Henning, and he would kick back as much as $5,000 to the teams if their players signed with him. Sorkin, however, started losing his clients' money in risky stock ventures and attempted to make it back at the track. In the end, he was charged with seven counts of grand theft in excess of $360,000 from five New York Islanders – Nystrom, Henning, Gary Howatt, Bob Bourne, and Jude Drouin – and two members of the ABA's New Jersey Nets. The original charges were for thirty counts of grand theft and $600,000, but Sorkin copped a plea and got just three years in jail. He'd been the best man at Nystrom's wedding. He lost $125,000 of Nystrom's money.

Tiger Williams, who would go on to play fourteen seasons in the NHL, recalls a meeting in which Sorkin was introduced to the WCHL's Swift Current Broncos as their designated agent. Sorkin was nicely into his spiel when Williams stuck up his hand and asked, "Are you telling us we *have* to sign with you?" Sorkin hummed and hawed and finally said, technically, the players could sign with anyone they wanted. The Broncos then travelled to Flin Flon and Williams, one of the team's best players, was told by coach Stan Dunn he wasn't playing that night. Williams, who didn't take crap from anyone even back then, said, fine, if he wasn't playing he was going right to the newspapers, because he knew what was happening.

Williams played that night and didn't hear anything more about Sorkin.

That was not an isolated case. Mike Rogers, who would play

five years in the WHA and seven in the NHL, was a top prospect with the Calgary Centennials in the 1973-74 season. He wanted Herb Pinder as his agent, but Centennials owner, GM, and coach Scotty Munro had selected David Schatia as the team's agent.

"I said I wanted to go with Herb," Rogers says. "Munro said, 'Do you want to play in the playoffs?' I mean, I'm a nineteen-year-old kid, this is my draft year, and I've got this threat hanging over me. What do you do?

"Munro said, 'Don't worry, I'll look after you,' but I didn't like the way it was handled. I went back to Herb. Believe me, there were a lot worse stories than mine."

This, then, was the world in which the WHA operated, and while the rebel league had its own sins to answer for, at least they were honest about their intentions. "There are some players who are ready to play pro long before they're twenty and many who are not, but no one has the legal right to deny an athlete the opportunity to draw the salary a team is willing to pay him," said Davidson. "I am not pretending any noble motives. All of us, owners, coaches, players, are in it to make money. If an eighteen-year-old is ready to play at the top, we want him, because he can help us."

Maybe they spoiled some young careers, and maybe they should have been more judicious about handing out contracts to teenagers. But if the WHA exploited these kids, they also paid them while they did it.

Ron Delorme, the Vancouver Canucks' director of scouting, has been assessing talent for the team for fifteen years. Prior to that, he played pro hockey in the NHL and WHA for ten years, and prior to that he played in the WCHL during one of the most fertile periods in that league's history. He's a hockey lifer, a man who's seen literally thousands of players come and go during his career in the game, and his opinion is sought after in NHL circles.

Delorme, who played against Dennis Sobchuk in the WHA and the WCHL, has this to say about him. "We were in awe of him. You look at the things scouts look for in a player, and he had it all. He could skate. He could handle the puck and make plays. He had a cannon for a shot. And he was tough. He had so much talent. You have to ask what happened to him, and I come back to the league and the era. The WHA was really good for some players, but it wasn't so good for others."

Sobchuk wasn't a complete bust in his WHA career, but neither did he come close to achieving the stardom the sooth-sayers predicted for him when he was a teenager. He now lives a comfortable life in Bellingham, Washington, due in large part to his WHA money. And while he makes no apologies for his career and the path he chose, he also understands why he never lived up to the potential.

Says Sobchuk of his younger self, "When I talk about that guy now, I talk about him in the third person, because I don't know who he is. I lived a movie. I thought they wanted a char-acter, so I gave it to them. I had these Jesse James dusters. I had the floppy hats. I smoked these small cigars like Clint Eastwood. *The Hockey News* called us the Cincinnati Kids. We thought we were something."

And for a while, he was something. He was among the first generation of under-age signings by the WHA, a group that included Mark and Marty Howe, Wayne Dillon, Jacques Locas, and Tom Edur. He was the player around whom the Stingers would build their franchise, a new star for the new league. He was also a kid from Lang, Saskatchewan, who was given a million bucks and asked to take on a responsibility for which he was completely unprepared.

If Sobchuk is remembered now, he's remembered, like so many of the WHA under-agers, as a cautionary tale, a player whose talent was ruined by all that money and all those expec-tations. The same thing happened, the theory goes, to Pat Price.

And Dillon. And Locas. And others. Some would survive the egregious excess of their early years and put in long careers. Some, like Sobchuk, would not.

"It might have been different if I would have gone to an established team and learned from some older guys," says Sobchuk. "I think about that. But I also look back on my memories – the fun I had, the guys I played with. I wouldn't trade that for anything. My only regret is it went by so fast."

In the 1972-73 season, Sobchuk, then a nineteen-year-old, six-foot-two, 185-pound centre, counted 67 goals and 147 points as a junior with the Regina Pats, along with 128 penalty minutes. There was already talk that he'd be the first player taken in the 1974 NHL draft. But Sobchuk had spent two full seasons with the Pats, and there was this new league that was throwing money around like a drunken sailor.

Sobchuk was playing baseball at the 1973 Canada Summer Games in British Columbia when he and his agent, Norm Caplan, met with two of the Cincinnati Stingers owners, Brian Heekin and Bill DeWitt, Jr. The Stingers, who'd been rejected in the most recent round of NHL expansion, had found a home in the WHA and were building a magnificent new arena in the Ohio city with the money of Bill DeWitt, Sr., who had owned the Cincinnati Reds. That was the good news. The bad news was it wouldn't be ready for two more years, but that didn't deter the Stingers owners or Sobchuk.

"I thought, Great," says Sobchuk, "my first team doesn't exist and it doesn't have a building. But they told me they'd sign my brother Gene, as well as my father as a scout. We started listening, and they made this incredible offer [ten years, $100,000 per year].

"The NHL couldn't touch me at that point. They said I was going to be the first pick, but that was a different era, and it didn't take much to go from the penthouse to the shithouse. All I knew was they were offering me more money than I knew existed."

Sobchuk would sign the deal in Montreal and return to the Pats for the 1973-74 season. At first, the WCHL recoiled at having a professional in their midst, but they also realized Sobchuk was the best player in the league and a draw every-where he went. The Pats would win the Memorial Cup that year with a team that included future Hall of Famer Clark Gillies, Greg Joly, who became Washington's first pick of the 1974 NHL draft, and future NHL goalie Ed Staniowski.

At the end of the season, however, there was still no team in Cincinnati, which would have posed a problem to any league but the WHA. Reasoning that Sobchuk had signed a league con-tract, the WHA treated him as league property and asked him where he'd like to play the following season. Sobchuk's brother Gene had played with Seattle in the old Western Hockey League and raved about Phoenix. As luck would have it, the Roadrunners were starting up that year.

"I asked the DeWitts, and they said sure," shrugs Sobchuk. "So I became a Roadrunner."

And his education in the WHA had begun. One of Sobchuk's teammates in Phoenix was veteran hellraiser Howie Young, a man whose exploits could fill this book and a hundred others. Young had been a legend everywhere he played, from Detroit with the Red Wings to virtually every minor-league stop in the hockey world.

"Howie Young was my first roommate," says Sobchuk, still laughing at the memory. "Here I was, fresh off the farm from Lang, Saskatchewan, and my first roommate was Howie Young. He could drink. He was a rodeo cowboy. He'd acted in a Frank Sinatra movie. He rode motorcycles. He'd start telling me stories and I'd get scared. I'd lock my door at night."

And those were the nights Sobchuk was allowed to stay in his room. By virtue of his years in the old WHL, Young had built up a stable of regular female companions whom he would entertain on a frequent basis. The first night Sobchuk walked into his room, Young was in the company of one of his lady friends.

"He said, 'Kid, you're outside,' which meant I had to grab my mattress and sleep in the hallway," says Sobchuk. "It wasn't the only night that happened. You become humble pretty quick around those guys."

Young wasn't the only character on the Roadrunners. There were grizzled minor-leaguers like Bob Barlow and NHL journeyman Gerry Odrowski. Jim "Shitter" Niekamp patrolled the blueline. Sobchuk also had an ample supply of running mates in tough guy John Hughes, Cam Connor, and Dave Gorman. Sandy Hucul, a born-again Christian, coached the team. Interesting juxtaposition, that.

The Roadrunners played at the old War Memorial in downtown Phoenix but practised at another locale. For morning practice, the team would dress at the War Memorial and Sobchuk's crew would pile into his dune buggy and drive through Phoenix in full hockey gear to the practice rink. After practice, they'd repair to their bar of choice without changing.

"We got some strange looks, but we really didn't care," Sobchuk says.

Sobchuk says he learned a lot about the game that first year in Phoenix. He learned, for example, about team meetings. "We had them at bowling alleys. Two reasons: the coaches never thought to look there, and there was usually a women's league."

He also learned that highly paid rookies shouldn't call attention to themselves. In keeping with his image of himself, he started that first year wearing a headband. It didn't last long. "I was a hot dog," he admits. "But I had to take the headband off to save my ribs. Every game I had it on, some old guy would skate up to me, go, 'Fucking kid,' and spear me in the ribs. That went on for about twenty games before I took it off."

Finally, Sobchuk learned it was one thing to be a tough guy in junior, and another to be a tough guy in the WHA. He recalls one game in Phoenix when the Fighting Saints were at the height of their reign of terror.

"They started their five toughest guys, and it was like a street gang," he says. "Jack Carlson, Gordie Gallant, Curt Brackenbury . . . Sandy goes down our bench and taps Cam Connor, John Hughes, and two of our other tough guys. Then he taps me. I don't know what he was thinking. My heart just dropped. So they drop the puck and it's ninety seconds of pure hockey. My heart was in my mouth the whole time, and I was never so relieved when a shift ended.

"One thing you learned as a rookie in the WHA. You never made eye contact."

Sobchuk survived that year in Phoenix in fine style, scoring 32 goals and picking up 77 points. Sandy Hucul, for his part, was named coach of the year, and the expansion Roadrunners finished eight games over .500.

Sobchuk's WHA career would begin in earnest the following season in Cincinnati. After they were rebuffed in the NHL expansion of 1972, the DeWitts went about trying to force their way into the senior league with a merger. They built the gleaming new Riverfront Arena. They poured money into the team, signing Rick Dudley away from Buffalo and junior stars Jacques Locas, Claude Larose, and Blaine Stoughton. It wasn't an easy sell in the new market. "We used to joke we'd get the lead sports pages for two weeks from January 15 to February 1. Then the Reds would head for spring training and we'd be at the back of the section again," Sobchuk says. But the DeWitts were leaders in the merger movement, and they appeared to be in it for the long haul.

In the summer of 1977, Bill DeWitt, Jr., and Howard Baldwin were convinced they'd worked out a deal with the NHL that would allow six WHA teams – Cincinnati, Houston, New

England, Edmonton, Quebec City, and Winnipeg – into the senior circuit. The terms of that agreement were much more favourable to the WHA teams than the pitiful terms of surrender under which they'd eventually enter the NHL. They would have kept their players under the DeWitt-Baldwin plan. They would have formed their own division and played most of their games against themselves. They would have been absorbed into the mainstream of the NHL over five years.

"We thought we'd worked out something that would benefit everyone," says Baldwin.

That deal was voted down by one vote when Harold Ballard of Toronto and Paul Mooney of Boston mobilized the established league's anti-WHA forces. In the end, that vote stiffened the resolve of some WHA teams. "We vowed to hit the NHL where it hurt most, with young players," says Baldwin. But the vote also killed the DeWitts' NHL aspirations. The Stingers had loaded up for the 1977-78 season, adding Robbie Ftorek, a legitimate WHA superstar, Pat Stapleton, and young goalie Mike Liut. By December, however, Sobchuk was sold to Edmonton and the next year the Stingers would accept a payoff to drop out of the merger process.

"We really thought hockey would work in Cincinnati," says Sobchuk. "There was so much excitement around the team when we started."

A lot of it was centred around Sobchuk. The Stingers gave him number 14, which was interesting, because that was the number worn by the Reds' Pete Rose and Bengals quarterback Kenny Anderson. Sobchuk was taken to a Bengals practice to meet team owner and Ohio legend Paul Brown. Brown told him, "I can't take you down to the field. We don't have one guy making $50,000."

Sobchuk also put up some numbers and became the Stingers' most popular player. His first year in Cincy he totalled 32 goals and 72 points. His second year, he had 44 goals, 96 points, and made the All-Star Team. When he was dealt to Edmonton, it was widely assumed he'd be the player around whom new Oilers coach Glen Sather would build his team. But three years after his 96-point season, he was out of professional hockey in North America.

"Looking back, it's so easy, because you know where you went wrong," says Sobchuk. "I went from coulda-been, to shoulda-been, to has-been like that. My direction wasn't totally focused on hockey. I was this flamboyant kid. I thought I was a personality. You forgot what got you there."

The injuries didn't help. Sobchuk broke his wrist in Cincinnati. He tore up his shoulder in Edmonton, and after three operations his clavicle was removed. But Sobchuk also knows those injuries were symptomatic of a larger problem.

"We had Rick Dudley and Robbie Ftorek [in Cincinnati], who were exactly the opposite to me," he says. "They'd stretch and work out after practice. I headed to the bar. I wonder why their careers lasted longer."

Still, he packed a lot into his short, star-crossed career. Sobchuk tells a story from his days with the Stingers when he was sidelined with the fractured wrist. Dressed in civvies, he was watching the game from between the players' benches when Dale Smedsmo – Shmo to his teammates – was victimized by an opposition goal.

"He was a bit of a loose cannon," Sobchuk says charitably, before adding, "I'm just standing there, and he comes over the bench and he swings his stick, meaning to break it over the boards. He hits me instead and knocks me out. The guys on the other team are watching this and they go white. I guess they figured if he'd do that to the million-dollar kid on his own team, he'd do anything. I think we ended up winning 7-3."

The million-dollar kid, now fifty and at peace with himself and what might have been, still laughs at that one.

In the same way every young man with an acoustic guitar who could write a song was the next Bob Dylan in the 1970s, every young defenceman who could skate and carry the puck was the next Bobby Orr.

Orr revolutionized the game when he graduated from the Oshawa Generals to the Boston Bruins as an eighteen-year-old, but he also sent every scout in hockey looking for a blueliner who could play like Superman and lead the league in scoring. The problem was, as his former teammate John McKenzie says, "There's only one Bobby Orr. No one else could do the things he did." But that didn't stop hockey men from trying to find another one.

One of the first next-Bobby-Orrs was Pat Price, a young man from Trail, B.C., who played junior with the Saskatoon Blades and had the great good fortune to arrive about the time the war was heating up between the WHA and the NHL. Price would go on to have a rock-solid fourteen-year pro career with seven teams as a stay-at-home defenceman, but that career was a testament to his adaptability, not his talent.

"It was too much, too soon, and I didn't have enough guidance," says Price, who now sells cars in Trail. "But when you're nineteen, who thinks of that? Everyone was telling me how great I was, and they were throwing more money at me than I could have imagined. I showed my dad the cheque for my signing bonus, and he said, 'There's something wrong with this. There's too many zeros on it.' It was for $250,000, and that was more money than he ever made in his life."

Price, like Sobchuk, was considered the total package when he played with the Blades. In coach Jackie McLeod's wide-open system, and playing with future NHLers like Bob Bourne and Dave Lewis, Price rang up 27 goals, 95 points, and 147 penalty minutes in 1973-74, his fourth season in Saskatoon. Lewis, now the coach of the Detroit Red Wings, calls Price the best junior he's ever seen. "I think that was part of his problem," says Lewis.

"He was too good for our level. He could do whatever he wanted on the ice."

By the time the Memorial Cup was played in Calgary that year, Price was also the object of a frenzied bidding battle between the expansion Washington Capitals, who owned the first pick of the NHL draft, and the WHA's Vancouver Blazers, who'd been purchased by multi-millionaire Jimmy Pattison the year before and were looking for a star to sell to their new market. In Calgary, Price and his family took a hotel room while his agent, David Schatia, went back and forth between Caps GM Milt Schmidt and Blazers head coach and GM Joe Crozier. Schatia would then report back to the Price family on the state of negotiations, and Price couldn't believe what he was being told.

"I had no intention of signing with the WHA," says Price. "My dream had always been to play in the NHL. But my agent said he'd give Joe one last shot. It was already crazy. It was like, What kind of car do you want? A Ferrari? We'll get you a Ferrari. Clothes? Stereo? No problem. I'd just turned nineteen and they were giving me everything I wanted.

"Then the question came: How much is Pele making? Isn't he the highest-paid athlete in the world? I ended up signing for $1.3 million over five years with a $250,000 bonus. My agent told me I could play for five years, retire, and live off $80,000 a year for the rest of my life.

"I didn't want to make the move, but Vancouver was the only place I'd play. I walked out of there with a certified cheque for $250,000. How does anyone relate to that? I was nineteen and I had a quarter of a million dollars. I wanted to take everyone out to dinner, but there was no place to cash the cheque. My mom was just mad because she couldn't see me play on TV."

Pattison was determined to take the Vancouver market away from the Canucks, but he had a small window to make an impact on the West Coast, and his efforts, while well-meaning, were doomed to failure. The Canucks were just three years out of expansion and coming off a 53-point season in 1972–73. Two years later, during Price's rookie campaign, they fashioned an improbable 86-point season and finished first in the Smythe Division. After that year, Pattison would move the team to Calgary, where it would survive for two years as the Cowboys. But there seemed to be something off about the franchise from the start.

At the Blazers' very first press conference, Pattison laid out a sumptuous spread at the Bayshore Hotel. Coach Phil Watson, who'd moved with the team from Philly, looked at the buffet and called out to Johnny McKenzie, "Pie, look at this. Fucking caviar! And it's seven bucks a tin!"

Pattison also attempted to capitalize on the Blazers' nickname by executing a marketing strategy based, well, on fire. There were bonfires inside and outside the rink. Fire-engine sirens sounded to celebrate goals. Blazers employees wore plastic fire helmets, and the cheerleaders, the Blazer Belles, wore, what else, hot pants. Remarkably, this bold initiative never took, and by the end of their second year in Vancouver the Blazers couldn't draw flies. Pattison, however, didn't get rich by throwing good money after bad, and according to Vancouver legend he made some changes around the team. A couple of hockey men were said to have walked into Pacific Coliseum when one noticed the concessionaires were new. "What happened?" he asked. "Jimmy brought in volunteers from his church," the other answered. They walked a few more steps and heard the organist playing "Just a Closer Walk with Thee." "He hired the organist from his church, too," the second guy said.

Price, like Sobchuk in Cincinnati, was supposed to be the great star who would single-handedly draw fans to Blazers games. He wasn't that. Only a handful of players in the history of the game have been that for their team. In time it might have worked, and in time Price might have developed into a great two-way defenceman. But he wasn't going to do it as a nineteen-year-old fresh out of junior.

"There was all this talk about him being a superstar, but he was just a kid making big money who was thrown in with men," says McKenzie. "It was a real tough position for him."

And Price didn't make it any easier for himself. About a month and a half after he signed his contract, the young blue-liner hopped in his new Ferrari and headed for Vancouver. He was going a hundred miles per hour when it started to rain. He slowed down to ninety but hit a puddle, spun out of control, and flew off the road. Miraculously, he wasn't hurt.

"It was obviously too much car for a nineteen-year-old to handle, but I thought it was just right for me," Price says. "I had that car for six weeks. They took it away and gave me a Monte Carlo."

When training camp started, Price, Sobchuk, and Ron Chipperfield, another Western kid the Blazers had signed, were allowed to work out with the WHA All-Star Team that met the Soviet Union in an eight-game series. Prior to game three in Winnipeg, Price was entrusted with taking a phone call for Gerry Cheevers concerning the health of his father-in-law. The phone rang in Cheevers's hotel room, and Price, anxious not to miss it, came sprinting down the hallway in his platform shoes which, regrettably, were in vogue at the time, and wiped out.

"I couldn't believe it," says Price. "Platform shoes. I thought I was okay, but when I got to the rink they checked me out and, sure enough, I had sprained my ankle. That was it for me for the series."

Price would play 68 games with the Blazers that year, totalling 5 goals and 34 points. By any reasonable standard, that was a good year for a nineteen-year-old rookie. But it wasn't quite the production hoped for from the next Bobby Orr.

He would also sour quickly on the Blazers and the entire WHA experience. He clashed with Joe Crozier, an old-school coach who worked through intimidation. The Blazers were a bad team, and Price's contract made him an easy target. In one game, New England tough guy Nick Fotiu was roughing up Blazers scoring star Danny Lawson when Price stepped in. Predictably, the ensuing fight was one-sided, and none of his teammates came to his aid.

"That was a turning point," Price says. "I was always told you stand up for your teammates. About two nights later, Ulf Nilsson gave me a two-hander and no one did a thing. I stood up in the dressing room between periods and said, 'What's going on? Where were you guys?' I was told to shut up.

"It was hell. I was partly to blame, but it was just a bad fit."

And it never got better. A story made the rounds that Blazers veteran Andy Bathgate, an NHL Hall of Famer with the New York Rangers, tried to instruct Price in one of the game's finer points. Price, who'd earned the nickname Pat the Brat by then, is supposed to have said, "What do you know, old man? Get the fuck away from me." Price denies it ever happened, but he acknowledges that given his frame of mind at the time he might have snapped at Bathgate.

"I've heard that one a million times," Price says. "But, honestly, Andy was one of the reasons I signed with Vancouver. He was like a buffer between Joe and me, and I admired him a great deal. I might have got frustrated once and snapped, but I had a lot of respect for Andy."

He couldn't say the same thing about a number of his other teammates. Price had kept in touch with Lewis and Bourne, his buddies from the Blades, who were now playing with the New York Islanders. They painted a rosy picture of NHL life on Long Island with coach Al Arbour and an up-and-coming young team. They kept telling Price he'd made a mistake and he should be playing in the NHL.

Price, for his part, didn't need a lot of convincing. A settlement was reached with the Blazers, who were glad to get out from under his contract, and the next Bobby Orr signed with the Islanders, where Denis Potvin, who could make a legitimate claim to being the next Orr, was playing. Price played four years on the Island and was traded to Edmonton in 1979-80, the year the Islanders won their first of four straight Stanley Cups. Two years later, Edmonton traded him to Pittsburgh, which was two years before the Oilers' dynasty started. He then settled into four years with the Quebec Nordiques and retired after tours with the Rangers and North Stars. He never counted more than 11 goals or 42 points in a season, but under Arbour's tutelage he managed to reinvent himself as a reliable stay-at-home defenceman with a physical edge. In the end he wasn't Bobby Orr, but neither was he the flake who cracked up his Ferrari and injured himself falling off his platform shoes before he ever played a game in the pros.

"I have no doubt that if I had been more focused and disciplined it would have turned out differently," says Price. "But everything was wide open back then. It was the old boys, and everyone went to the bar after the game. If you didn't you'd get fined. There was a saying: Don't take a bad game home with you. Leave it in the bar.

"I was a kid. What did I know?"

If there was ever a man who embodied the spirit of the WHA, it was John F. Bassett, the owner of the Toronto Toros and Birmingham Bulls and the leader of the rebel league's raiding party on teenage talent. Even now, almost twenty years after his death, Bassett remains a larger-than-life figure, the scion of one of Canada's most powerful families, an athlete, an entrepreneur, a movie producer, a rogue, and a character of irresistible appeal. He died in 1986 at age forty-seven after fighting cancer for the better part of a decade, but he extracted every available morsel of adventure and excitement from his short, rich life. Bassett was the closest Canada ever came to producing its own JFK, and he is a beloved figure to the men of the WHA.

"I'll never understand why God called Johnny so soon," says Don Regan. "I've met some fascinating people in my life, but he's at the top of the list. If you couldn't have fun with John Bassett, you weren't alive."

There are, of course, a million stories about John F., but this one tells you all you need to know about the man. When Bassett owned the Memphis Southmen of the World Football League, Elvis Presley asked him for his autograph.

"You have to understand, John was a former college goalie and a Davis Cup tennis player," says Toros and Bulls coach and GM Gilles Léger. "He'd been a reporter on the *Toronto Telegram*, and his father had been a part owner of the Leafs. So you add it up and you've got a person who has a background in sports, a background in ownership, and a background in the media. He was the perfect owner and a great guy. He had a way of making everything exciting."

His colleagues in the WHA could certainly attest to that.

Bassett jumped into the new league at the end of the first year, when he bought the Ottawa Nationals from Nick Trbovich for $1.8 million, moved them to Toronto, and renamed them the Toros. The Nats had already relocated to Toronto temporarily for the playoffs after a tumultuous first season in the nation's capital. Now the move was permanent, but the ride under Bassett was as wild as anything the franchise experienced in Ottawa.

The Toros' new owner was the son of John W.H. Bassett – owner of the *Toronto Telegram*, founder of Baton Broadcasting and its flagship station, CFTO, in Toronto, and Harold Ballard's partner, both in business and sparring, in the Toronto Maple Leafs. John W.'s eldest boy didn't lack for confidence or ambition, and it was apparent from the start that he had every intention of taking on the Leafs, one of Canada's enduring institutions. If he ultimately failed, it wasn't from lack of effort.

"I was at the WHA meeting in Toronto where he bought the franchise from Nick Trbovich," says Regan. "Everyone was there but the prime minister, and John got up and said, 'We're going to buy this franchise, and I want to know what you're going to kick in.' Then he literally passed around a hat. He wanted a million, and when it came back he had notes for $1.1 million, so he got the team. It's still the greatest sales job I've ever seen."

While the Toros' board of directors included a couple of members of the Eaton family and future Leafs owner Steve Stavro, Bassett's subsequent sales job on Ballard wasn't quite as successful. John F. reasoned that Toronto's omnivorous hockey market was large enough for two professional teams, and if his intent wasn't to knock the Leafs and Ballard out of the box completely it was because he felt the NHL and the WHA could both thrive in Toronto. In theory, that notion was fine. In practice, Toronto had only one big-league facility, Maple Leaf Gardens, and it was operated by a man, Ballard, who'd feuded with Bassett's father and didn't feel too kindly toward the rebel league. The Toros played most of their first season at the dingy Varsity Arena, where they managed to draw little more than four thousand fans per game. At the time, Bassett was making brave noises about building a rink nearby in Mississauga, but in the end he had to do business with Ballard. He was not negotiating from a position of strength.

The Toros' lease agreement at the Gardens was, on some levels, predictable, and on others set impressive new standards for Ballard's small-mindedness. The Toros paid $25,000 a game in rent. They were given the locker room assigned to the visiting teams playing the junior Toronto Marlies. For WHA games, Ballard had the padding taken off the players' benches.

"Even if John had sold out every game, he couldn't have made money," says John Garrett, who played goal for the Toros and the Bulls after the Minnesota Fighting Saints folded.

"He brought a team into Toronto to compete against Harold Ballard, then negotiated a lease with Ballard," says Léger, laughing at the memory. "Who else does that?"

Bassett didn't go down without a fight. In the Toros' second year, he stunned the hockey world by signing former Maple Leaf star Frank Mahovlich, Czech star Vaclav Nedomansky – the first great player from Eastern Europe to defect to North America – and national hero Paul Henderson, who was just two years removed from the most dramatic moment in Canadian sports history. When Henderson returned from the Soviet Union after scoring the game-winning goal in the 1972 Summit Series, Ballard had publicly promised he'd negotiate a new, long-term deal with his winger. Two years later, Ballard offered Henderson a five-year deal and told him, "You don't deserve this, but I'll be damned if I'm going to lose another player to that league."

Henderson told Ballard to stick the offer up his ass.

"That was before I became a Christian," Henderson says.

"I'd lost all my respect for Ballard," he continues. "I didn't think there was any way we were going to win the Stanley Cup as long as he was in Toronto. It had already started, and you knew it was going to get worse. I just didn't think it was going to be that bad.

"You look at the way he treated Ron Ellis, Darryl Sittler, Lanny McDonald, Roger Neilson. He didn't want anyone bigger than him in Toronto, and it killed that franchise. I look back, and when he lost his wife, he lost his keel. He wasn't the same man."

Life with the Toros was easier on Henderson's nerves in one respect and just as trying in another. The hero of 1972 made his reputation as a strong two-way winger, and his scoring outburst against the Russians had run against the grain of his career. When he signed with the Toros, he tried to play the same team game with a strong defensive conscience. He didn't have a lot of company in that regard.

"I knew we'd score some goals, but we didn't have a team," says Henderson. "You have to have some defencemen, and our goalie [Gilles Gratton] was from Mars. It was a carnival."

Adding to the franchise's carnival atmosphere was a series of teenage phenoms whom Bassett made prematurely wealthy even as he thumbed his nose at the hockey establishment. Bassett was aware he was stirring up a hornet's nest when he signed under-age players, but he was also aware the law was on his side. At one point he famously observed that, as far as the junior leagues were concerned, "I will continue to defy their laws until they start conforming with the laws of Canada. These kids can go to jail and drink booze. I don't see how a little hockey could hurt them."

The Toros' first big under-age signing was Toronto Marlies star Wayne Dillon, a playmaking centre who was supposed to be Wayne Gretzky four years before Wayne Gretzky became Wayne Gretzky. Dillon played two seasons in Toronto before he and Pat Hickey, another OHA star, were signed away by the New York Rangers. He never panned out.

Undaunted, Bassett then went after eighteen-year-old Mark Napier of the Marlies in the summer of 1975. Amid howls of protest, Napier signed a three-year deal worth $200,000 a year, and NHL president Clarence Campbell immediately said his league would no longer honour its agreement with the CAHA. The WHA, for its part, said it wouldn't sign any more under-agers, which was a bad lie.

"I just couldn't see where going back for two more years of junior would do me any good," says Napier. "In a lot of respects, going to the WHA was perfect. It was a step below the NHL, but it was certainly better than junior, and the money was a lot better."

Napier would play three seasons with Bassett, moving with the team to Birmingham at the start of Year 5, before he signed with the Montreal Canadiens. Like so many of the WHA's under-age signings, he didn't quite become the superstar every-one expected, but he would put in a solid fourteen-season NHL career and scored 40 goals each in back-to-back seasons with the Habs in the early 1980s and won Stanley Cups with Montreal in 1979 and Edmonton in 1985.

With a few exceptions, the under-agers who signed on with the WHA went on to have long careers in the NHL. Obviously, their talent had something to do with that longevity, but as Sobchuk observes, the WHA demanded a certain toughness of spirit and body. If you could survive it, you could survive just about anything.

Napier wouldn't be Bassett's last foray into the junior ranks. The Toros, to no one's surprise, were crushed by the lease with Ballard, and after a brief attempt to save the team – "He had the players making phone calls to sell tickets," says Garrett. "Try that today" – Bassett relocated to Birmingham, Alabama, where he had some business connections and where he found a more favourable rental agreement with the Birmingham Civic Center.

He also found one of the strangest markets in the history of professional hockey. Houston, San Diego, Phoenix, and some of the WHA's other more exotic locales could at least lay claim to a history of high-level minor-pro teams. Birmingham, however, had little history with the game before the Bulls arrived, and despite drawing respectably in their three years, there remained something incongruous about hockey in the Deep South. The "Battle Hymn of the Republic" and "Dixie" were played before Bulls games, and fans waved Confederate flags in the stands. That was kind of funny. But it wasn't so funny when Bassett agreed to terms with Tony McKegney, an elite prospect from the Kingston Canadians who's also African Canadian, in the summer of 1978. When word leaked out that the Bulls were about to sign McKegney, there was an immediate backlash from the Bulls' season-ticket holders. "Bassett was getting all these calls," says Léger. "My office was next to his, and I kept hearing him go, 'Same to you, buddy,' and he'd slam the phone down."

Bassett ended up working a deal that sent the young winger to Buffalo and the NHL.

"I'm quite shocked," McKegney said at the time. "I never really considered my colour as being a major factor in hockey. I thought all those kinds of feelings were over with ten years ago."

The Bulls were also never more popular than in Year 6, when Glen Sonmor, the man who built the Fighting Saints, assembled the greatest collections of wackos and nutbars in WHA history, which is saying something. When asked which team of his creation was scarier, the Fighting Saints or the Bulls, Sonmor pauses, then says, "I think we probably had more tough guys in Birmingham. I think for sheer terror, you couldn't beat that Birmingham team.

"This was Bear Bryant country," he continues, referring to the legendary football coach. "They used to ask him what kind of team he'd have, and he'd say, 'We'll put the hurt on them.' They asked me the same thing about our team, and I said the same thing. That endeared me to Birmingham."

It was against this backdrop, then, that Bassett tried to sell Canada's game, and he did it with his typical flair. In their first year, for example, Léger noticed the stories in the local papers reflected a surprising knowledge about the game. He called Bassett's attention to the favourable coverage the new team was receiving and his boss just laughed.

"It turned out John was writing the stuff and sending it in," Léger says.

John F. was just as serious about building a team in Birmingham as he had been in Toronto, and in the Bulls' second year he sparked another furor when he signed Ken Linseman away from Kingston. Linseman had challenged the NHL's draft in the summer of 1977 before he signed with the Bulls, but in their continuing efforts to make nice with the CAHA, the WHA banned Linseman from playing in Birmingham. Linseman sought and won an injunction that allowed him to play, and that decision remains one of the landmark legal rulings in the evolution of the eighteen-year-old draft.

The following summer, Bassett sold off Linseman, Garrett, Napier, and a young defenceman named Rod Langway and used the money to blow the lid off the under-age issue. In the WHA's last season, the Bulls signed six junior stars: goalie Pat Riggin, defencemen Gaston Gingras, Rob Ramage, and Craig Hartsburg, and forwards Michel Goulet and Rick Vaive. Wayne Dillon, ironically, came back from the NHL and played on that team, as did two more under-agers: future Bruin Keith Crowder and future Nordique Louis Sleigher. Collectively, they became known as the Baby Bulls.

"When you look at it, we brought every kind of player you could think of to the South," says Léger. "The first team we had there had all the stars: Mahovlich, Nedomansky, Henderson. The second team had all the tough guys. And the third one had the kids who could actually play. It was really a year-to-year thing, and we never knew if we'd be around. But every year, John would call and say, 'Looks like we're back in business. Let's build a hockey team.'"

Now, you could argue the 1977-78 Bulls weren't a hockey team so much as the Mongol horde on skates, but the signing of the Baby Bulls remains the signature stroke of Bassett's career. It was bold and controversial. It was also brilliantly conceived: Goulet would become a Hall of Famer; Ramage, Hartsburg, and Vaive were All-Star-level players. And, most importantly, it guaranteed the merger between the NHL and the WHA.

"The NHL didn't want one team to get them all, and they certainly didn't want John to sell them," says Bill Watters, the Baby Bulls' agent, who signed all six players to identical one-year, $60,000 deals. "That only left the merger."

"My wife and I felt like parents to those kids," says Henderson, who turned thirty-six in the Bulls' final season. "What a bunch they were, crazy as bedbugs, but they had talent and they learned a lot that year. You just had to look at Ramage and Hartsburg and you knew they were going to be great players. I enjoyed that year as much as any year I had in hockey. I just went out and had fun."

Playing under head coach John Brophy, who was an interesting figure in his own right, the Baby Bulls held their own that season, finishing ten games under .500. Brophy had coached the immortal Long Island Cougars in the 1973-74 NAHL season, and it's widely believed he's the inspiration for the Paul Newman character in *Slap Shot*. After coaching the Bulls, he returned to the minors, enjoyed, if that's the right term, one brief stint as the Maple Leafs' coach in the late 1980s, then returned to coach in the minors. Brophy finally retired after the 2002-03 season at age seventy. He played twenty seasons in the minors without playing one NHL game. He coached in the minors for twenty-four seasons and he and Scotty Bowman are the only two coaches with 1,000 professional wins.

Ramage, Hartsburg, and Gingras would form the core of Brophy's defence in the Bulls' final season. Vaive, in many respects, had the most eventful year, scoring 26 goals and leading the WHA with 248 penalty minutes. The nineteen-year-old right winger learned first-hand that season that many of the league's veterans hadn't forgotten the havoc raised by the Bulls in the previous year. He spent much of his first professional campaign answering for old debts.

"We'd go into these cities and it would be payback for what Birmingham did the year before," says Vaive. "I had to stand up, because I wasn't the most skilled player, and I always thought I had to earn my space and respect."

But he could have picked an easier way to do it. Vaive recalls one game against the Oilers when he started a spirited dialogue with Edmonton coach Glen Sather. This, naturally, led to an appearance by Oilers enforcer Dave Semenko, who hammered Vaive into unconsciousness in the ensuing fight.

The Bulls were returning to Edmonton in five days, so the rookie was left behind to nurse his wounds in Edmonton. The next evening he was lying on his hotel bed with cotton stuffed up his nose when the local station showed a replay of the fight.

"I was lying there going, 'Oww, oww,'" says Vaive. "It's like I felt the punches all over again."

Vaive, like his young teammates, would survive that year and eventually prosper. The WHA, in fact, took much of its shape and character from the kids in its last season. Wayne Gretzky opened the year in Indianapolis before he was sold to Edmonton. Mike Gartner scored 27 goals with Cincinnati. The Stingers also had a rugged young winger named Mark Messier, who didn't quite enjoy Gartner's success that season but would eventually find his place in the game. The Winnipeg Jets had a flock of great young talent, including Kent Nilsson, Terry Ruskowski, and Morris Lukowich. And there were the Baby Bulls.

"You look at that group of players and you think, What if we had been able to stay together?" Vaive says. "With some good drafting and a good organization, who knows? It's an interesting question.

Like almost everyone who played in the rebel league, Vaive still cherishes his memories from his year with the Bulls. His first roommate was the aforementioned Henderson – imagine a kid from Charlottetown rooming with the guy who scored The Goal – and in the Bulls' first game on the road, Vaive scored the game-winner in overtime, then went out and celebrated. He got back to the room around 2:00 a.m. and learned from an unamused Henderson that a reporter from P.E.I. hadn't stopped calling in an attempt to interview the Bulls' new hero.

"Needless to say, I had a new roommate the next night," Vaive says.

Vaive also developed a relationship with Bassett, and he was amazed when the team's owner took a personal interest in his young charges. John F. was still talking about getting into the NHL at the start of the last season, and even if there wasn't a merger, there were other kids he and Léger had their eyes on. There was this young defenceman in the Quebec junior league named Ray Bourque. There was a big centreman in Regina named Doug Wickenheiser. There was another defenceman they liked named Kevin Lowe. And they'd signed some of the Baby Bulls to contract extensions during the course of the year.

"By mid-season, he knew we weren't going to be one of the teams involved in the merger," says Vaive. "But his health was good that year and I think he really enjoyed having the young guys around."

His health wouldn't hold up. Bassett was first diagnosed with cancer during the 1976-77 season, when Léger was coaching the team. "He came into the dressing room and said there were going to be some changes made," the old hockey man says. "I became the full-time GM and took over a lot of John's duties. Pat Kelly coached the team for the rest of the year."

Bassett, as would be expected, fought the good fight for the better part of ten years. In February of 1985, he was diagnosed with two brain tumours, and in April he went public with his illness.

"I'm convinced attitude is number one, and you're going to see the greatest attitude anyone ever had with these things," he said.

On May 15, he died.

Harold Ballard, his long-time nemesis, reached his hand out to John F. in those last weeks. Léger also visited his old boss and brought him a turtleneck sweater. "Here was a guy who had everything, and he thought that was the greatest thing he'd ever received," says Léger.

When they were with the Toros, Léger and Bassett had been in the habit of going to lunch once a month for lobster sandwiches and martinis as they discussed ways to keep their team alive. Now Bassett's wife made the two men lobster sandwiches, and they ate, sipped martinis, and talked the afternoon away.

Too soon it was time for Léger to leave. It was the last time he saw John Bassett alive.

# CHAPTER 8

# "They brought the Quebec flag with them everywhere they went."

From the day they were conceived by Marius Fortier and the owners of the junior Quebec Remparts to the day they were sold to Colorado for $73 million, there was something improbable about the Quebec Nordiques. The market they played in was far too small to support a major-league franchise. No one really cared about them outside of their isolated region. They never had enough capital. Players refused to play there. They even spoke a different language than the rest of the hockey nation. The Nordiques just seemed to live in their own little world, and in the end that world could not sustain them.

But the Nordiques always had one thing they could count on, one thing that saw them through seven years in the WHA and sixteen years in the NHL. Maybe it wasn't enough to compensate for all their other shortcomings, but for twenty-three seasons the Nordiques survived on their fans' almost irrational passion for hockey and their unconditional love for their team. The all-powerful Montreal Canadiens were based in bilingual

Montreal, were owned by Molson, and their management was largely anglo. The Nordiques were of the Quebec people – *chez nous*. Their players were virtually all francophone. Owner-ship and management was French. They wore the fleur-de-lys, the symbol of Quebec, on the shoulder of their uniforms. At times, they seemed to wear it over their hearts.

"I think we represented the ordinary people in Quebec," says Richard Brodeur, Nordiques goalie for all seven years of the WHA. "We had sympathy from the people because of that. We had all these kids who played in the Quebec league who never would have had a chance to play with the Canadiens. They identified with our team."

"They represented the province, absolutely," says Jacques Demers, a Montrealer who coached the Nords in their last WHA season. "They had that impact with the francophones. The Canadiens were the NHL and they had great stars, but there was something special about the Nordiques. They brought the Quebec flag with them everywhere they went."

After the Nordiques survived the WHA's wild seven-year ride and made it to the NHL, it felt as if the good times would never end. Then they had to watch the Colorado Avalanche parade down the main street of Denver with the Stanley Cup that should have been theirs. Maybe Quebec City didn't have money to build a new rink with fancy luxury boxes and premium seats and underground parking and all the other artifices of today's NHL. But if you ever sat in Le Colisée for a game, you know they had something else. The NHL still doesn't know what it lost when it left Quebec City and Winnipeg, and they're too busy trying to force-feed the game to the Nashvilles of the world to understand it now. But they lost something they haven't been able to get back.

So did Quebec.

"It was great that Quebec got a team in the NHL, but it was sad when it moved to Denver," says Serge Bernier, a fine Nords centreman, who now works in construction in the Gaspé. "A lot of us sacrificed our careers to come back and play in Quebec and build up the Nordiques. Now we have nothing."

For a while they seemed to have it all. It would take two and a half seasons for the Nordiques to get it right, but when they did, they built something of beauty and substance in the old town. At the start of Year 3 of the WHA, after they failed to steal franco-phone icons Guy Lafleur and Gilbert Perreault from the NHL, they scored a major coup when they signed junior sensation Buddy Cloutier from the Remparts. Midway through that year, they acquired the mercurial Marc Tardif from Michigan and Christian Bordeleau from Winnipeg, and the Nordiques had a team that spoke to the soul of Quebecers. They were passionate and artistic, occasionally unpredictable and temperamental, but they were never dull. They won the Avco Cup in Year 5 when they beat the powerful Winnipeg Jets, and maybe they should have won more. But at their best they played beautiful hockey, and to the people of Quebec, that was as important as winning.

It just took them a while to play that beautiful hockey.

Following the Rocket Richard fiasco in Year 1, and follow-ing failed attempts to land Perreault, Guy Lapointe, and Pierre Bouchard, the Nordiques were still searching for a face to sell their franchise when Lafleur popped up on their radar screen. The former Remparts star from Thurso, Quebec, was a tran-scendent figure in Quebec City, as popular to his generation of fans as the great Jean Béliveau had been in the early 1950s. When the Flower was selected first overall by the Canadiens in the 1971 draft, he was identified as the heir apparent to Les Glorieux's long succession of French-Canadian superstars. But it didn't happen right away for Lafleur in Montreal. In fact, it almost didn't happen at all.

Lafleur had just turned twenty when he joined the Habs, and his first three years in the NHL he struggled in head coach Scotty

Bowman's demanding four-line system. He scored 29 goals his rookie year in Montreal, the next year 28, and just 21 in his third. He was booed at the Forum in those early years, and his relationship with Bowman wasn't always easy. At one point, Béliveau had him over for dinner and told him to stop acting like a baby. By March of his rookie campaign, Lafleur was telling friends he missed Quebec City. His future father-in-law, Roger Barre, was a shareholder in the Nordiques, and Lafleur was close to Réjean Houle, who jumped to the Nords from Montreal in 1973-74.

Late in the 1972-73 season, all signs pointed to Lafleur signing with the Nordiques. In March, Nordiques management met with Lafleur's agent, Gerry Patterson, in Montreal and lowballed him in their first offer. They then came back with a five-year deal worth $125,000 a year and were willing to go up to $150,000.

In Montreal, meanwhile, the Habs held an organizational meeting to determine if their young star was worth all the trouble. This was an era when the Canadiens didn't break the bank to sign their players. They let J.C. Tremblay go to the Nordiques, they let Ken Dryden sit out for a year over money, and they would lose Houle and Tardif to the WHA. The mighty Habs had never worried about restocking their team, so why should they start now? There was also some question about how good Lafleur would prove to be. Bowman thought he'd be a good player but never more than a second-liner, "a Bob Nevin type," the great coach said. Others felt it wouldn't do to lose to the new league a player the Canadiens had selected as their next great star. General manager Sam Pollock would make Lafleur a ten-year, $1-million offer. In early April, the Canadiens announced they'd locked up their star.

Two years later he scored 53 goals in Montreal.

Lafleur would later admit that had the Nordiques plunked down their best offer immediately, he probably would have signed. He was aware he was losing $50,000 a year by signing with the Habs, but he had security, and just as importantly he had an opportunity to become the man in Montreal. Still, the Nordiques took something out of the process. While they were wooing Lafleur, they made contact with Houle and would sign the former Junior Canadiens star before Year 2. Houle, like Lafleur, had been the first pick of his draft year, in 1969. Montreal owned the second pick of that draft and they used it to select Tardif, another star on the Junior Canadiens. In time, he would also sign with the Nordiques.

"It was a big marketing coup, because we took something away from the mighty Montreal Canadiens," says Brodeur of the acquisition of Houle and Tardif. "That didn't happen back then."

The Nords would sign away another member of the Canadiens family prior to Year 2, but this one almost precipitated a disaster in Quebec City. Jacques Plante was one of the greatest goalies of all time. He was also an innovator and a brilliant hockey mind whose book on goaltending, *Devant le filet*, is still one of the defining works on the position. When the Nordiques signed him to a ten-year contract as coach and GM before the 1973-74 season, they thought they had found a hockey man who'd give their franchise the credibility they so desperately sought. But Plante was also a raging eccentric and a bit of a loner, and by the end of the season the Nords were happy to see the last of him.

"We didn't have the happiest room that year," says Brodeur.

Plante's year in Quebec started reasonably well, and the Hall of Famer put in long hours with the understaffed team. That year, however, Plante discovered cross-country skiing, and his new hobby began to consume as much of his time as his hockey team. The Nordiques coach would often blow off practices to go skiing in the Laurentians, leaving Tremblay and Jean-Guy Gendron to run the team.

Brodeur recalls watching Plante waxing up his skis in Le Colisée before an important stretch of games. "I thought, That's all right as long as he shows up on the ice," says Brodeur. "But then the practice started and there's no Jacques. Jean-Guy and J.C. had to run the practice, and it pissed them off."

Brodeur, at least, would learn a great deal about goaltending from Plante that season. The master taught him how to go down on one knee with his stick in front of him, the way 90 per cent of the goalies play in today's NHL. He taught him about angles. He taught him about the psychology of the position.

"He used to tell me, 'You see the guy come in from an angle, and you've got him,'" Brodeur says. "'You don't move. He's got to think about where he's going to make his move. And forwards don't like to think.'

"He had a vision for the game."

He just had a hard time communicating that vision. By the end of the season, Plante was routinely late for games and the directionless Nordiques missed the playoffs by one point. They also lost $500,000, and the team began to look for ways to rid themselves of their unpredictable coach.

Plante saved them the trouble. After watching the WHA for a year, the forty-five-year-old goalie concluded he could make more playing in the league, and with substantially less aggravation than his coaching duties caused him. He walked away from the last nine years of his deal, the Nords gave him $5,000 as a parting gift, and Plante signed a one-year deal with Edmonton for $150,000.

"I'll catch them with my bare hands," Plante said of the calibre of shooters he'd face.

And he wasn't far wrong. In 1974-75, his last season of professional hockey in North America, he recorded a 3.32 goals-against average with the Oilers in thirty-one games. There were just six goalies in the league who played more than 30 games who had a better GAA.

The same year Plante made his comeback, Jean-Guy Gendron retired as a player and stepped behind the Nords' bench, which at least gave the team some stability in the coach's office. But they were struggling on the ice as well as off. The Nordiques hadn't made the playoffs in either of their first two seasons and attendance was starting to decline. They had Tremblay and Houle to offer their fans, but not much else. They needed help. And they would get it in the form of the natural selection that aided so many of the WHA's stronger franchises.

It now seems that Marc Tardif was destined for the Nordiques and the Nordiques were destined for him, but they took their time finding each other. Like Lafleur, Tardif was a brilliant individualist who had trouble fitting in to Bowman's system in Montreal. For starters, he wasn't too keen on playing defence, nor was he eager to learn. He had his own ideas about how the game should be played, and he quickly developed a reputation for being moody and uncoachable. His contract with Montreal expired at the end of the 1972-73 season, and that year Bowman, seeing the writing on the wall, told him, "Stop thinking about all the money you're going to make in the World Hockey Association and sign with the Canadiens."

Tardif responded, "Why don't you mind your own business?"

In 1972, the Habs had also drafted Steve Shutt from the Toronto Marlboros, and Shutt was projected as the team's first-line left winger. It came as no surprise, then, when Tardif signed a three-year deal worth $450,000 with the Los Angeles Sharks prior to Year 2. The contract included a brand new Mercedes.

"My timing was pretty good," says Tardif. "My contract was over at the end of the season and Los Angeles started talking to me. It was a great experience. I was from Granby and I'd played in Montreal, and I could say about two words of English at the time. Maybe it was a tough decision, but I was twenty-three and I thought, If I don't do it now, I'll never do it."

Tardif would score 40 goals with the Sharks that season, but the following year the team moved to Detroit to play out of Cobo Hall as the Michigan Stags, and the flashy young winger wanted no part of Motown. When Bill Hunter approached him about playing for Team Canada against the Russians in the fall of 1974, Tardif said he'd suit up if Hunter would help get him out of Michigan. A month into the season, the Stags weren't drawing flies and they were as eager to unload Tardif's big ticket as he was to get out of Detroit. Houle had been monitoring the situation for the Nordiques and started to recruit his former junior teammate. Nords GM Maurice Filion made a special trip into Detroit, met Tardif in a scary part of downtown, and told him the Nords would do anything to get Tardif and if he played in Quebec City he'd be a hero to the entire province.

The second part of Filion's sales pitch was accurate, but the first part wasn't entirely true. Nordiques' management wasn't 100 per cent sold on Tardif. They'd just committed big bucks to Cloutier, and Tardif had floated through the Canada-Russia series and the first part of the regular season. The Stags also wanted a package built around Pierre Guite, a tough, two-way left winger who was a fan favourite in Quebec City. After some deliberation, the deal was made and the Nordiques and Tardif agreed to a four-year extension at $140,000 a year. About the same time, the Nords acquired Christian Bordeleau, whose ice time in Winnipeg had been reduced when the Jets signed Ulf Nilsson, and the two newest Nordiques were put on a line with Cloutier.

There are still fans in Quebec who maintain the Nordiques' trio was better than the Nilsson–Bobby Hull–Anders Hedberg line in Winnipeg.

"Marc was the final piece," says Bernier. "We were a pretty good team after that, and Quebec City became a great place to play. You can ask anyone. It's special when you play in front of your home fans in your home province, but what made it really special is we were a winning team."

Tardif would score 38 goals in 53 games with the Nords in Year 3. The next season, the line would dominate the league as the Nordiques' average attendance grew to 9,885 fans, an increase of 3,000 over Year 1. Tardif led the league in Year 4 with 71 goals and 148 points. Bordeleau totalled 109 points. Cloutier, whom Tardif calls the most talented player he ever played with, had 60 goals and 114 points. The Nords' power play that season featured the big line with Bernier and Tremblay on the points and clicked at a surreal 30.3-per-cent success rate. They also added toughness in Gordie Gallant, Curt Brackenbury, and Steve Sutherland. Houle, in what was his last season in Quebec, scored 51 goals.

"It's funny the way it worked out," says Tardif. "Houle was the reason I went to Quebec. Two years later he was back in Montreal and he never left. I'm still in Quebec City. But I wouldn't trade it for anything. Things just clicked right from the start in Quebec."

Well, there's one thing Tardif would like to change. The high-flying Nordiques met the Calgary Cowboys in the first round of the playoffs that season in what, on paper, looked like a monumental mismatch. Owner Jim Pattison had moved the Vancouver Blazers to Calgary that year, and the Cowboys finished eighteen points behind the Nords in the regular-season standings. Their offence was led by forty-goal scorers Ron Chipperfield and Danny Lawson, but the Cowboys' lineup paled in comparison to the star-studded Nordiques roster. The series was supposed to be a walkover for Quebec. It would be remembered for different reasons.

Cowboys coach Joe Crozier had played senior hockey in Quebec for Punch Imlach, and upon arriving in the old town Crozier decided the series needed some publicity. Before the first game he took winger Rick Jodzio, who was given the job of shadowing Tardif, and some of the Cowboys' tougher players to a boxing club and had pictures taken of them sparring. Subtle.

They then upset the Nords 3-1 in the first game of the series before all hell broke loose in game two.

Early in the contest, Gallant jumped Jodzio and both players were given five-minute majors. Tardif scored while Jodzio was serving his penalty. Later in the first period, Tardif had positioned himself along the boards in his zone when Jodzio came off the Calgary bench and made a beeline toward the Nordiques star. According to Brodeur, who was playing goal that night, Jodzio got within ten feet of Tardif, launched himself, cross-checked the Nordiques winger in the face, then started to punch the defenceless player.

"Jodzio had one thing on his mind," says Brodeur. "When he jumped on Marc, I jumped on him, then somebody jumped on me, and the riot started. Wayne Wood was playing goal for Calgary and he came down to our end, and I was glad to see him. We just held on to each other and watched the war."

The ensuing brawl lasted for twenty minutes and ended only when Quebec police appeared by the players' benches and escorted both teams to their dressing rooms. Eleven players were ejected, including Gallant and Lawson, who both left the penalty box to join the melee. Referee Steve Dowling issued 179 penalty minutes, 110 to the Nordiques. Tardif was taken off the ice on a stretcher.

"It was the worst thing I've ever seen in hockey," says Maurice Filion.

The aftermath wasn't much better. The Cowboys, who would win the series, immediately accused the Nordiques of exaggerating their star's injury. Jodzio denied he cross-checked Tardif. Crozier blamed Gendron for failing to control his team. The Nordiques, for their part, threatened to withdraw from the series unless Jodzio was suspended for life. Crozier was suspended for the rest of the series, and WHA vice-president of hockey operations Bud Poile resigned. Given the geopolitics involved with the two teams, the coverage of the incident took on a shrill, bigoted tone that got even more shrill when the Nordiques claimed they saw league president Benny Hatskin with his arm around Jodzio in the Calgary press box prior to game three.

It's now clear that Tardif suffered a major brain trauma and was one of the first acknowledged victims of a serious concussion. He didn't skate for the next four months and only resumed training at the end of the following summer. When he did return, he suffered from dizzy spells and struggled to regain his old form. He scored 49 goals in 62 games the next year but then came back to lead the league with 65 goals and 154 points in 1977-78. He says he was never the same player after Jodzio attacked him, however, and at least one of his teammates agrees with him.

"It's not something I like to talk about and I only remember a part of it," Tardif says. "It changed me after that. I was, I would say, a more careful player. I played with some very good players, and my numbers were good, but it was tough, that's for sure."

"He was in the hospital with a concussion and they said he's faking it," says Brodeur, the emotion still evident in his voice almost thirty years after the fact. "That's real smart. Marc was never the same player after that. We all knew it."

Jodzio, for his part, was suspended indefinitely by the league and charged with assault. Eventually he was fined $3,000 in Quebec court and Brodeur was called to testify against the Cowboys winger.

"It was a sad day for hockey," Brodeur says. "A sad, sad, day."

But it would get better in Quebec. Even with a reduced Tardif, the Nordiques were still good enough to capture the Avco Cup the following year. Cloutier had a huge regular season with 66 goals and 141 points. He and Bernier led the playoffs with 14 goals, and Bernier, who was named the MVP of the playoffs, led all scorers with 36 points. In the final, they knocked off the mighty Jets in a wildly entertaining series that produced 59 goals in seven games. The Nords won game seven in Quebec 8-2 with Bernier, Tardif, and Cloutier combining for three goals and ten points.

"They were great games to watch, but they weren't great for the goalie," Brodeur says of that series. "You'd just take your medication before the game, because you knew you were going to face forty shots from some very good shooters."

"I won the Stanley Cup twice in Montreal, and my feeling in winning the Avco Cup was just as good," says Tardif, the star who transformed the franchise. "It was really a big, big thing for Quebec City. It was an exciting time. The Colisée was packed every night and the people loved us."

They especially loved Buddy Cloutier, who would score 75 goals for the Nords in 1978-79, the last season before the merger. Quebec's homegrown star, however, would never be the force of nature in the NHL that he'd been in the WHA. Scoring goals was obviously a more demanding skill in the established league than it had been in Cloutier's first few years with Nords, but anyone who saw Cloutier play maintains he could have been as big a star as Lafleur had he taken the game more seriously. He scored 42 goals in the Nords' first season in the NHL but suffered an injury the next. He was out of the NHL by the time he was twenty-eight.

"Buddy Cloutier had the tools to be one of the great stars in hockey," says Maurice Filion. "He was spoiled too young, I guess."

But that didn't diminish the Quebec fans' affection for their shooting star one iota.

"He was from St-Émile, which is just outside Quebec City, and he was this fun-loving kid who had a lot of friends," says Brodeur. "Maybe too many. He could score goals any way you wanted, and he had all the talent in the world. There were some nights he'd say, 'I'm going to score three goals,' and he'd go out and do it. There were other nights where you'd see him pouting on the bench and you'd go, 'Not tonight, I guess.' He was a pure French-Canadian goal scorer, and they loved him in Quebec."

They also loved J.C. Tremblay in Quebec, and if they ever build a Mount Rushmore to the Nordiques, the magical defence-man should be the first face they carve out of the rock. Tremblay was already thirty-three when he joined the Nordiques in Year 1, and for the next seven years he was the foundation on which the team was built. He was an undersized blueliner who wasn't the best skater and who routinely recorded less than twenty penalty minutes per season. But he was also one of the most intelligent defencemen ever to play the game, one of the best-ever passers at any position, and an indefatigable workhorse who, Marius Fortier swears, played sixty-three minutes one night in an over-time game. Fortier also says he saw Tremblay control the puck for all two minutes of a Nordiques penalty kill.

"J.C. was perfect for our team, because he was strong and independent," says Fortier. "Nothing bothered him."

"He never got the credit he deserved for what he did in Quebec," Brodeur says. "He had to average forty-five minutes [of ice time a game] at his peak, and he was a magician. He could pick guys out in traffic like no one I've ever seen. And he did it in the NHL as easily as he did it in the WHA."

Brodeur goes on to tell a story from an early Nordiques train-ing camp where a young speedster was put on the ice with Tremblay. During a scrimmage, the kid broke free on the wing as Tremblay was crossing the red line with the puck. The old master took one look at the kid, pulled up, then circled in the neutral zone. On the bench the kid asked Tremblay why he hadn't passed him the puck. "Because your stick wasn't on the ice," Tremblay said. "Put your stick on the ice and you'll get the puck." Sure enough, the Nordiques were playing a game the next week, the kid got a step on his man, Tremblay put the puck on his tape, and the youngster scored.

On another occasion, Brodeur was playing in goal when Tremblay carried the puck behind the Nordiques' goal as a forechecker closed in. Just as Brodeur was about to alert his teammate about the coming pressure, Tremblay flipped the puck over the Nordiques' net and picked it up on the other side. "It scared the hell out of me," says Brodeur. "But he knew where everyone was, and he knew he could get away with that."

Despite Demers's exhortations for him to play another season, Tremblay would retire after the Nordiques' last year in the WHA and, fittingly, never played for another team. On many levels he was a difficult man; he could be moody and distant, and his teammates called him "Grumpy." But over the years Demers managed to break down the wall Tremblay built around himself and discovered not only a brilliant hockey mind but also someone who wasn't as cold as he pretended to be.

"He was very quiet, but after you got to know him, he had a good heart," says Demers. "I guess there are two sides to some people, and I thought that was the case with J.C."

Demers believes that, had Tremblay stayed with the Canadiens, he'd now be in the Hall of Fame. As it was, he moved to Switzerland when his playing days were over and scouted for the Habs, who drafted Saku Koivu in part because of Tremblay's recommendation. The old defenceman had moved back to Montreal in 1994 when he was diagnosed with cancer in his one good kidney. In the fall of that year, he underwent surgery to have the cancerous part of his kidney removed. He died two months later at age fifty-five.

"It happened very fast," says Demers, who visited with Tremblay the day before he died.

But he didn't go out alone. Hundreds would attend Tremblay's funeral at Mary Queen of the World Basilica in Montreal, everyone from Canadiens president Ronald Corey to Nordiques president Marcel Aubut, to Hall of Famers, to WHAers, to hockey fans who sat in the back of the cathedral and prayed for the soul of the man who'd given so much to the game.

"He's the one who made the Nordiques' franchise," Demers says.

In the end, that might have been the most fitting epitaph for Tremblay.

## CHAPTER 9

# "It was one of the greatest lines to ever play the game."

**B**obby Hull was aware he hadn't selected the path of least resistance when he signed with the Winnipeg Jets, but by the end of his second year, the romance of his trailblazing experience was starting to wear as thin as his hairline.

The Jets of Year 2 finished five games under .500 and were blitzed by the Houston Aeros in four straight in the first round of the playoffs. Hull scored 53 goals that season, but the next-closest Jet was Norm Beaudin with 27. At one point, in order to spread out the team's scoring, Hull took himself off his regular line with Beaudin and Christian Bordeleau and skated with Danny Spring and Ron Snell. Suffice to say, no one bothered thinking up a nickname for that trio.

"After a while I learned why a lot of these guys couldn't make it in the NHL," Hull says, before adding, "That first year I rarely had a meal with the team. I was shuttled in and out of towns to speak to the chambers of commerce. I must have talked to everyone in Winnipeg four times that first year. My dad told me what would happen, but I thought, What the hell, nothing ever bothered me before. But I hadn't gone through anything like that before.

"By that third year I was just about done. I went to Billy Robinson [the Jets' chief scout] and Jerry Wilson [team doctor and a former junior star] and told them we had to do something about the menagerie we'd collected."

A world away, something *was* being done. While the Golden Jet was bemoaning his lot with the Jets, events were taking place in Sweden that would unite Hull with two young Swedes, Anders Hedberg and Ulf Nilsson. These two, along with another Swede, defenceman Lars-Erik Sjoberg, would arrive in Winnipeg that year and form the nucleus of the best WHA team ever. They would also break down the prejudices against European players and introduce elements of artistry and imagination that, when combined with the best aspects of the North American game, would forever change the face of hockey. You can argue whether the Hull-Hedberg-Nilsson line – the Hot Line – was the best line in the game's history, but they were inarguably the most influential. They played together for just four years, but when they were done practically every NHL team was trying to capture the magical combination of speed, skill, and creativity the line possessed. Glen Sather built his Edmonton Oilers dynasty on the Jets model. The modern transition game was pioneered by Hull and his colleagues, as was the practice of interchanging forward roles on the rush. The numbers they accumulated in their four seasons together are staggering, but they played in a league that didn't have a television contract, which means most of their legacy is anecdotal and almost mythic. In the end, that only seems to add to their aura. And if the NHL never saw the best of Hedberg and Nilsson, in much the same way the NBA never saw the best of Julius Erving, it makes their four years in Winnipeg that much more memorable.

"They revolutionized the game," says André Lacroix, the seven-year WHA veteran. "They said, Just because you play left wing doesn't mean you have to go up and down your wing like a robot. You can use the whole ice. It was exciting."

"They were unbelievable," says Glen Sonmor, the long-time WHA and NHL coach and general manager. "It's a pity the NHL never saw the best of the two Swedes. They never wanted to give our league any credit, but they were as good as any line I've ever seen."

"There was no line in our league who even came close to them," says Joe Daley, goalie with the Jets for all seven years of the WHA. "You had to compare them with players they didn't play against, but they were the best I ever played with or against."

Hull played on three of the most famous lines in hockey: the Million Dollar Line in Chicago with Red Hay and Murray Balfour; the HEM line in Chicago with Phil Esposito and Chico Maki; and the Hot Line. He says the two Swedes were, hands down, the best he ever played with.

"The first time we went up the ice together it was like we'd never played with anybody else," says Hull. "It was one of the greatest lines to ever play the game. It made the game fun for me again."

It also made the game fun for everyone who watched them.

As with all great stories, there is an element of serendipity in the tale of Hull's union with the two Swedes that adds to its appeal. Dr. Jerry Wilson was one of the best junior prospects in all of Canada during his playing days, but a knee injury ended his career and sent him into medicine, where he eventually became an orthopedic surgeon. In the fall of 1973, he was given a $30,000 grant to conduct research at a Stockholm sports institute, where his research assistant was a young winger on the Swedish national team named Anders Hedberg. Wilson, who was from Winnipeg and the father of future NHLer Carey Wilson, wasn't officially connected with the Jets but was close to several members of the organization, particularly Billy

Robinson, the chief scout. Hedberg, for his part, was playing for Djurgarden in the Swedish elite league at the time, and while he was curious about the game on the other side of the ocean, it wasn't his burning ambition to play in North America.

"I didn't know much about the NHL or the WHA in those days," says Hedberg, now the director of player personnel for the Ottawa Senators. "Teams were just starting to tour. There was no television and there wasn't much of an exchange of ideas. We played Canada in an exhibition game in '72 [before Team Canada went on to Russia] and we kept hearing this term *superstar*. We didn't know what it meant, but it seemed they were playing the same game as us and skating the same speed."

Others weren't so sure. Despite the epic Canada-Russia series of 1972, the hockey world of that time had a narrow, dismissive view of European players. Ulf Sterner, a member of the Swedish national team, played four games with the New York Rangers in 1964-65 before he returned to his homeland. Defenceman Thommie Bergman, who would play with the Jets, came over and played a full season with the Detroit Red Wings in 1972-73. Defenceman Borje Salming and winger Inge Hammarstrom joined the Toronto Maple Leafs the following season. Slowly, attitudes were changing, and the Europeans had some champions in North America, but they were still regarded with suspicion and mistrust. The enduring image of all Swedish players was forever cast when Leafs owner Harold Ballard said of Hammarstrom, "He can go into the corner with eggs in his pockets and come out without breaking any of them."

The Jets, however, weren't in a position to be choosy prior to the 1974-75 season. With Hull growing increasingly sour on the Canadian prairies, Wilson struck up a relationship with Hedberg – "It was a case of two hockey guys hitting it off," Hedberg says – and was invited out to some of Djurgarden's games. There, the good doctor quickly formed the opinion that the chasm between the North American and European games wasn't as wide as some had suggested. The best Swedish players could not only survive in the NHL and the WHA, he concluded, they could thrive. About the same time, Wilson received a letter from Robinson saying the Jets needed help and he should keep his eyes open for players. Wilson approached Hedberg, who told him he preferred the idea of playing in the NHL, but he'd listen. Hedberg then gave Wilson the name of a slender young centre playing for AIK, Ulf Nilsson, and a defenceman playing for Leksand, Lars-Erik Sjoberg. Wilson eventually contacted the other two on behalf of the Jets.

Again, the Jets had help from outside forces in landing the Swedes. Nilsson had been on Buffalo's negotiating list, and Sabres GM Punch Imlach had gone to the 1974 world championships in Helsinki to scout him. Nilsson, however, had taken some cough medicine before the tournament, tested positive for a banned substance, and never played. Sjoberg, meanwhile, was on the Minnesota North Stars' list but cracked a rib early in that same tournament and missed the first week of play. The Stars' scout went home and recommended the defenceman be taken off the team's list. Sjoberg returned to the Swedish lineup later in the tournament and was named outstanding defenceman for the championship.

Hedberg was on Toronto's negotiating list, and even though the Leafs would offer more money, he was intrigued with the idea of playing in Winnipeg with Hull and with his fellow Swedes. As chance would have it, Dennis Sobchuk, the WHA's young million-dollar star, had just toured Sweden with his junior team, and the Regina Pats were drubbed in a series of exhibition games.

"I thought, If they give Dennis Sobchuk a million dollars, I can play over there," says Hedberg. "I also thought, What the heck, if I don't make it in Winnipeg, I can always play in Toronto."

"It's gratifying to know I was an inspiration to such a great player," Sobchuk responds dryly.

Hedberg and Nilsson also needed representation in North America, and Wilson recommended a young lawyer of his acquaintance, Don Baizley, who'd done some work with the Jets' Fran Huck. The two players and Baizley met with Billy Robinson at the Viscount Gort hotel coffee shop in Winnipeg and a deal was struck. Sjoberg would sign up later. The Jets had taken a huge step into the unknown.

"We talked about it among ourselves, and we decided it would be so much better if we could go together and influence a team with the European style of play," says Nilsson. "I think I would have had trouble if I went by myself to Buffalo. The more we talked about it, the better Winnipeg sounded."

The Jets weren't finished with the great European experiment. Robinson, whose role in hockey history has been underreported, made three trips into northern Europe prior to the 1974-75 season and would eventually add Finns Veli-Pekka Ketola and Heikki Riihiranta and Swedish goalie Curt Larsson. Thommie Bergman, the original pioneer, would join the team midway through that season. Wilson and Robinson then returned home with their new players and the belief that the Jets were on the leading edge of an exciting new movement in hockey. Others thought they were insane.

"The first impression from everybody in North America was this was a joke," says Wilson. "But once it started, it just took off. There's no question it was Bill's initiative. He kept it alive."

"My biggest problem was convincing [Jets owner] Benny Hatskin to spend the money to go over there," Robinson says. "He kept saying, 'Why the hell do you want to go over there? How much is this going to cost me?' But I had a friend in the travel business and he'd get me these cheap flights to Copenhagen, then I'd make my own way from there. I've often wondered what would have happened to our team if I didn't know that travel agent."

For all of Hatskin's budgetary concerns, the Swedes would prove to be one of the best bargains in hockey history. Nilsson and Hedberg were signed to two-year deals that started at $60,000. Sjoberg signed for a little more, but he was thirty when he played his first year with the Jets. Robinson said his team didn't pay a nickel to the Swedish hockey federation for the three stars. Hedberg and Nilsson would later sign deals with the New York Rangers for ten times their original contracts with the Jets.

"I knew I was on to something, but I didn't really understand until I got them over here," Robinson says. "I stayed in the background. That was bad for me. It's not so much the recognition I missed but just the acknowledgment I played a big part in it."

Maybe the biggest part. Robinson and Wilson kept Hull informed of the negotiations, and the Swedes were promised they'd play on a line with the great left wing. When Hedberg pointed out he was a left-handed shot, Robinson said, "Great, now you're a right winger."

Before the Jets opened their training camp in Year 3, Hull was in sweats skating with the University of Manitoba team at Winnipeg's St. James Civic Centre when his new linemates arrived for a workout session. Hull was in one corner of the rink. Hedberg and Nilsson were in the other. Hull picked up a puck and took off on a line rush.

He still remembers that moment as clearly as any in his career.

"I just picked up the puck in the corner, and these two guys sprang from the other side," says Hull. "Then it was *bing-bing-bing* and in the net, and I just said, 'What the fuck have we got here?'"

"We were doing these line rushes against a college team, and we couldn't miss," says Hedberg. "I said to Ulfie after the practice, 'This is unbelievable! I wonder what Bobby is thinking?' Bobby had rushed home and called Jerry Wilson. He said,

'This is unbelievable! I wonder what the Swedes are thinking?' Honestly, we had goosebumps we were so excited about playing with each other."

Hull would soon leave for the WHA's 1974 series against the Soviet national team, and when he returned, Jets GM Rudy Pilous was already doubting the durability of the Swedes.

"He said, 'Wait till they start laying the body on them,'" Hull says. "I just said, 'Shit, Rudy, you just watch.'"

Pilous and the rest of the league got an eyeful. In their first game together, the new line scored forty-one seconds after the opening faceoff against the Vancouver Blazers, and Hull says Hedberg missed an open net later that same shift. After seven games, the Jets had a 6-1 record, Hull was leading the league in scoring with 10 goals and 17 points, Nilsson was third with 3 goals and 14 points, and Hedberg was sixth with 4 and 8. They would maintain that pace for the rest of the season, and while the Jets just missed the playoffs, they rejuvenated the franchise in Winnipeg and Hull's passion for the game. The season before the Swedes arrived, the Jets had drawn an average crowd of 6,102 per game. With the Swedes in the lineup, the average jumped to 8,586 fans. The year before, Hull had scored 53 goals and totalled 95 points. In his first season playing with Hedberg and Nilsson, he rang up 77 goals and 142 points.

"It was a new lease on life," Hull says. "I was ready to call it quits, then I finally found a couple of kids who could play the game the way I wanted to play it. My dad used to tell me, 'You've got the whole ice in front of you, why would you just go up and down your wing? Go where you want to go.' And that's exactly the way they played the game."

"It was like three great jazz musicians playing together," Wilson says. "It was three completely different personalities and three completely different styles of play. But they just seemed to fit together. No one knows why. They just did."

The line, in fact, was a study in contrasts. The Golden Jet is best remembered today for his booming slapshot and end-to-end rushes, but in the autumn of his career, Hull, one of hockey's greatest individualists, had developed an intelligence and instinct for the team game that was at the core of the line's success. Hedberg, who'd never really played with Nilsson before their arrival in Winnipeg, had blinding straightaway speed, was fearless going to the net, and could shoot the puck in stride as well as anyone in the game's history. Nilsson, meanwhile, supplied the X factor with his vision, creativity, and uncanny passing ability. They were three distinctive talents, but they played with one heart and one brain at the same inspired level. As Wilson said, no one knows why. They just did.

"I can't explain it," says Hedberg. "I don't think anyone can. That was part of the magic."

"I knew Bobby's name, but I didn't know anything about the way he played or his personality," he continues. "I think that helped us. We weren't intimidated about playing with the great Bobby Hull. And Bobby *was* great. He kept saying, 'Just keep playing the way you've always played.' And that's what we did."

It helped that they'd brought Sjoberg with them. The squat blueliner, who would become the first European to captain WHA and NHL teams, had already put in a full international career as captain of the Swedish national team when he arrived in Winnipeg. A seasoned, polished performer, he was one of the most nimble skaters ever seen and carried himself with a confidence that was not understated.

Sjoberg could back up his swagger with a complete, brainy game that Hedberg describes as "simple but brilliant." His numbers were never blinding, but he had the ability to start the Hot Line off on the rush and, more importantly, to cover the many holes his freewheeling colleagues left on the ice.

"Everyone talked about Borje Salming [on the Swedish national team] at the '76 Canada Cup, and he was great, but, defensively, Lars-Erik was our best player," says Hedberg. "You just couldn't beat him because he was such a great skater. He was so quick in the corners and he never made a mistake with the puck. He was our reliable guy back there."

And he knew he was good.

"Shoe didn't see anything from minute one that said [the three Swedes] weren't going to be stars," says Baizley. "He was nothing if he wasn't confident."

That first season, Sjoberg and young, mobile defenceman Mike Ford played behind the Hot Line in a five-man unit. Hull turned thirty-six that year and it was one of his greatest as a pro. He scored 50 goals in the season's first fifty games, his 50th finishing off a hat trick against Houston. Hedberg accounted for 53 goals and 100 points in his rookie campaign, and Nilsson totalled an incredible 94 assists and 120 points. This, remember, was their first year together. They'd get even better over the next three years.

"You might think my face is red from embarrassment," Toronto defenceman Rick Cunningham said after the Toros had been scorched by the Hot Line. "Actually, it's windburn."

In the line's second year together, Denver Spurs head coach Jean-Guy Talbot threw out a checking ensemble against the threesome that featured rookie Ron Delorme and the irrepressible Bill Goldthorpe on the wings. Goldthorpe had built his reputation as a penalty killer in the minors, and Talbot told his two checkers to follow Hedberg and Hull all over the ice. After a minute, Goldthorpe came to the bench out of breath with sweat dripping off his mug and rasped to Talbot, "Coach, I can't stay with them." "Try staying in your lane, then," Talbot advised. After the next shift, Goldthorpe returned to the bench, again out of breath and covered in sweat, and said to Talbot, "Fuck it. That didn't work either."

"Bobby always wanted to play that style with puck possession and moving the puck around," says Nilsson. "But it was hard playing centre for that line. If I passed to Bobby, I'd get shit from

Anders. If I passed to Anders, I'd get shit from Bobby. If I shot myself, I'd get shit from both of them."

"Ulfie was the brains of our line," says Hedberg. "He made it work with his vision and his ability to distribute the puck. He had no physique and he wasn't much of a skater, but he was very, very competitive. Peter Forsberg is a better skater, but I see the same competitiveness there. They'll be a step behind the play and they'll whack and hack their way back into the play. They both have that edge."

That edge also made the Swedes' lives interesting. Both Hedberg and Nilsson knew they'd encounter some resistance in North America, but they weren't prepared for what they faced night in, night out. This was an era when the Philadelphia Flyers of Broad Street Bullies fame won Stanley Cups with a particularly vicious style of play. The WHA, moreover, had only a handful of players who could match the Swedes' skill, and the rest of the league attempted to level the playing surface in the predictable manner. Hull remembers one game in San Diego around the middle of their first season together when the Jets beat the Mariners 9-7. Nilsson picked up five assists and finished the game looking, in Hull's gentle turn of phrase, like "ground hamburger." Hull also sounded off publicly after that game about his linemate's treatment. It wasn't the last time it would happen.

"It was bad, really bad," says Nilsson. "Guys would get suspended for two or three games now for some of the things they did, and they barely got a penalty in our league."

"They took a shit-kicking that first year," Hull says. "They talk about toughness and competitiveness. I really think those two guys were the toughest players I ever played with."

They had to be, because the Jets weren't over-endowed with toughness in 1974-75. The following year they would add the formidable Ted Green to their blueline, and Barry Long and Dave Dunn arrived two years later. In Year 6, the Swedes' last

season in Winnipeg, the Jets finally landed the ultimate deter-
rent in Kim Clackson, and that made life easier. Still, you
wonder what would have happened to the next generation of
European players if Hedberg and Nilsson had been scared out
of the WHA in their first season.

"I wasn't thinking too much about that," Nilsson says. "I was
just trying to survive."

"Thommie Bergman helped," says Hedberg. "Borje Salming
helped. We helped. If you want to be on the leading edge of the
plough, you're going to have to get dirty. It was a time when
teams thought they could win by intimidation. But it wasn't in
my personality to be scared. There's no way that was going to
bother us, and, believe me, lots of people tried."

After that first year, Hedberg went home to Sweden for the
off-season determined to learn how to fight. But when he and
Nilsson returned, Green, who'd just joined the Jets from New
England, let them in on a little secret. The veteran defenceman
told the Swedes it drove the Whalers crazy that they couldn't be
thrown off their game. They'd whack. They'd hack. But they
couldn't slow down Hedberg and Nilsson, and that frustrated
them no end. There were a lot of ways to prove you were tough,
Green said. Their way made the deepest impression.

"I've played and been around a lot of great players, but I have
a great deal of respect for Ulf Nilsson and Anders Hedberg," says
Green. "They had to play through a lot of crap and they had the
strength of character to do it without changing their game. I'm
not sure how they survived. A lot of Canadians wouldn't have
taken that abuse and played the game the way these guys did. It's
because of them the NHL is such a global game now."

For all the notoriety gained by the Hot Line in their first year
together, the Jets still missed the playoffs, and there persisted the
notion that no team could win playing the effete style the
Europeans favoured. After the 1974-75 season, Rudy Pilous sat

The two players most responsible for the WHA's survival: Bobby Hull and Gordie Howe. (© *Bruce Bennett Studios*)

Howe was forty-five when he came out of retirement, and his comeback was largely regarded as a novelty act by the hockey world. He would lead the Aeros to back-to-back Avco Cups in his first two years with the team. (*M. DiFiacomo/ © Bruce Bennett Studios*)

Marty and Gordie Howe after New England Whalers owner Howard Baldwin signed the Howe clan out from under the NHL's Boston Bruins. (© *Bruce Bennett Studios*)

Gordie and Mark Howe played on the same line with the Aeros, forming the most dangerous two-man partnership in the WHA. Mark was the triggerman on the line, Gordie was the playmaker. (© *Bruce Bennett Studios*)

The Hot Line. There might have been better lines in the game's history than Hull, Anders Hedberg, and Ulf Nilsson. There haven't been any as influential. (© *Bruce Bennett Studios*)

The Quebec Nordiques' ascension started when they acquired Marc Tardif from the Michigan Stags. Tardif's game epitomized the Nords' wide-open, attacking style. (© *Bruce Bennett Studios*)

Defenceman Rob Ramage, complete with his Great Gazoo helmet, was one of six underage juniors signed by Birmingham Bulls owner John Bassett. Ramage was also the first player taken in the NHL draft following the merger. (© *Bruce Bennett Studios*)

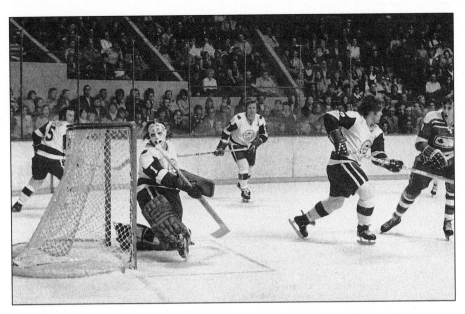

Whalers goalie Al Smith in a game against the Ottawa Nationals from Year 1. Smith was named the WHA's outstanding goalie in Year 6. After his retirement, he built an interesting body of work as a writer. (© *Bruce Bennett Studios*)

The Nordiques' J.C. Tremblay attempts to control a rebound as the New York Golden Blades' Andre Lacroix hovers around the net. Lacroix would record 106 assists with the San Diego Mariners the following season. (© *Bruce Bennett Studios*)

Mike Gartner was one of the many under-
agers signed by the WHA in their final season.
Playing on a line with slick centreman Robbie
Ftorek, Gartner scored 27 goals with the
Cincinnati Stingers. (© *Bruce Bennett Studios*)

Paul Stewart, the Ivy-League-educated tough
guy, gave the Stingers some much-needed
muscle before he became an NHL referee.
(© *Bruce Bennett Studios*)

Jacques Demers coached four different WHA
teams before he graduated to the NHL and
led the Montreal Canadiens to the '93 Stanley
Cup. (© *Bruce Bennett Studios*)

Glen Sather took the blueprint for his
Edmonton Oilers' dynasty from the Jets' team
of Hull, Hedberg and Nilsson. (© *Bruce
Bennett Studios*)

Wayne Gretzky in his
Indianapolis Racers'
uniform. Gretzky lasted
all of eight games with the
Racers before Nelson
Skalbania sold him to Peter
Pocklington and the Oilers.
His original nickname was
Brinks. (© *Bruce Bennett
Studios*)

Gretzky in the Oilers'
locker room shortly after
they dropped the sixth
game of the Avco Cup
final to the Winnipeg Jets,
the last game in the
WHA's history.
(© *Bruce Bennett Studios*)

down with Jerry Wilson and reviewed the team. The Europeans all received passing grades, and in the case of Hedberg, Nilsson, and Sjoberg, exceptional ones, while most of the North Americans got failing marks. Pilous then drew the remarkable conclusion that there were too many Euros on the team. A stunned Wilson said, "Walk me through this again. These guys have passing grades. These guys have failing grades. And the reason we missed the playoffs is we have too many of these guys?" When Wilson reported Pilous's assessment to Hull, the Golden Jet spat out, "In a pig's ass," and Billy Robinson went out and signed two more Swedes, Willy Lindstrom and Mats Lindh, for the 1975-76 campaign.

That fall, the Jets became the first North American club team to tour Europe when they conducted a nine-game pre-season exhibition series. They finished with a 5-3-1 record, including a win over the Swedish national team, then returned home and raced to a 15-6 start. They would eventually finish the year with 106 points, tied with Houston for the league's best mark, before they ripped through the playoffs with an astounding 12-1 record, their only loss coming against Calgary. It was as impressive a season as any WHA team would ever record. It was also not without incident.

The issue of violence against the Swedes became an ongoing theme with the Jets that second season, and Hull acted as the Europeans' advocate even as the rest of the league howled in derision. The Golden Jet sat out an October 24 game against Denver, then held a teary press conference the next day, claiming he'd staged a one-game protest against violence in hockey. Later that season, the Jets beat Quebec 10-3 in Winnipeg, and police had to be called to break up a brawl. After sweeping Edmonton in the first round and dispatching Calgary in five games in the second, the Jets met the Aeros, winners of the two previous Avco Cups, in the final in what should have been one of the most memorable series in WHA history. The Jets, however, took out the Aeros in four straight, winning the fourth game 9-1. The Hot Line accounted for three goals and eight points in the deciding contest.

"Those guys used to take a beating, but they came right back at you," says Mark Howe. "They were the ones who knocked us off our perch and I have a lot of respect for Anders and Ulfie. They changed the game."

The Aeros team that year may have been better than their two Avco Cup teams. In addition to the three Howes and the other mainstays from the championship teams, they'd added eighteen-year-old winger John Tonelli to play with fellow youngsters Terry Ruskowski and Rich Preston. The first game of the series drew 15,256 fans to the Summit in Houston and ended when Hull scored the game-winning goal late in the third period. Game 2 drew 14,794 fans in Houston and ended when Hull again scored the game-winner late in the third period. By the time the series moved back to Winnipeg, the Aeros were a spent force, and the Jets romped to victory in consecutive games before sellout crowds. Nilsson, Hull, and Hedberg finished one, two, and three respectively in playoff scoring, and Nilsson was named the playoff MVP.

Hull, however, remembers that season for another moment.

"We scored this goal in Phoenix," says Hull, still smiling at the memory. "It was the perfect goal. We came out of our end, made about five passes, and it was in the net. When we got back to centre ice, you could have heard a pin drop. Then the fans gave us a standing ovation, because they knew what they'd just seen."

By their third season together, the Hot Line had become the talk of the WHA, if not the talk of the hockey world. That pre-season, Hull fractured his wrist when he was hit from behind by the St. Louis Blues' Bob Gassoff as the Jets were spanking the NHL club 6-2. Hull would play in just thirty-four games that season, but Hedberg went nuts, scoring 51 goals in his first forty-seven games to become the first WHA or NHL player to score fifty in less than fifty. While he was chasing the record, Hedberg cracked his ribs in late January and missed two games. He had them taped, came back, and scored four goals in an 11-1 win over Edmonton, four more in an 8-2 win over San Diego, and three more in a 6-4 win over Calgary. He injured his knee after his first goal against the Cowboys and came back and scored two more. He would miss the next two weeks with strained knee ligaments.

"I know when my name goes into the record book, people will read Maurice Richard, fifty goals in fifty games, and Bobby Hull, fifty goals in fifty games," Hedberg said at the time. "Then they'll read Anders Hedberg and say, 'Anders Hedberg? Who's he?'"

He wasn't far wrong, although the rest of the hockey world was starting to take notice.

"Anders Hedberg playing in the WHA is like Secretariat running in the state fair," said Bruins GM Harry Sinden.

Year 5 was eventful for the Jets for reasons other than Hedberg's assault on the record book. That December, they met the touring Czechoslovakian national team in Winnipeg, fell behind 4-0 heading into the third period, and rallied to win 6-5 as six different players scored in the final frame against goalie Vladimir Dzurilla. Later that month, the Jets became the first professional club from North America to take part in the prestigious Izvestia tournament in Moscow. They finished their four games against the Swedish, Czech, Finnish, and Russian national teams with a 1-2-1 mark and the players received $2,000 apiece – $500 per game – for their efforts. Hull held a press conference in Moscow attended by some fifty Russian journalists and broadcasters. Still, one voice declared the Jets' participation an unmitigated disaster.

"Sending a second-rate team to a high-calibre tournament like the Izvestia was foolish on the part of everyone concerned," sniffed Alan Eagleson. "The Russians have gained a lot of political advantage from this foolishness. Already they're running around saying they've beaten the best team in the WHA. It makes everything look second-rate, and a lot of what we've done in the international arena has gone for naught."

Eagleson, of course, was the czar of international hockey at that time and viewed those games as his property. Literally. That spring, the Canadian entry at the world championships was beaten 11-1 by the Russians. The Russians, meanwhile, sent over a touring side that winter that featured seventeen of the players who'd met the WHA All-Stars in 1974. In the highlight of the tour, that team edged the Jets 3-2 with Alexander Yakushev scoring a pair of goals and goalie Vladislav Tretiak stopping twenty-eight of thirty shots.

"You are lucky," Konstantin Loktev, one of the Russian coaches, said after the game. "You have beautiful players in Winnipeg."

As for the rest of the WHA, not so much. A Greek chorus rose from the league's coaches that year concerning the preferential treatment afforded the Jets by league powers. Referee Bill Friday was routinely referred to as Lars-Erik Friday for his perceived bias toward the Jets. Edmonton coach Bep Guidolin said, "They've got professional rules for us and amateur rules for Winnipeg." Quebec coach Marc Boileau said, "There's a rule book for the WHA and one for the Winnipeg Jets." Calgary coach Joe Crozier said, "It seems when you play the Jets, hockey becomes a non-contact sport."

The Jets, for their part, weren't quite as passive in the face of the constant aggression as they'd been the previous two years. In a pre-season game, Guidolin and Jets coach Bobby Kromm got into a punch-up when Oilers defenceman Barry Long crosschecked the Jets' Mats Lindh after he scored a goal. In another game early in the regular season, the Nordiques' Curt Brackenbury pummelled Dan Labraaten, the Jets' newest Swedish import, and Kromm immediately accused Boileau of targeting Jets players. The next time the two teams met, Kromm and Boileau started throwing punches at a pre-game meeting that was held to discuss the WHA's new rules emphasizing less-violent play.

"What Anders and Ulfie went through was enough to send anyone back," says Jets goalie Joe Daley. "Some nights it was just godawful. There were some real jaloonies in that league, but the Swedes kept playing their game and, as time went on, we added to our team and we could play it any way you wanted."

The Jets weren't solely dependent on the Hot Line by Year 5. Labraaten was placed on a line with Lindstrom and shifty centreman Peter Sullivan, and with Hull out for half the season that unit had a huge year. Lindstrom scored 44 goals and finished with 80 points. Between all the international exhibition games and the playoffs, as well as the regular season, he played in 123 games that season. (Read that last sentence again slowly.) Sullivan had 31 goals and 83 points. Labraaten survived his run-in with Brackenbury and finished the year with 24 goals and 51 points in just sixty-four games. They would lose the final to Quebec City that season, but the next year the Jets added Clackson and another incandescent talent in Kent Nilsson and demolished the league.

"Just look at the players we had on that team," says Hedberg as he begins to tick off the names. Since their days with the Jets, Riihiranta and Ketola have both been high-ranking members of the Finnish hockey federation for years. Green has coached in the NHL for more than twenty years. Checking winger Bill Lesuk was the director of scouting with NHL teams in Winnipeg, Phoenix, and Chicago. Lindstrom, Labraaten, Bergman, and Sullivan are all high-level scouts. "That was no ordinary team," Hedberg concludes.

The Europeans "borrowed from our style of play and we certainly borrowed from theirs," says Green. "The end result was, the game was better. We were ahead of the curve in a lot of areas: tactics, systems, conditioning. One of the reasons I got a chance to coach in Edmonton was because Glen Sather respected the way the Jets played and he wanted to know more about what went on inside the team. Glen built his team off the Winnipeg Jets."

It was a pretty good model. Hull, who was close to retiring before the Swedes arrived in Winnipeg, would score 197 goals in the 264 regular-season games he played with Hedberg and Nilsson. When the Swedes left for the New York Rangers following the 1977-78 season, Hull, who was also in the throes of a messy divorce from his wife, Joanne, retired. He made a half-hearted attempt at a comeback the first year of the merger, and even attended a Rangers training camp a couple of years later in the hopes of rekindling the fire with his former linemates. By then, however, he was forty-two and the Swedes were having problems of their own in Gotham.

"We were never really able to play together in New York," says Hedberg. "Ulfie was never healthy. In the end, we didn't play the way we wanted to, and we didn't have Bobby Hull on our left wing."

In his retirement, Hull has also seemed lost. While he's been able to coast by on an assortment of autograph sessions, personal appearances, and after-dinner speaking engagements, the honour and respect which should be his have been missing. Hull can blame himself for most of his problems. In 1998, while in Moscow, he made international headlines when a series of remarks that revealed a less-than-enlightened world view were attributed to him. He subsequently denied those remarks and threatened to sue the reporter who wrote the story, but the damage had been done. ESPN, the American cable giant, then profiled Hull as part of its *Sports Century* series. The lengthy piece focused to a large degree on Hull's troubled relationship with Joanne. His relationship with his five children with Joanne is also strained, and Hull once told a magazine writer, "My only regret is that I lost my family. Of course, I should have lost my wife a long time before."

"I know there've been situations that haven't painted me in the best picture," Hull now says. "It's not the first time it's happened in my life. I've had some experience with adversity."

But no matter what else Hull is, his contribution to the modern game is immeasurable. He single-handedly blew open the market for players and allowed his generation and succeeding generations an opportunity at a real payday. Because Hull jumped to the WHA, the reserve clause was challenged and defeated. His partnership with Hedberg and Nilsson broke down the preconceptions about European players and opened the door for the next wave of Euros. The game they played in Winnipeg, a hybrid of European speed and skill and North American straight lines and tenacity, liberated hockey from barbarism and created the template on which the best of today's game is played.

Hull, in short, did for hockey what Curt Flood, Dr. J., and Joe Namath did for their sports, but his contribution to the game has seldom been acknowledged by the NHL and the NHL Players' Association. He also took hockey to markets at which the established league thumbed its nose, and he remains as responsible as anyone for today's thirty-team NHL.

You can judge if that's a good thing or a bad thing.

"Every player on every team should bow down to him on their knees," his old Chicago teammate Stan Mikita said when Hull retired. "He did more for us than any player in history. Nobody else could have done that."

"Everything I've done in my career was for the betterment of the game," Hull says. "I don't need anybody to tell me that. I know what I did and what our line did."

And his linemates know what Hull did for them.

"Bobby had an individualistic personality, and I know he's not a stranger to controversy," says Hedberg. "But he was incredibly strong and supportive as a teammate. You couldn't ask for a better friend or a teammate."

As for the Swedes, their contribution to the game has been similarly marginalized. Their brilliance is undeniable, as is their pioneering work with the Jets. Yet not only are they excluded from the Hockey Hall of Fame, they're not a part of the discussion. It is the *Hockey* Hall of Fame that stands in Toronto, not the NHL Hall of Fame. On that basis, Hedberg and Nilsson should walk through the front door and take their place among the game's immortals.

"It really bothers me we're not in the Hall of Fame," says Nilsson. "I just look at what we did for the game in North America. I don't know many people who did what we did. It's brutal, just brutal."

# "They provided some beautiful moments."

W hen Harry Neale was growing up in Toronto, he used to have fights with the neighbourhood kids over who would be Gordie Howe in their endless ball-hockey games. Of course, only one of them could be Gordie Howe, and as often as not Neale ended up playing that role. That didn't make it any easier for the New England Whalers coach when his hero, now age forty-nine, appeared at the Whalers camp in the fall of 1977 with his two sons.

"I was scared to death I was going to have to be the coach who had to tell Gordie Howe he was through," says Neale. "I mean, I'd seen him play in Houston, and he was great. But he was going to turn fifty that year.

"Thankfully, Gordie made sure that wasn't a problem."

Howe would finish the season with 96 points. Neale still regards it as the greatest achievement he witnessed in his coaching career.

This was just one of many noteworthy developments in the WHA's 1977-78 campaign, the last season in which the rebel league would pose any threat to the NHL, and in many respects the greatest season in the history of the league. The Hull-Hedberg-Nilsson line was at the peak of its power in Winnipeg, and the two Swedes would be pursued by virtually every team in the NHL that season. The Cincinnati Stingers had loaded up for the merger, and while they didn't make it to the finish line, they iced the best team in the history of the franchise in Year 6. Glen Sather was starting to build his team in Edmonton based on the Jets model. The Birmingham Bulls would unleash one of the most memorable teams in hockey history on the unsuspecting league. Most remarkable of all, no team folded during that last good year, and by their standards at least there was order and stability in the WHA.

It started with the Howes' arrival in New England. Hockey's first family hadn't left Houston on the greatest terms, and that summer the Boston Bruins and their general manager, Harry Sinden, had made a huge pitch for Mark and Marty. Mark was close to signing with the Beantowners, who were prepared to accommodate his father with an executive position in another company. But if Mark jumped to the NHL, it would have meant the end of Gordie's playing career, and the young star wasn't going to have that on his conscience.

"Boston was offering me twice what I was making, and I would have gone, but I stayed for Dad," says Mark. "It was really close, but I couldn't do that to my family. That just wasn't going to happen."

In the meantime, the Bruins lost to Montreal in the Stanley Cup final in 1978 and again to the Habs in a seven-game semifinal the following season. What might have happened with Mark Howe in their lineup?

"I talked Mark into going to Hartford and I wish I hadn't," says Marty. "It was a huge mistake. I was there ten days and I wanted to get traded. But Dad wasn't going to play with the

Bruins, and at the last minute Boston reneged on the guaranteed money, so we decided to go to Hartford."

Despite his elder son's misgivings about the Whalers, 1977–78 may have been the most remarkable season of Gordie Howe's remarkable career. Neale, apparently, wasn't the only WHAer who was worried about Gordie heading into that year. Terry Ruskowski, Howe's former teammate in Houston, said at the start of Year 6, "I think Gordie is ruining his image as a great hockey player. I wish he would retire." There were also concerns about his arthritic wrist, and they intensified when he failed to score a goal in the pre-season. But when they dropped the puck in the regular season, and the live ammunition started flying, the ageless wonder ripped off 9 points in his first six games and never looked back. He turned fifty that March. He also played in seventy-six games, more than either of his two boys, and finished ninth in the league in scoring.

"It wasn't his talent for the game or his toughness, and believe me that was impressive enough," says Neale. "It was his passion for the game. He never got tired of practising, let alone playing."

Neale tells a story from that year in which the Whalers played three games in four nights. When the team landed in Edmonton for the third game of the stretch, Neale ordered Howe to take off the morning skate. "I'm serious about this," the coach said. "We need you to be fresh." Knowing that wasn't going to be enough, he had the trainers pack away Gordie's equipment. Neale then arrived for the morning practice session to find six or seven players on the ice, including Howe in another player's equipment.

In training camp that year, Neale opened workouts with a two-mile run. The patriarch of the Howe clan had never been one for jogging – his goal every year was to show up for camp one pound lighter than the weight at which he'd finished the previous season – and he developed shin splints after his roadwork.

Neale excused his hero from the run the next day, but he also explained things to his team.

"I told everyone, 'Gordie isn't going to run today, and I'm going to make you guys a deal. If any of you play for me until you're fifty, you won't have to run either,'" Neale says with a cackle.

Gordie's sons, meanwhile, saw a different, more complete picture of their father that year. The previous season, after the Fighting Saints II had folded, Whalers president Howard Baldwin bought Dave Keon, Johnny McKenzie, Steve and Jack Carlson, Louis Levasseur, and others. When the Howes arrived in Hartford, Keon and McKenzie, whose wars with Gordie went back to the days of the NHL Original Six, cornered Mark and Marty and delighted in telling them stories about their father.

Keon, for example, told of one of his first seasons as a young centre in Toronto when he put the hook into Gordie one too many times. His veteran teammates on the Leafs told Keon to watch himself. Keon protested, "There's no problem. I'm just going for the puck." "That's the point," the older Leafs said. "It's Gordie's puck. He doesn't like it when you try to take it away from him." Sure enough, the next shift Keon got a little too close to number 9, an elbow flashed, and the Leafs centre woke up about thirty minutes later in the hospital.

Then there was this one from Neale. Gordie used to take the faceoffs for his line, and in a game against Winnipeg he found himself across from Kent Nilsson. Nilsson was a sublime talent, but he wasn't the bravest soul in the world, and he was well aware of Howe's reputation. Neale looked at the faceoff circle and saw, to his utter astonishment, Howe waving his stick under Nilsson's nose. When the shift ended, Neale went over to Gordie and asked what he was doing.

"I was just asking him if this bothered him while he was taking a faceoff," Howe answered.

The father was every bit as protective of his two sons as he'd been in Houston. At one point in the season, Neale looked at Gordie sitting on the bench with one hand in a bucket of hot water for his arthritis and the other in a bucket of ice. Neale asked him what was wrong, "Aw, I've got this hand thing," Howe said, showing his coach a hand that was like a balloon. "I'll be all right." A couple of days later, Mark took a shot off his foot and Gordie saw him favouring it. "You better take practice off," he advised his son.

"Their relationship was very much father-son on the ice," says Larry Pleau, who played with the Howes that year. "He watched over his kids, and if Gordie didn't like the way his boys were getting treated, there'd be trouble."

Just ask Robbie Ftorek. On New Year's Day, 1978, the Whalers were playing the Cincinnati Stingers when Marty pinched in at the blueline and Ftorek, attempting to lift his stick, hit the defenceman in the face. According to Neale, Howe was on the ice with the trainer while play was still going on, and when Marty was put in the hospital for observation that night, his dad stayed over with him.

The two teams met again in the last game of the regular season with the Whalers needing to hold the Stingers to two goals or less to win the coveted WHA trophy for the fewest goals allowed. With about five minutes left, the Whalers were winning 6-1 and the puck went into the corner with Ftorek in pursuit. A nanosecond later, Gordie arrived, Neale heard the crowd gasp, and Ftorek lay crumpled on the ice while Howe went to the penalty box for five minutes.

"Now I'm pissed off they might score," says Neale. "I've got to say something to him. It's my job as the coach, but I'm dreading it. I finally said, 'Gordie, you can't do that with five minutes to go in the game.' He said, 'You're right, Harry. But I couldn't let that bastard get away with what he did to Marty on New Year's Day.'"

One final story from the Howe archives. The boys had made a deal with their father that they'd call him Gordie at the rink. One night, the Whalers were playing in Quebec, when Mark saw a hole and took off as Gordie was battling for possession of the puck. In the heat of the moment, Mark called out, "Dad!" and Gordie looked up and hit him with a sixty-foot pass on the tape. Mark went in, flicked his wrists, and put the puck in the top corner of the net.

Says Neale, "They provided some beautiful moments."

Robbie Ftorek's issues with Gordie Howe aside, the shifty American centre was one of the league's most recognizable stars, and when the Stingers signed him to a new deal before the 1977-78 season, it was interpreted as a clear sign the DeWitts were building for the NHL.

It didn't work out that way, but the Stingers of Year 6 were still one of the more intriguing teams in WHA annals. Their captain was Rick Dudley, a strong two-way winger who was also one of the toughest players in the league. Dudley, who played with a wild mop of black hair poking out from his helmet and a full beard, would become an NHL GM, one of the most respected talent scouts in the game, and a bright, articulate voice in the NHL.

At least one WHA veteran finds the transformation interesting.

"I listen to him now, and I can't believe it's the same guy," says Bill Friday. "He was a real cementhead in our league."

"I've never seen anyone who could snap like Duds," says Barry Melrose, a defenceman on that Stingers team. "He was one of the scariest individuals I've ever been around. He'd be going along just fine, then something would happen to set him off, and watch out.

"[Stingers forward] Claude Larose used to do an imperson-ation of him, and he had him down to a T. Duds had a distinc-tive style of skating, and Claude would go around the ice just like him. Then he'd stop and pretend to hear something in the stands. Then he'd launch himself into the stands and start swinging at these imaginary fans. It used to crack us up."

The difference between Dudley and so many of his WHA confreres, however, was that the Toronto product could play. In Year 6, he toiled on a line with Richie Leduc and Blaine Stoughton (immediately dubbed the LSD Line, this being the 1970s) that became one of the league's best units. That year the Stingers also had Mike Liut in goal, a young defence built around Melrose, Barry Legge, and Craig Norwich, and a potent offence triggered by Ftorek and the LSD Line. The only element they were missing was heavyweight toughness. That situation would be rectified after one of the most famous brawls in WHA history.

On Thanksgiving Day, 1977, the Stingers travelled to Birmingham, where Glen Sonmor had just acquired Dave Hanson and Steve Durbano in a trade with the Detroit Red Wings and had recalled Frank Beaton from the minors. The Bulls' starting lineup that night featured Durbano, Beaton, Serge Beaudoin, Gilles "Bad News" Bilodeau, and Bob Stephenson. The Stingers countered with Ftorek, Del Hall, Jamie Hislop, Ron Plumb, and Legge.

If you can guess where this is going, congratulate yourself on your grasp of the obvious.

Twenty seconds into the game, a line brawl started. The five Stingers had the same chance as five pygmies in an elephant stampede. Beaudoin started pounding on the five-foot-ten, 160-pound Ftorek. Bilodeau squared off against Hislop, who wasn't much bigger than Ftorek and totalled all of 17 penalty minutes that season. Durbano battled Plumb, who never accumulated more than 66 penalty minutes in any of his eight professional seasons. After peace had been restored, however, referee Peter Moffat incredibly gave the Stingers the extra penalties and Dudley went ballistic. Stingers coach Jacques Demers threw sticks on the ice and tried to get at Bulls GM Gilles Léger. After the game, Demers was still livid: "This proves to me Glen Sonmor is not a hockey man. I put real live hockey players on the ice. He put out goons."

"The thing I'll always remember about that fight is they had this minister come out and say a prayer before the game," says Melrose. "He's at centre ice, going, 'And God please protect these players and deliver them from harm and watch over them.' And the minute they drop the puck this war breaks out. Duds went crazy that game, and after that we changed the look of our team."

Dudley and Demers would each be suspended one game for their part in the riot, quickly dubbed the Thanksgiving Day Massacre, and Dudley went to management, demanding they find a heavyweight. The call went out to the North American Hockey League, where Paul Stewart, who'd failed in a three-game tryout with Edmonton the year before, was gleefully plying his trade. Stewart, who used to train with boxing champ Aaron Pryor, had fought most of the WHA's tough guys in previous years in the NAHL, and no one had to explain to him why he was being summoned to Cincinnati. The Stingers offered him a three-game tryout. He held out for five games. And one of the more interesting careers in hockey was born.

Stewart was an Ivy League graduate from University of Pennsylvania who had a degree in Asian history and who loved to fight.

"Paul Stewart was as tough as any player I've ever seen," says Dudley. "I did it for a purpose, but he actually liked to fight. He'd fight anyone, anywhere, at any time, and you had to admire him for that."

Stewart's first game was against the relatively meek Indianapolis Racers and he didn't get a shift. The next day he asked Demers about his lack of ice time. "Don't worry," the coach told him. "We're in Birmingham tomorrow. You'll play."

"It was all the guys I'd fought in the North American league, so I knew what I was up against," Stewart says. "To quote Yogi Berra, it was *déjà vu* all over again. They were trying to intimidate me in the warmup: 'We're going to kick your ass.' I just said, 'You'll know where to find me.'"

That night, in his version of the natural hat trick, Stewart fought Beaton, Bilodeau, and Beaudoin. A couple of nights later, the Stingers were in Hartford, and Whalers GM Jack Kelley – "He was like an uncle to me," Stewart says – warned the league's newest gunslinger about Jack Carlson.

"Kelley told me he's the toughest guy in the league, don't try him," Stewart says, "I said, 'Sure thing.'"

That night, Stewart scored a goal in his first shift, which is memorable, because it was the only goal he scored that season and one of just five he'd score in his WHA/NHL career. The next shift, Carlson came out on the ice, and Stewart soon found himself in a more familiar role.

"Out comes Jack, they drop the puck, and we go toe-to-toe at centre ice," Stewart reports. "My brother was there, and he said the crowd was roaring when it started. Then it got real quiet, and all you could hear was *thwack, thwack*. We went at it for two minutes, and there was no holding on. When we were finished, Bill Friday came up to us and said, 'That was the greatest fight I've ever seen.'"

"He was different," says Friday. "After every fight he'd ask me, 'Bill, how did I do? Did I beat him?' After the Carlson fight I told him it was the greatest fight I'd ever seen, and he was happier than hell."

In the penalty box, Carlson informed Stewart that he'd been lucky in their first go-round and upon their release there would be a further encounter. The five minutes elapsed. The two players returned to the ice. And off they went again.

"It wasn't as good as the first fight, but it was still pretty good," says Stewart. "I knew I'd earned some respect, because there wasn't a third fight."

After the game, Stewart approached the Stingers' management about a contract. He was given $25,000 for the rest of the season with a $1,000 signing bonus. "It was just before Christmas and I wanted to buy some presents, so they gave me $1,000 in cash," he says. Stewart would play forty games with the Stingers that season. He scored one goal, added five assists, and accumulated 241 penalty minutes.

"That was me," he says with a shrug.

The next season, he played twenty-three games with the Stingers before Demers took him to Quebec in 1979-80 in the first year after the merger. In one game against Boston that season, Stewart fought Terry O'Reilly, Stan Jonathan, and Al Secord.

When his playing career ended after the 1979-80 season, Stewart began refereeing high-school hockey games around Boston. In 1983, he called NHL referee-in-chief Scotty Morrison about a job and was advised to enrol in Bruce Hood's referee school. He was placed in the NHL's training program, ended up working sixteen years as an NHL referee in The Show, and retired at the end of the 2002-03 season.

"When he became a referee, I told him, Paul, you should make a hell of an official, because you know the rule book so well," says Friday. "You broke every rule in there."

Stewart's grandfather had been an NHL referee, and his father had worked at the collegiate level. The one-time tough guy worked over a thousand NHL games before he retired and, no, he doesn't see anything contradictory about the way he played and his officiating career.

"I wasn't the greatest player myself, but I had a passion for the game and I wanted to see it played well," Stewart says. "I think I understood why people went to the games. And I always felt fortunate to be a part of it."

Stewart wasn't the only player who battled with the Bulls that year. As mentioned, when Sonmor arrived in Alabama, he orchestrated the first interleague deal between the WHA and NHL when he sent Vaclav Nedomansky and Tim Sheehy to Detroit for Dave Hanson and Steve Durbano. Nedomansky and Sheehy were skill players. Hanson and Durbano were not. In addition to saving the Bulls some half a million dollars in contracts, the deal also sent a pretty clear message about the direction they were headed.

"You look at that trade," Hanson says, "and it tells you all you need to know about the kind of team Glen wanted."

Hanson had no illusions about the game that got him to the WHA, but Durbano was a different story altogether. At his best, he was a big, mobile defenceman who had some offensive ability and a considerable mean streak: Scott Stevens, if you will. At his worst, he was one of the most destructive forces ever let loose on the ice, and that was to the other team *and* himself. His original nickname was Durby, which soon became Demolition Durby, and that captured the essence of the man perfectly.

"He was big, mean, he could shoot the puck and make a play," says Garrett. "But he'd just snap and he'd be out of control. He could play any system you wanted for a while, but then it was see-you-later. He was off on his own."

It was a strange world Durbano inhabited. His former teammates say keeping him on track was a demanding job at the best of times, but any chance the big defenceman had at normalcy disappeared about the time he married Lisa. Garrett tells of the first meeting between his own wife, Sharon, and Lisa Durbano. It was at the wives' lounge in Birmingham, and the conversation went something like this.

*Lisa*: You're a pretty girl.

*Sharon*: Thanks.

*Lisa*: You should get your tits done, like mine.

Whereupon she lifted up her top to reveal her surgically enhanced bosom. Apparently, she'd got her money's worth.

Later that year, the Bulls were in Winnipeg, and Durbano was out carousing when Lisa called the team's hotel, looking for her husband. Durbano's roommate, Phil Roberto, answered the phone and told Mrs. Durbano her husband was out. "Have him call me when he gets in," she instructed. Durbano, alas, didn't return until the next morning. When he called his wife, she informed him she'd killed the family dog and was in the process of burning the furniture.

"Durby loved that dog," reports Garrett.

The Stingers played the Bulls soon thereafter, and every time they went past the Birmingham bench, they began to bark.

Durbano would play just one more season after the 1977-78 campaign, and when his playing days ended, his life spun out of control. In 1983 he was arrested and sentenced to seven years in prison for trafficking cocaine. Upon his release he was caught shoplifting. In 1995 he went back to prison after he attempted to recruit an undercover police officer into an escort service he operated.

Durbano died in 2002 in Yellowknife of liver cancer. He was fifty.

"I talked with him a couple of times about it," says Steve Shutt, a Hall of Fame left winger and Durbano's teammate on the Toronto Marlies. "He knew what he was getting into. He couldn't get out of it. I don't know why. I watched him, grew up with him, watched him waste it away. He just couldn't control himself. It's too bad, really, because he had genuine talent. He didn't have to be a fighter. He could play the game."

But at least he played with some kindred spirits on the Bulls that season. Individually, the Birmingham hitmen ran up some impressive penalty totals. Collectively, their stats boggle the mind. Frankie Beaton: 56 games, 6 goals, 279 penalty minutes. Serge Beaudoin: 64 games, 8 goals, 115 penalty minutes. Gilles

Bilodeau: 59 games, 2 goals, 258 penalty minutes. Steve Durbano: 45 games, 6 goals, 284 penalty minutes. Dave Hanson: 42 games, 7 goals, 241 penalty minutes. The Bulls also rang up $23,650 in fines and lost forty-two man-games to suspensions. Durbano himself was suspended for eighteen games in total as a result of four separate incidents.

"We went from the finesse team to the goon show," says Mark Napier. "When Glen took over, he realized they wanted wrestling in Birmingham. It was scary enough practising against that team. I can imagine what it was like playing against them."

But at least they played to an appreciative audience. The veteran hockey writer Al Strachan recalls going to a game in Birmingham that season against the New England Whalers. Before the game, "The Star-Spangled Banner" and "Dixie" were played. The Bulls' cheerleaders – the Cobblettes, who were named for a nearby bar – formed two lines on the ice and the players were introduced. Dave Keon then scored four minutes in to give the Whalers a 1-0 lead, and that was enough hockey for the crowd. They started chanting, "Bring in the goons, bring in the goons," and Sonmor obliged by sending out a line with Bilodeau, Stephenson, and Beaton. Bilodeau immediately jumped Marty Howe. The next shift, Hanson went after Whalers defenceman Bill Butters. The crowd went wild. This was hockey night in Birmingham.

That Bulls team included the patrician Frank Mahovlich, who would go on to become a Canadian senator, and Paul Henderson, who'd just become a born-again Christian, and the two veterans stood out among their teammates like Dennis Rodman at an Amish wedding. Mahovlich had a pet turtle named Sammy, which he doted on. At Christmas, Henderson passed out Bibles to his teammates. Henderson still cringes at the memory of that team. So does everyone who played against them.

"It was a good thing I was on that team or they would have killed someone," says Henderson. "I must have stopped a hundred fights that year. Most of those guys were good guys off the ice. Well, Durbano was just crazy. But you put a pair of skates on some of them and their eyes would go glassy."

In the first round of playoffs that year, the Bulls would meet the Winnipeg Jets in the WHA's version of going from the ridiculous to the sublime. As good as the Winnipeggers had been in the first three years Hull, Hedberg, and Nilsson played together, the Jets of 1977–78 were clearly the best team ever assembled in the rebel league. That season they added Kent Nilsson, a forward from Ulf Nilsson's hometown of Nynasham and an Atlanta Flames draft pick. Ulf described his namesake thus: "He skates like Anders, shoots like Bobby, handles it like me, but doesn't try very hard all the time." If there ever was an accurate description of the Magic Man, that was it. That year, his first as a pro, the twenty-one-year-old totalled 42 goals and 107 points, giving the Jets four 100-point scorers in their lineup. Willy Lindstrom also scored 30 goals from the second line, and Sjoberg ended the season plus-60. All told, the Jets averaged just under five goals a game in the regular season, went on a fifteen-game winning streak in February, and lost one game in the playoffs in rolling to their second Avco Cup in three years. That year the Montreal Canadiens won their third of four straight Stanley Cups, losing just ten regular-season games and two playoff games in the process. Following the season, the Jets would issue a challenge to the Canadiens. The WHA was always big on challenges and, of course, this one went unanswered. But Hull maintains a series between his team and the Habs would have produced some of the most memorable hockey in the game's history.

"You look at those two teams," Hull says. "I have no doubt that our line would have outplayed the Lafleur line, and our other lines would have held their own. We were probably shy a defenceman or two, and they had the Big Three then [Larry

Robinson, Serge Savard, and Guy Lapointe], but just think about the hockey. We wanted to show the fans the game the way it should be played."

Now, you'd dismiss Hull's posturing as so much hot air except for one thing. On January 5, 1978, the Jets faced the mighty Russian national team at Winnipeg Arena and beat them 5-3 in a game Hedberg says was every bit as good as the Canadiens' fabled 3-3 tie with Red Army on New Year's Eve, 1975.

"If that game had been televised nationally, they'd still be talking about it," says Hedberg.

That night, the Hot Line played head-to-head against the Russian's great line of Valery Kharlamov, Alexander Maltsev, and Boris Mikhailov and went plus-five against them. Hull, in perhaps his greatest game ever, scored three goals and added an assist; Ulf Nilsson scored twice and picked up two helpers; Hedberg drew two assists. The sellout crowd of 10,315 floated out of Winnipeg Arena that night.

"I played against them quite a few times with the Swedish national team, and we always lost," says Hedberg. "But that night our line beat them 5-0 and our fans went crazy. You couldn't imagine a more proud, excited group of fans.

"We only played four years together, and it was always exciting. We had this incredible support from the community. It was a small market, but it had this world-class hockey team and they were very proud of it. It was a special relationship, one you don't often get in professional sports."

And one that was in the process of ending. The day of the game, New York Rangers general manager John Ferguson and his star centre, Phil Esposito, flew into Winnipeg to negotiate with Don Baizley, agent to the two Swedes. "I can't believe we flew in here to talk two guys into leaving this place," Esposito said while trying to stay warm on a bitterly cold day. Hedberg and Nilsson had signed five-year extensions after their original deals with the Jets, but they also had out clauses after two years.

The Jets had the right to match any outside offer, but even with a new ownership group taking over the team late in the season it was obvious to all concerned that the two stars had priced themselves out of Winnipeg. Yes, there was some talk of a public Save-the-Swedes movement, and the new owners bravely said they'd match any offer for Hedberg and Nilsson. But in the end, and in a sad foreshadowing of the Jets' ultimate fate, the franchise simply couldn't afford to keep its two stars.

"This was all new to us," says Baizley. "We thought it was going to be good, but we didn't know it would be that good."

Oh, it was good all right. Of the NHL's eighteen teams, fifteen were involved in the bidding. Bobby Orr flew in from Chicago to woo the Swedes. Bobby Clarke dropped in from Philadelphia. On any given night, the crowd in Winnipeg would include NHL GMs, scouts, and personnel directors. In December, the Swedes asked Jets coach Larry Hillman for a day off, flew to New York with Baizley, and had dinner with Ferguson, Rangers president Bill Jennings, and Sonny Werblin, the president of Madison Square Garden. At one point, Ulfie said if the offers got up to $200,000 a year, they were gone. The offers soon hovered around half a million per player. When Hedberg and Nilsson went to the WHA All-Star Game in February, players pleaded with them to stay, because they were afraid they'd lose their jobs.

The bidding was soon narrowed down to two teams, the Blackhawks and the Rangers. For a time, the phones stopped ringing and Baizley started worrying. "I thought the jig was up," the agent says. "I thought they'd decided they weren't worth the money. My stomach was churning."

Then the Rangers came back with an offer of $600,000 per player per year. The WHA initially made noises about pooling their resources to keep the Swedes, but when Jennings let it be known the Rangers could go higher, the league dropped out.

"We'd just taken over, and the first thing we know, New York is making this huge offer to Hedberg and Nilsson," says Barry Shenkarow, one of the Jets' new owners and its future president. "We had a right to match, but there's no way. We told the Rangers, We're going to match, but if you want to work something else out, maybe we can do a trade. They called our bluff."

"It was more exciting than sad," says Hedberg. "The league was shaky, and we didn't know there was going to be a merger. We still had friends in Winnipeg and their attitude was, 'You've got to take advantage of this opportunity.' There weren't any bad feelings. It was like they were proud of us."

They were all of that. In May, after the Jets had disposed of the New England Whalers to win the Avco Cup, the *Winnipeg Free Press* ran a series of fans' letters to Hedberg and Nilsson.

"I'm trying to express my gratitude towards you," wrote Audi Sims. "I pray you may be loved and respected by the people in New York and all those with whom you come in contact. I don't think they'll be able to match our love and respect because we love and respect you more than these words, or any words, can ever express."

The Bulls, not unexpectedly, weren't similarly disposed to the Jets and their departing stars. Before the series, and with the Manitoba capital worked into a lather over the impending confrontation between good and evil, a Winnipeg TV type grilled Glen Sonmor on his team.

"No one has ever been able to control Steve Durbano," the TV wiener said. "What makes you think you can do it?"

"What makes you think I want to control Steve Durbano?" Sonmor answered icily. And thus the table stakes for the series were set.

In game one, the Jets scored five power-play goals as they blitzed the Bulls 9–3 in a game that will forever be remembered in Winnipeg for L'Affaire Hair. Early in the first period . . . well, why not let Dave Hanson tell it.

"I looked at that series as my opportunity to go out and make an impression," Hanson says. "So I went out there on my first shift, and I thought I had Bobby lined up, but he flattened me. The next time I tried it again, and I might have got my elbows up a bit, and we went at it.

"So we're fighting, and the place is going crazy. Then all of a sudden it was like someone flipped a switch. The noise stopped. Everyone else stopped. I looked in my hand, and there it was: Bobby's toupée. I threw it down and it just lay there."

Hanson had, indeed, yanked off the great man's rug, which immediately raised a fine point of the WHA rule book. The league issued automatic match penalties for pulling hair in a fight. Friday, however, assessed Hanson a minor and major, because, technically, he hadn't pulled on Hull's real hair. Hull, for his part, left the ice holding his toupée and returned for the second period wearing a Jofa helmet. This development filled Hanson with regret.

"When I finally got out, I lined up next to Bobby and said, 'Bobby, I'm so sorry,'" Hanson says. "He said, 'Don't worry about it, kid, I needed a new one anyway.'"

Game two was more of the same, with the Jets winning 8–3 on the strength of four more power-play goals. "The only way to stop the intimidation was to score goals on the power play," says Hedberg. But it also helped that the Jets had added Kim Clackson to their lineup that season.

Clackson was obtained from Indianapolis on the recommendation of Pat Stapleton, and if he wasn't the toughest player in the league, he wasn't far from it. The twenty-three-year-old defenceman would play a semi-regular shift with the Jets that season, accumulating 203 penalty minutes in just fifty-two games. He was an undersized heavyweight, sort of the Tie Domi of his era, and, like Domi, he had a remarkable capacity to take a punch before he started throwing. In the end, he was every bit as good at his job as Hull, Hedberg, and Nilsson were at theirs, and he might have been just as important to the Jets.

"Our team changed when we got Clackson," says Joe Daley. "We said, We'll play hockey, but if you want to goof it up, you'll have to talk to Clackson. He was one of the strongest men I've ever seen."

Clackson was ejected in the first period of game two for his part in a fight with Gilles Bilodeau. Hanson, Phil Roberto, and Bilodeau, meanwhile, were all tossed, and Bilodeau received a match penalty for kneeing, resulting in the Jets having a two-man advantage for seven minutes in the game. At one point in the contest, Birmingham had eleven players on its bench and seven in the penalty box.

"We'll see if they all come to Birmingham," Sonmor said after game two.

After the Gong Show in Winnipeg, game three went off without incident, and the Bulls actually earned a 3-2 win on a late goal by Cam Stewart set up by, *ta-da*, Durbano. The Bulls were partly inspired by a clipping on their locker-room bulletin board in which Jets defenceman Ted Green offered the following opinion of their team.

"They've got a stupid coach who's a goon himself. He knows nothing about the execution of technique. The only thing he knows about hockey is to get the toughest, meanest, dirtiest, funniest-looking guys, put them on the ice and call them a hockey team."

Actually, that was a fairly accurate description of the Bulls, but in game three the two teams combined for just three minors over the final two periods. Game four marked a resumption in hostilities — a sign greeted Hull, "HAIR TODAY, GONE TOMORROW" — and Hanson and Clackson fought twice before Jets coach Larry Hillman, GM Rudy Pilous, and Bulls owner John Bassett got into a screaming match at the end of the game. The

Jets blitzed their crude colleagues 5-1 before finishing them off in game five.

"They took a tremendous amount of abuse and still won," said Bulls captain Dale Hoganson. "They showed us they have jam."

"[Hedberg and Nilsson] are not only great hockey players but they're smart," said Sonmor, in character to the end. "Smart because they're leaving Winnipeg. Winnipeg is one of the places I'm happiest to leave, too."

On the series, the Jets scored twelve power-play goals, and Hedberg and Hull each totalled 6 goals and 3 assists in the five games. The win earned them a bye into the league final, which also meant they had to sit around for nineteen days while the Whalers and Nordiques battled it out in the semis.

"I'm just glad we're playing hockey against them," said Neale of the Jets after his Whalers took out the Nordiques. "They'd wipe us out in golf."

The Whalers arrived in the finals after an eventful season of their own. In the early morning of January 17, with the league breaking for the All-Star Game in Quebec City, the Hartford Civic Center's roof collapsed under the weight of a huge snowfall. A college basketball doubleheader had been played there the night before.

"I don't want to think about what might have happened," says Howard Baldwin.

Baldwin and Neale were in Quebec City when their home rink cratered, and Baldwin, in particular, had played hard the night of the disaster. They phoned him at five in the morning and at first he thought someone was trying to play a practical joke. When he was finally convinced that there was a huge problem, he hopped on a plane and flew back to Hartford.

"I couldn't believe it when we flew over the thing," says Baldwin. "It was like Godzilla stepped on it."

"I got this call first thing in the morning from my wife," Neale remembers. "She said, 'The roof fell in.' I said, 'Will they be able to fix it by the weekend?'"

Not exactly. The Whalers moved back to Springfield for the remainder of the season, but the whole incident was a blessing in disguise for the franchise. The roof's collapse allowed the team to rebuild the Civic Center up to NHL specs, and when it reopened for the 1979-80 season, Hartford had a 15,635-seat rink.

"I'm still not sure what we would have done if the roof *hadn't* caved in," says Baldwin.

The Whalers had other problems in the spring of 1978, and principal among them were the Jets, who didn't exactly grow rusty during their long layoff. With the Hot Line producing only sporadically, Winnipeg still won the first three games of the final, including game three by a whopping 10-2 count. Game four in Winnipeg was pushed back to Monday of the May 24 long weekend, which allowed Neale to raise a rallying cry for his troops.

"Boys," he said, "this is your one chance to fuck up a parade."

The Jets clinched the Avco Cup anyway with a 5-3 win. Hedberg scored two goals and added two assists in the deciding game. Ulfie had three helpers. Hull scored the game-winning goal. It was the last game the line would play together.

"We knew we were the best team that year and no one was close to us," says Hedberg. "Our mission was to win the Avco Cup. It was like our teammates decided, We're not going to send Anders and Ulfie off without this thing."

"It was sad, but I was happy for them," says Hull. "I was at the end of my career. I wanted them to show the NHL what kind of players they were."

The Whalers' goalie in games three and four of the final was Al Smith, who was named the league's top netminder. Smith had backstopped the team to the Avco Cup in the WHA's first year and returned to the rebel league that season after a two-year stint with the Buffalo Sabres. He is remembered today as one of the most intriguing characters to play in the WHA, which, you should understand by now, is saying something.

Neale says his goalie was a hippie when the concept of hippiedom wasn't exactly embraced by the hockey world. He read. He watched foreign movies. He wrote. This marked Smith as an oddball to his peers.

"He was a little to the left of the right side of the railroad tracks," is how Larry Pleau puts it. "He had his own ideas about things, but he was a competitive guy and a good teammate."

He also had a wicked sense of humour. The Whalers had Swedish twins on their team named Thommy and Crister Abrahamsson, who had to drive through a tough Latino neighbourhood on their way to the rink in Hartford. One day, they got trouble from some punks hanging out on a street corner and told Smith about it. The Whalers goalie thought about their problem for a minute, then said, "This is what you do. The next time you drive through there, you raise your middle finger to them. That's the sign that you're friends in Puerto Rico."

Neale says the twins had to rip through a red light the next day to escape the angry mob.

After he retired, Smith attempted to carve out a career as a writer and drove a cab to support his various projects. He wrote a novel entitled *The Parade Has Passed*, in which a star forward from the WHA, Lonnie "Lahdee Dahdee" Daniels, hitchhikes to the funeral of his former coach, Red Eastman, who's been murdered in a brawl. Fifty copies of the book were printed. Sales didn't hit double digits.

Smith also wrote a play, *Confessions to Anne Sexton*, which he mounted with the money he received from his NHL pension settlement – "my Carl Brewer money," he called it. *Confessions*, which was about a former goalie who makes a trip to New York with a friend to take in an Impressionist art exhibit, was supposed to run for four weeks in a downtown Toronto theatre, but it shut down after three. One reviewer, who gave the piece a generally positive review, wrote, "The rule used to be as long as the audience outnumbered the performers, the theatre was obliged to put on a show." He noted six people showed up that night. Allen Abel, who profiled Smith in *Sports Illustrated*, attended one night on a complimentary ticket. There were two other patrons in the theatre for that performance and they both left at intermission. Mark Brender, a writer for *The Hockey News*, went to one of the last nights of the run and the show was cancelled because he was the only person in the audience. A crowd – if that's the right term – of seventeen showed up on opening night. It was the biggest house to take in the play.

"It's an awful thing," Smith said of his writing jones, before adding, "I haven't cheated. I've put in my time and made enormous sacrifices. It's not some delusion. It's not some fantasy."

"He believed he was a writer," says Abel. "He saw himself as a craftsman of the written word."

And he was willing to drive hack to support his craft. Neale, who became one of the most recognizable broadcasters in Canada, recalls getting into a cab outside Union Station one night. The driver said, "Hi, Harry." Neale grunted a hello, then looked a little more closely at the man behind the wheel. It was Smith.

Pleau stayed friendly with his former teammate and would leave him tickets at Maple Leaf Gardens when he coached the Whalers. "He chose his own path, and there were things he wanted to do with his life," says Pleau. "That's the way he lived. On his own terms."

And that's the way he died. A malignant tumour was found in Smith's pancreas in December 2001, and the old goalie was given three to six months to live. He lasted eight and spent most of his last summer going to movies and visiting art galleries with his friend Jim Keon, Dave's brother. He was also working on another novel, *The Tragedy of Lake Tuscorora*, when the cancer began to take its toll. His son Adam, an English major, had read all of his father's work and pronounced most of it terrible. But there was one fourteen-page section in *Tragedy* which, against all odds, Al Smith nailed. He was on his deathbed when his son told him about those fourteen pages and how they'd moved him.

Smith, who was in considerable pain, opened his eyes and said, "Really?"

"It was pretty good that I got a chance to tell him, and it was even better that I meant it," Adam Smith said.

His father died a writer. You sense that's all he ever wanted.

# CHAPTER II

# "He surprised me. He surprised everyone. Forever."

Nelson Skalbania freely admits it wasn't the game that drew him to the WHA. It was the action around the game, and in that respect he was fairly typical of the men who owned franchises in the rebel league.

In the mid-1970s, Skalbania, a structural engineer who fell into real-estate development and made a fortune, did a lot of business with Edmonton Oilers co-owner Dr. Charles Allard about the time Allard was growing weary of his team. Allard encouraged Skalbania to buy in, telling him he couldn't lose more than $300,000 a year and, depending on a merger, could make a ton. Skalbania had money to burn in those days, and he thought, I can live with that. He lost $300,000 in his first month.

"I was a jock, and this kind of fell into my lap," Skalbania says. "But it wasn't exactly a dream of mine to own a hockey team."

No, Skalbania didn't love hockey, but he loved the art of the deal, and that put him in good company in the WHA. He recalls sitting around a league meeting – "We were meeting every month, because there was always a crisis" – and he was about to pay $200,000 as a down payment on two thousand apartments in Toronto. Peter Pocklington heard about that, gave him a cheque for $400,000 on the spot and the two men made a killing. At a league meeting in Palm Springs, Cincinnati owner Bill DeWitt, Jr., cut Skalbania in on a real-estate deal in San Francisco and they lined their pockets.

"Some of us are friends to this day, and it's been twenty years," Skalbania says. "The fun we had. If we would have stuck to making money with each other, we would have been very wealthy. Instead we turned around and poured it all into our hockey teams."

Yes, it was a crazy time. One night in Edmonton, Skalbania was having dinner with Pocklington and Pocklington's wife, Eva, and mentioned he could use a partner with the Oilers. Pocklington reached over the table, took a diamond ring the size of a golf ball off his wife's finger, and gave it to Skalbania as down payment. Skalbania then went over to Pocklington's house and took ten paintings, mostly Group of Seven stuff, off the walls and drove away in a Rolls. To close the deal he received more paintings and two more Rollses.

"I never got a fucking cent from him," Skalbania says, still laughing at the memory. "But the more he owned of the Oilers, the less I had to pay in losses."

By the start of Year 6, Pocklington owned half the Oilers, and Skalbania, to ensure there would be seven teams in the league, had bought the Indianapolis Racers. Things were quiet in Indianapolis when the new owner arrived – too quiet for Skalbania's liking – and he immediately started looking for a deal to grab the market's attention. Following that first season with the Racers, he was talking to John Bassett about his plight when Bassett, owner of the Birmingham Bulls, told him about this kid he wanted to sign. The problem was, Bassett was in the process of signing six other under-agers, and he didn't have enough money left to sign the best one in Canada, a kid named

Wayne Gretzky who'd just played his first OHA season in Sault Ste. Marie. Bassett had even tried to sign the kid after the World Junior Championship in Montreal, but his dad, Walter, wouldn't go for it.

"I wasn't exactly a knowledgeable hockey guy, but John was urging me to sign him," says Skalbania. "So I listened to John."

And without knowing it, Skalbania bought the Hope diamond.

Wayne Gretzky's year in the WHA is barely a tumbleweed on the landscape of the Great One's career. He spent one season with the rebels, putting up extraordinary numbers for a seventeen-year-old kid playing with men, but before he knew it he was playing in the NHL, which was where he wanted to be all along.

Gretzky's year with the zanies is remembered today largely as a source of questions and answers in the popular field of Wayner trivia. Q: Who did Wayne Gretzky score his first professional goal against? A: The Edmonton Oilers. Q: Who were the two players traded to Edmonton with Wayne Gretzky? A: Peter Driscoll and Eddie Mio. Q: What award did Wayne Gretzky win in the WHA which he never won in the NHL? A: Rookie of the year.

Even Gretzky admits his contribution to the history of the WHA is minute.

"I'm proud of my small part," he says. "The legacy of the WHA is really Gordie and Bobby Hull and Johnny Bassett. I was just a small part of it."

Except for one thing. You could dismiss Gretzky's year in the WHA as a fluke of history – like Moses Malone's ABA career or Jim Kelly's USFL career – had it died there. But in looking at that season, at the forces that were brought together in Edmonton and their subsequent impact on the game of hockey, Gretzky's one-year WHA career is anything but inconsequential. It was the start of the greatest individual career in NHL history and one of the greatest teams in NHL history, and both the player's and the team's roots run deeply through the renegade league. It was only one year, but a lot happened in that one year, and even if there's a tendency to dismiss Gretzky's season in the WHA as unimportant, number 99 doesn't.

"I look at the guys I played with that year: Ace Bailey, Cowboy Flett, Ron Chipperfield, Dave Dryden," says Gretzky. "A lot of those guys had played with guys like Lafleur, Orr, and Clarke, and they understood the pressure. They made things a lot easier for me. It was the right situation with the right team and the right coaching staff.

"You just grow up faster when you're around men," he continues. "I don't think I would have evolved that quickly as a player if I'd stayed in junior. On the hockey side, it was a great stepping stone. I went from the OHA to the WHA to the NHL, and it was like a natural progression."

The Indianapolis-to-Edmonton part of the story wasn't quite as natural, in fact, but it was consistent with the WHA. Gretzky would discover that during his first meeting with Skalbania.

The year before he turned pro, Gretzky had served notice of what was to come when, as a sixteen-year-old, he ripped off a 182-point season with the OHA's Sault Ste. Marie Greyhounds. He now says the watershed moment of that season, and a turning point in his early career, was the 1978 World Junior Championship in Montreal, where he led a star-studded Team Canada in scoring with 17 points in just six games. After the tournament, Bassett offered Gretzky a contract to play out the year in Birmingham, but Walter Gretzky insisted his son finish the season in the Soo. Bassett would turn his attention to the Baby Bulls the next summer and direct Skalbania to the young prodigy.

"I wasn't expecting to leave that early," says Gretzky. "I was so young. But I started to think a little differently after the World Junior tournament. I was thrilled just to make the team, and it turned out to be a tremendous tournament with all these great players" – Team Canada included Bobby Smith, Mike Gartner, Craig Hartsburg, Rob Ramage, Rick Vaive, Stan Smyl, and Ryan Walter – "but when I made the team and played that well, I started to think about turning pro.

"I wanted to jump to Birmingham, but my dad was adamant about finishing the year in the Soo. Then in May we met with Nelson, and the pieces just fell in place. My whole goal was to play pro, and I just felt that in life you only get so many opportunities and this was one of them. I was a huge fan of Gordie Howe's and Bobby Hull's, and they were talking about so much money. In the end, it was easy. I'm outta here."

Except, of course, it wasn't that easy, because nothing in the WHA was ever that easy.

After Bassett persuaded Skalbania about the wisdom of signing the teenage phenom, the Racers' owner flew Gretzky out to his Vancouver home with Walter, Gretzky's mother, Phyllis, and his agent, Gus Badali. Skalbania picked them up at the airport in his Rolls, and the car promptly broke down. Skalbania then summoned another Rolls on his car phone – a car phone? who had a car phone? – and it too broke down. While they were waiting for another mode of transportation, Skalbania leaned in to Walter Gretzky and advised, "Walter, never buy a Rolls."

Walter Gretzky had worked for Bell Canada most of his adult life and never made more than $32,000 a year, according to his son.

"My dad just said, 'I don't think you have to worry about that, Nelson.'"

And that was just the start of the fun. When they arrived at Skalbania's house, the Racers' owner set about to determine if the young hockey player kept himself in shape and took him on a six-mile run.

"I was a runner then, so six miles wasn't that difficult for me," Gretzky says. "I don't know what would have happened if I didn't make it."

"I just figured if he could make it through six miles, he wasn't going to collapse on me," says Skalbania.

The next order of business was negotiating the contract, a process that, says Gretzky, took about five minutes. Then it was on to Skalbania's private jet. Skalbania had scheduled a stop in Edmonton for a press conference because the NHL draft was set for the next day and he wanted to spread word of his coup as quickly as possible. En route to Edmonton, Gretzky wrote down the terms they'd negotiated in Vancouver – "Nelson said he couldn't write while the plane was flying," Gretzky explains – and when it came to the issue of the team to which he was selling his services, he had to write down both Indianapolis and Houston, because Skalbania was sniffing around the Aeros. In Edmonton they were met by Jim Matheson, a hockey writer for the *Edmonton Journal*, and Rod Phillips, the Oilers' play-by-play man. This was the press conference. Gretzky, Skalbania, and the two media types proceeded to a nearby hotel, where they spent the next hour. Finally, it was on to Indianapolis.

Gretzky is asked if, anywhere between the Rolls breaking down, the six-mile run, writing out his own contract, and the stop in Edmonton to announce his signing with Indianapolis, he had second thoughts about Skalbania.

"I didn't know what to think," he says. "I was just so excited about the chance to play pro hockey. When Gus said we're going to Vancouver, I thought, That's strange. I think I know hockey, and I don't think there's a WHA team in Vancouver. Then Indianapolis came up and I had no idea where Indianapolis was."

He'd soon find out.

Gretzky's contract was a seven-year personal-services deal with Skalbania worth $1.7 million. His first job with his new boss was a ribbon-cutting ceremony at a Prince George, British Columbia, brewery Skalbania had just bought, because, naturally, you want an under-age kid to open your brewery. He then arrived in Indianapolis, where a wildly successful marketing campaign was being built around the teenage star.

"I think our season tickets jumped from 2,000 to 2,300 when we signed Wayne," says Skalbania. "That was all. A seventeen-year-old kid, no matter how good he was, wasn't going to sell tickets in that market."

In truth, a twenty-five-year-old Gretzky probably wouldn't have made an impact in Indy. Paul Deneau, Bill Dineen's old pal from Houston, put the franchise in operation in the 1974-75 season when the new Market Square Arena opened. Initially, by WHA standards at least, the team drew well, and under Jacques Demers they reached the Eastern Division final in 1976-77, averaging 9,295 fans per game along the way. The next season, Skalbania's first as owner, Demers decamped for Cincinnati and Ron Ingram and former NHLer Bill Goldsworthy coached a spotty assortment of players to a last-place finish in the eight-team league. Attendance would drop by almost three thousand fans per game, and by the time Gretzky arrived the franchise was running on fumes.

"It was awkward in Indianapolis," says Gretzky. "I was a seventeen-year-old kid trying to make his way, and there were players on that team a lot better than me. But they were marketing the team around me."

Gretzky, as always, is being modest, because even then there wasn't a Racer within a million miles of him. He was the player the team should have been built around. The problem was that Racers coach Pat Stapleton, a veteran of many NHL and WHA campaigns, took one look at the teenager and reasonably assumed it was unfair to place the franchise on his scrawny shoulders.

Gretzky, like Derek Sanderson in Philadelphia, would play just eight games with the Racers, totalling three goals and three assists. His first two goals were noteworthy, however, because they came against the Oilers about the time Skalbania was trying to cut his losses with the Racers. They also came while Gretzky played on a line with Angie Moretto and Kevin Nugent. There's a trivia answer for you. Here's another one. His original nickname in Indy was Brinks.

"I talked to Pat before the game and asked him about this kid," says Dave Dryden, the Oilers' goalie that night. "Pat said he's not so sure. He hadn't scored a goal and the magic wasn't happening. That night he scored twice and I remember thinking what a lot of goalies thought when Wayne scored on them: I should have had those two. He didn't overpower you. He didn't make you look bad. They just went into the net."

A week after that game, with the Racers hemorrhaging red ink, Skalbania decided to reduce his losses and move Gretzky. There were two teams vying for his services: Edmonton and Winnipeg. The Oilers had the advantage of having seen Gretzky play, and their coach, Glen Sather, was convinced he was the real deal. Goldsworthy had also ended up in Edmonton that season, and he advised Sather that young winger Peter Driscoll and goalie Eddie Mio were the best players on the Racers.

"I was just playing," says Gretzky. "I wasn't aware there was a problem. Three days before the trade, Nelson called and said, 'You've got a choice: Edmonton or Winnipeg.' I didn't know much about either team, but Gus was sold on Edmonton. They had a new arena and a better chance to get into the NHL. So it was Edmonton."

Again, it wasn't that easy. In Winnipeg, a new ownership group was in its first full year of operation, and the Jets had just whipped out $500,000 to purchase the contracts of thirteen Houston Aeros. But even with that commitment, Winnipeg was still in the hunt. Barry Shenkarow, one of the Jets' new owners, had been told by his new general manager, John Ferguson, that Gretzky would be a star, and Shenkarow and Jets president Michael Gobuty flew to Indianapolis to meet with Skalbania.

They offered him $250,000 and a one-sixth franchise share for Gretzky. Pocklington offered substantially more cash.

Skalbania took the money and ran.

"Rudy Pilous [the Jets' old GM] told us Gretzky would never play in the NHL and Fergie said, 'Get him. He'll be great,'" says Shenkarow. "Michael and I flew to Indianapolis to meet with Nelson. He had this deal worked out with Peter for all this money and Nelson wanted the money. Peter and Nelson had a unique relationship. It was like the Wild West with those two. The ordinary rules didn't apply."

According to legend, there was one final twist to the Jets' participation in the Gretzky deal. During their negotiations, Skalbania supposedly challenged Gobuty to a game of back-gammon for Gretzky's services. Gobuty lost, and that's how Gretzky became an Oiler. It's a great story; unfortunately, it's the only WHA tale that isn't true. Well, not altogether true.

"Nelson offered to play me one game of backgammon, our franchise for Gretzky," says Shenkarow. "I just said, 'Uh, no.'"

"Obviously, it wasn't the right decision, but at the time it made sense," Shenkarow continues. "We had no idea about the NHL. Paying that kind of money for a player in the WHA was illogical. We'd just spent all this money on the Houston players. Gretzky represented a big gamble to us."

As it was, he represented a huge loss for Skalbania. The deal with Pocklington was recorded as a straight cash transaction: Skalbania was to receive $850,000 for Gretzky, Driscoll, and Mio. Skalbania says he never received $850,000. He also says that as part of the deal he waived a $500,000 option he owned to buy back in to the Oilers in the event of an NHL merger.

The capital, moreover, was supposed to give Skalbania the wherewithal to finish the season in Indianapolis, and after the trade he said, "I'm going to continue this season come hell or high water." Stapleton, for his part, said, "Wayne Gretzky has an excellent future as a hockey player, but from our position we can't wait for a player to develop. The number-one guy we'll miss is Mio."

They didn't miss him for long. On December 15, which was supposed to be a payday, Skalbania folded the Racers.

"I was pissed off," says Skalbania. "By the time I sold Wayne, I'd had enough of hockey. I had this private jet, and every time I flew into Indianapolis I had to bring a cheque with me. It wasn't a lot of fun owning a team in a strange town which wasn't crazy about hockey and paying out those losses."

Neither was losing the Hope diamond.

"I wasn't smart enough to see how good he was," Skalbania says. "He surprised me. He surprised everyone. Forever."

Two years before Gretzky's arrival, and under the luckless Skalbania's stewardship, the Oilers were in worse shape than Keith Richards. Bill Hunter was never the general manager he believed himself to be, and when Skalbania bought the team he removed the old lion from the corner office and replaced him with former Bruins coach Bep Guidolin. That summer, Glen Sather's contract had also expired with the Minnesota North Stars. The journeyman forward asked for a new two-year deal. The Stars offered one year. Sather, who made his summer home in Banff, then called Joe Crozier in Calgary, and was told the Cowboys' team was set but that Guidolin was looking for players in Edmonton. The Oilers would ultimately give Sather the two-year deal he wanted and a whole lot more.

Sather, typically, is ambiguous when he's asked if his goal was always to coach and manage. He says his experience in running hockey summer schools gave him a good background when Guidolin offered him the coaching job. He also says coaching was the farthest thing from his mind when he arrived in Edmonton.

Others aren't so sure.

"He always knew what he wanted to do and where he wanted to go," says Oilers defenceman Al Hamilton. "Even as a player he was hanging around management, trying to soak up knowledge."

But if Sather's motives were unclear, his direction when he assumed control of the Oilers was not. In the 1976-77 season, the Oilers played the Winnipeg Jets twelve times, and Sather had the best seat in the house to watch the Jets' flowing puck-control game. He immediately decided that was the game he wanted to play in Edmonton, and when Gretzky was dropped in his lap he had the perfect centrepiece for his creation.

"They had a great transition game," Sather says of the Jets. "That was the way I structured our team. We took them to Finland and Sweden for training. I watched a peewee team, and they practised the same way the Jets practised. I took a lot of those transition drills, a lot of the stuff you see in the NHL today. That was really the beginning of that system. At that time, no one played that way."

If it's any consolation to Sather, no one plays that way in the NHL today, either.

"The thing about the WHA is it offered opportunities," says Dave Dryden. "My brother [Ken] played with Slats in Montreal, and he said, 'He's got a lot of confidence and he's smart,' and that was pretty accurate. He was a horse trader and he was good at picking up information by asking the right questions and talking to the right people. Once he got behind the bench, I really liked the way he handled things. He didn't over-coach. He was clear and direct. Then, when we got Wayne, he made sure he was surrounded with the right guys who'd teach him the right things."

Sather, in fact, seemed born to coach, and that was apparent to Guidolin. At his first camp with the Oilers, Guidolin made Sather the captain of the team and told him he'd run most of the practices. The veteran grinder also enjoyed one of his best offensive seasons as a pro, totalling 19 goals and 53 points in eighty-one games. Sadly, that was more a commentary on the rest of the Oilers than on Sather's talents. Toward the end of the season, with the Oilers mired in fifth place in the division, Guidolin called Sather into his office.

"He said, 'They're not responding to me. You're going to coach the team,'" Sather says. "I said, 'I'm not really interested in coaching the team.' He said, 'You're coaching or you're sitting in the crowd.' So I became the player-coach that day."

Under Guidolin, the Oilers were eleven games under .500. Under Sather, they went 9-7-2. In his first game as player-coach, Sather scored the game-winning goal in overtime against the Jets and immediately said, "One win doesn't make me a genius." He also said, "The only rule I have is if you do something to hurt the team, like staying out and drinking the night before a game, then you're in trouble." It was a simple philosophy, but it seemed to speak to the Oilers. They won their final two games of the season and beat out Calgary for the final playoff spot in the Western Division. The Cowboys would fold in the off-season. It was the beginning of a warm hockey friendship between the two cities.

That summer, Skalbania and Pocklington fired Guidolin and turned the team over to Sather. The Oilers of 1977-78 weren't appreciably better than they had been the preceding season, finishing one game under .500 and fifth in the eight-team loop before they were bounced in the first round of the playoffs. But that year they started to add some pieces. Ron Chipperfield came over from the Cowboys and would become the team's captain in its first NHL season. Paul Shmyr was acquired when San Diego took a dirt nap. Blair MacDonald rejoined the team from Indianapolis and Brett Callighen played his first full season in Edmonton. Those two would become Gretzky's linemates the following year. The Oilers also signed a monstrous young enforcer from the Brandon Wheat Kings named Dave Semenko.

They were all there when Gretzky arrived the following season. It was a fortuitous bit of timing for all concerned.

"You could see he was a quality kid, and that helped him with our team," says Dryden. "When you've got a young kid making that kind of money it can go two ways. I think our veterans saw the kind of kid he was and they decided to help him. He certainly helped a lot of them."

But first he had to get to Edmonton, and, as always with the WHA, that was a bit of an adventure.

Gretzky, Driscoll, Mio, and their gear took off from Indianapolis in a chartered Lear jet, which was interesting, because (a) they didn't know where they were heading, (b) no one had paid for the plane, and (c) Gretzky was terrified of flying. The three players had been told a deal had been made and they were going either to Edmonton or Winnipeg. The pilot then asked the trio the altogether reasonable question "Who's paying for this bird." After a nervous delay, Mio produced a credit card. That card had a $500 limit, but the pilot accepted it, then took off with the two older players in the passenger seats and a pale Gretzky huddled into the rumble seat surrounded by hockey sticks.

"I think he thought they would protect him," says Mio.

The Lear soon touched down in Minneapolis, where the players learned Edmonton would be their destination. It then landed at the Edmonton International Airport, conveniently located about thirty miles from the city, which was unfortunate, because the media had gathered at the Edmonton Municipal, located in town. At that point, the pilot decided to hold out for full payment until a call was arranged to Pocklington, who assured one and all that the Oilers would be paying for the flight. The cost came to $7,900 and a relieved Mio immediately had his credit-card receipt torn in half.

"I should have kept it," says Mio, who would form a lasting friendship with Gretzky and stand as best man at his wedding. "That would have made a great souvenir."

But Gretzky would provide other mementos to Mio and all of Edmonton over the next ten years. After the press conference that welcomed him to Edmonton, Gretzky met with Sather and asked for his junior number, 99. Sather had picked out number 14 for Gretzky and tried to tell him the goofy number he'd worn in junior would bring even more pressure. Gretzky said, "I'm going to have pressure anyway, I'd like to try it." When the teenager left the coach's office, Sather called in team captain Shmyr and said, "You're not going to believe this. The kid wants to wear number 99." Shmyr said, "It's the WHA. Who's going to notice?"

Gretzky moved in with Glen and Anne Sather his first three weeks in Edmonton, and the coach with the big ideas formed a bond with his preternaturally talented young centre. During one of their kitchen-table talks, Sather told Gretzky the Oilers were going to make it to the NHL, he was going to be his captain, and they'd win the Stanley Cup. Given the condition of the team and the league, he might as well have said, "I'm going to fly around this room backwards, then I'm going to turn into Queen Victoria in front of your very eyes." But Gretzky says simply, "I believed him."

On the ice, meanwhile, the trade paid immediate dividends as the Oilers beat the Jets 4–3 in overtime on, wait for it, Peter Driscoll's goal. They then went on a 9–3 spurt before they ran into a five-game losing streak on the road. The sixth game was in Cincinnati on December 12, and in the first period Gretzky's check scored. Sather then benched his young star for the entire second period before sending him out in the third with smoke coming from his ears. Gretzky would score three goals in that final frame and the Oilers won 5–2. Both men regard that game as a defining moment in the Great One's early development. It also cemented his relationship with the veteran Oilers.

"That was the last time he was benched in his career," says Sather. "I knew he was special before that. But he was like any other young guy. There are nights when you're on the road, you're tired and you don't feel like playing hard. I always thought that the coach's job was to push players, to get more out of them than they're willing to give you."

"A couple of the older guys, Ace Bailey and Cowboy Flett, came up to me and said, Keep your chin up," Gretzky says. "Then I scored three goals in the third period and I guess the rest is history. I learned a lot from that. You can go two ways. You can either mope about getting benched or you show you can play."

It was just one of the life lessons Gretzky would absorb that year. The Oilers surrounded the golden child with a collection of veteran hands who could see the kid's talent but would also instruct him in the time-honoured traditions of becoming a pro. In Hartford one night, the Wayner was caught with his head down for one of the four or five times in his twenty-year career and got drilled by Gordie Roberts. After the hit, according to Dave Dryden, Gretzky tossed his helmet down and skated off the ice. The next day at practice, Sather arranged a performance by Steve Carlson, who'd already established himself as the premier thespian on the Oilers by virtue of his work in *Slap Shot*. With Gretzky watching from the bench, Carlson came out in a number 99 jersey wearing you-know-who's Jofa helmet, performed a couple of theatrical pirouettes, then produced a dramatic swan dive whereupon a handful of the Oilers stood around his prostrate form pretending to take pictures.

Not a word was said to Gretzky. Nothing needed to be said.

Bill Friday also tells a story from that year in which Gretzky, who was developing a reputation as a diver, took a full gainer in Edmonton before the unimpressed official. With the home fans booing, Friday called over Hamilton and said, "You tell that kid if he wants to turn this rink into a swimming pool, I'll give him ten, and you tell him that right now." Hamilton passed on the message, and the next shift a sheepish Gretzky told the referee, "Mr. Friday, it will never happen again."

"I didn't feel like I had to sell hockey there," Gretzky says of the relief of playing in Edmonton. "I could just be a player. And the other players didn't look at me like, Who's this kid making all that money? I had some good people around me and they treated me like a teammate most of the time, but also like a seventeen-year-old kid sometimes, and that's what I needed."

It's also interesting to note that among that group not one of them will admit they had any doubts about Gretzky's talent. Sather says he saw it in the Oilers' game against Indianapolis earlier in the year when Gretzky scored two goals. Hamilton says, "He was a pimply-faced kid, but from the get-go you could see he had a gift. He had this uncanny ability to find holes and angles where no one else could find them, and he had a tremendous amount of poise for someone his age. After a while, you'd just shake your head at some of the things he'd do."

Dennis Sobchuk, who played that final WHA season in Edmonton, says, "You looked at this kid, and he was a kid, and you'd go, What's different about him? After a while the one thing I noticed is it was like trying to hit a feather when it's in flight. You can swing at it, but just when you're about to hit it, it moves. And he was always around the puck. He just knew where to be. The first couple of times you saw it, you thought it was just luck. After you watched it for ten games, you began to understand it wasn't just luck."

Still, not everyone was convinced. Jets GM Rudy Pilous has gone down in hockey history as the dolt who couldn't see Gretzky's ability, but he'd also coached the Chicago Blackhawks to a Stanley Cup in 1961 and he'd been around the game all his life. Tom McVie, another hockey lifer, coached the Winnipeg Jets that season and said he wasn't sold on the kid.

"Everyone else will probably tell you, 'Oh, yeah, I saw it right away. He was a genius on the ice,'" says McVie. "They're lying. To me, he looked like somebody's little brother. It looked like he was going to get fucking killed. But he made one pass that season that made me stop and think. He was behind the net with two guys, and he made this back pass to Blair MacDonald. I remember thinking, How did he know he was there?"

It wouldn't be the last time that question was asked about Gretzky.

Gretzky would turn eighteen on January 26 of that season, and Pocklington flew the young player's family in from Brantford to help celebrate. At centre ice, he signed a twenty-one-year contract with the Oilers, which would expire in 1999-99, get it? – the year he actually would retire. It's hard to determine the exact value of the contract, because it contained the usual WHA assortment of deferrals and side deals, but somewhere between $4 million and $5 million seems like a reasonable estimate. There was also a renegotiation clause after ten years. Today, of course, the contract seems laughable both in term and remuneration, but at the time it was groundbreaking and guaranteed the future of the working-class kid from Brantford.

"Looks like I'm here for life," Gretzky said as he signed the contract.

"I was just starting to come into my own, and a lot of the older guys were saying, 'Don't sign. You're going to be a lot better than you think,'" Gretzky now says. "But I come from a blue-collar family, and my dad kept talking about the security. It was a different era then."

After the game that night, the Oilers met at Shmyr's house for a team party to celebrate Gretzky's big day. Pocklington had sprung for a case of champagne and caviar, and Gretzky, who was finally able to drink legally, had more than a few beers with his teammates. A couple of guitars were also produced at some point, and Shmyr has a vivid memory of a slightly drunk, very happy Gretzky singing along with his teammates at four in the morning the night he turned eighteen.

"It was the first time he let his hair down around us," says Shmyr. "It was the first time we saw that side of him. He really was a nice, humble kid."

There were other reasons for Gretzky to be happy that year. Just prior to his birthday bash, the WHA hosted a three-game series in Edmonton pitting its All-Stars against Moscow Dynamo. The WHA All-Star Game had gone through a number of variations over the years: Eastern Division versus Western Division was the most popular, but there was one year when All-Stars from the Canadian teams met All-Stars from the American teams and another when the league All-Stars met the Avco Cup–champion Quebec Nordiques. By the time the All-Star break rolled around in Year 7, there were only six teams still standing, so an intraleague game would have been tricky. Instead, the league organized the three-game set with Dynamo, which was already in North America playing exhibition games against WHA teams.

That series would produce one of the most memorable lines in the history of the game.

Jacques Demers, who'd landed in Quebec that year, was named coach of the WHA All-Stars, and say this for the man, he recognized a moment when he saw it. Gretzky, of course, had grown up idolizing Gordie Howe, and he'd even struck up something of a relationship with hockey's Methuselah. When Demers was setting his lines, he put Gretzky between Gordie and Mark Howe, and the remarkable trio made magic against the Russians.

"I went up to Gordie and said, 'Mr. Howe, who would you like to play with?'" says Demers. "He said, 'You're the coach, kid. Whoever you say.' And I said, 'How about Wayne and

Mark?' It was important for me to do that for Gordie. It's one of those moments in your career you never forget."

Actually, it was one of those moments all three men, their teammates, Dynamo, and the fans who watched them in those three games will never forget. In game one, Gretzky, Mark, and Gordie each scored a goal and combined for seven points in a 4-2 win for the WHA. In game two, Mark and Gretzky scored goals and Gordie added an assist in another 4-2 WHA win. And in game three, the rebels completed the sweep with a 4-3 victory. Okay, the Legend Line was shut out in the final game, but that didn't for a minute diminish the beautiful symmetry and romance of a fifty-year-old Howe playing with his son and a seventeen-year-old Gretzky.

"How many guys can say they played on a line with Wayne Gretzky and Gordie Howe?" says Mark Howe. "You've got the best power forward who ever played and the best passer who ever played. My job was just to shoot."

Just before the series, Mark's father-in-law had passed away, and the younger Howe had been in Houston for his funeral. For game one, he flew all day, landed in Edmonton that afternoon, then scored one and set up two others and was booed when he was named the game's MVP.

He was never so happy to be booed in his career.

"Good players don't always play well together," says Mark. "I saw my dad and Bobby Hull in a lot of All-Star Games, and it was like oil and water. But playing with Wayne was different. It was like playing with Magic Johnson. You're running down the court and the ball shouldn't be there, but it is. That was Wayne. He'd hold the puck, then slide it into a place where a hole was developing, and you'd skate into it. Or you'd be in traffic and he'd find you when you weren't sure if he could see you. And there was no talking or yelling when we were on the ice. It was all instincts.

"In this game you look forward to playing with great players, and Wayne has such great respect for the history of the game," Mark continues. "I knew it meant the world to him to play with my dad."

Gordie Howe was eighteen when he played his first game with the Detroit Red Wings in 1946-47 and Syl Apps was still playing in the NHL that season. Thirty-two years later Howe was playing on a line with a kid not yet eighteen, a kid who would tear down the standard Gordie had set for greatness and erect his own. Two arcs intersected in Edmonton that year, and for three games hockey's past and its future met and the line was blurred between time and space.

"I didn't expect to be on the team, so when Jacques called me in and told me I'd be playing with Gordie and Mark, I almost fell down," Gretzky says. "Gordie was obviously my hero, and I had a chance to meet him as a kid and develop a bit of a relationship with him. Then to actually play with him — I just thought that was pretty special. It was a pretty good line."

When Gretzky, Driscoll, and Mio left Indianapolis, it opened up some roster spots on the Racers. Monitoring the situation from his home in Edmonton was Doug Messier, who'd played with Racers coach Pat Stapleton in Portland in the old Western Hockey League and whose seventeen-year-old son, Mark, was dominating the Tier II Alberta Junior Hockey League with the St. Albert Saints. As a sixteen-year-old, the younger Messier had recorded 74 points and 194 penalty minutes in fifty-four games with the Saints and suited up with Portland in the WHL playoffs that year. The elder Messier didn't know if his kid was ready for the pros, but he did know he was too good for the juniors. A call was made to Stapleton and Mark signed a deal for $30,000. He was making six bucks per win in St. Albert.

"Mark was six-foot-one, weighed 195 pounds, and he was a great skater," says Doug Messier, who's acted as his son's agent throughout his NHL career. "I was worried he'd be suspended most of the season, not because he was dirty but because he was aggressive and he'd just run over people."

Mark Messier was barely a blip on the WHA's radar screen. He played five games with the Racers before they folded, then moved on to the Cincinnati Stingers, where, playing on a line with Robbie Ftorek for most of the season, he recorded 1 goal, 11 points, and 58 penalty minutes in forty-seven games.

Messier was asked how he managed to score just one goal playing with the league's second-leading scorer.

"I don't know," he said. "I'm still trying to figure that one out."

Messier's lone goal that season, moreover, didn't exactly advertise a future Hall of Famer. According to legend, he flipped the puck in from centre ice during a game in Winnipeg and was on his way to the bench when it took a crazy bounce behind the Jets' goalie.

"It was a dump-in, and it wasn't a particularly good dump-in," says Mike Gartner, another Cincinnati under-ager.

"I went to dump it in and change and it hit a bad patch on the ice and went in the net," Messier says. "By the time it went in, I was sitting on the bench. Someone said, 'You just scored a goal.' I said, 'How did I do that? I'm sitting on the bench. Maybe I should try that more often.'"

But, as with Gretzky, there were developments in Messier's WHA season that would take on some significance as he morphed into one of the best players in the game's history. One of his teammates in Cincy that season was veteran Bryan "Bugsy" Watson, who would be hired as a scout by Glen Sather in Edmonton the following off-season. Sather, a family friend, also saw Messier play a dozen times that year and maintains he could see the potential in the bruising young winger.

Not everyone in the league, however, could make that claim.

"I bought him his first beer," says Paul Stewart, Messier's teammate in Cincinnati. "I remember we went to Sleep Out

Louie's, and he was dressed in these overalls with white socks. He looked like he just fell off a combine. Pete Rose was in there. He looked at me and said, 'Who the fuck is that?'"

"I knew Mike Gartner was going to be great, but Mess you weren't so sure about," says Barry Melrose, a former teammate. "He was big and physical, but there was nothing there to suggest what he would become."

What he lacked in finesse, however, he made up for in fractiousness. Many of the players who saw him that season compare the young Mess to a young Eddie Shack, a wrecking ball who'd charge around the ice like a rhinoceros in heat, indiscriminately hitting everything that moved. Dennis Sobchuk, who was playing for the Oilers at the time, remembers a game where Messier clobbered him on one of those search-and-destroy missions, then lumped him out in the ensuing fight. This, remember, was a seventeen-year-old playing with men. Someone, it seems, might have taken a chance on him with one of the forty-seven picks before the Oilers grabbed him in the summer of 1979.

"I played against him a couple of times, but I knew he was going to be good," says Gretzky. "He had the speed and size. I still can't believe all those NHL teams passed on him in the draft that year. It's like, What are you thinking?"

Two years after he was drafted by the Oilers, Messier would score 50 goals. He would be the last WHAer still playing in the NHL.

"The next year, when I went to the NHL, I really thought I had one up on the guys coming out of junior from those fifty-two games I played in the WHA," Messier says. "I felt playing pro hockey, playing against men, gave me the confidence, and I had an edge. It was a stepping stone for a lot of young players, and it was exciting. A lot of players will tell you they owe a lot to the WHA."

After his slow start in Indianapolis, Gretzky would finish third in the league in scoring with the Oilers. His 110 points put him behind only Quebec's Buddy Cloutier and Cincinnati's Robbie Ftorek. The Oilers, who led the league in attendance with an average crowd of 11,255, also ran away with the WHA's regular-season crown, finishing eleven points ahead of the second-place Nordiques and fourteen ahead of the third-place Jets. They then outlasted the New England Whalers in the first round of the post-season before they met the Winnipeg Jets in the last final of the WHA's seven-year history.

The Jets, in many respects, had a more eventful season than the Oilers in the WHA's final campaign. It started in the summer when the new ownership group purchased the contracts of the thirteen Houston Aeros, making their team, on paper at least, as strong as the Jets' powerhouse that ripped through the league the previous season. Kent Nilsson would finish the year with 107 points. Morris Lukowich, one of the Aeros, scored 65 goals. Peter Sullivan, likely the most underrated player in WHA history, rang up 46 goals and 86 points. Just prior to the Gretzky affair, they'd also signed John Ferguson, late of the Rangers, as their general manager, and Fergie would steer the Jets through the swamp that was the NHL merger.

But despite the new players and the new GM, Winnipeg struggled mightily through most of the season. The Houston players didn't mix well with the Jets' hold-overs. Head coach Larry Hillman was barely keeping the team over .500. By March, Ferguson was aware something had to be done to shake the team from its lethargy, and with just four weeks left in the regular season he gassed Hillman and brought in his pal Tom McVie to coach the team.

For the first and only time in his career, McVie was in the right place at the right time.

McVie might be the funniest, most likable man ever to stand behind an NHL bench, but in his eight seasons of coaching in the

NHL it seemed the hockey gods never tired of making him the butt of their private joke. His career record is 126-263-73. He finished over .500 in a season exactly once, with the New Jersey Devils in 1991-92. He also coached four of the worst teams in NHL history. The 1975-76 Washington Capitals, who were one year out of expansion, went 11-59-10. The 1983-84 Devils were 17-56-7. And the 1979-80 post-merger Jets went 20-49-11. McVie coached part of that season, then to prove it wasn't a fluke came back the next year when the Jets went 9-57-14.

"I got fired in Washington just before the [1978-79] season started," McVie says. "I was standing on my front porch for five months. It got to the point where the mailman crossed the street when he saw me standing there. The first two days everyone in hockey called to sympathize with me. It was almost exciting. Then the calls stopped. I'd check my phone to make sure there was still a dial tone."

Ferguson, his boyhood pal from Vancouver, finally called, and the timing couldn't have been better. Lars-Erik Sjoberg was returning to the Jets lineup after missing most of the season with a torn Achilles tendon. The Houston players were starting to fit into the team. When the Racers folded, Ferguson grabbed goalie Gary Smith, and Smith, who started the season as Gretzky's teammate, was in the process of playing himself into shape. Sort of. The group also responded to McVie's motivational message and his emphasis on conditioning.

"I wasn't a miracle worker, but it was like we had twenty-two Marines out there," says McVie. "We just whipped through the playoffs."

The Jets swept Quebec in the first round, then took out the Oilers in six to win the final Avco Cup. Willy Lindstrom led their balanced attack with 10 goals, and Lukowich and Rich Preston added 8 each. Kent Nilsson had 15 assists, and McVie threw out a checking line of Bill Lesuk, Lyle Moffat, and Roland Erikkson, which contained Gretzky. The Great One scored two goals and added three assists in the final, but he was shut out in Oilers' losses in games one and two on home ice, which was when the Jets essentially won the series.

"I was in way over my head," says Gretzky. "We had a pretty good series against New England [Gretzky had 15 points in the seven games], and I was starting to become the go-to guy, but I was still a kid playing in the final."

Preston would be named the playoff MVP, but how Smith, who won all eight games for the Jets, was overlooked is astounding. Smith – who was playing goal for the California Golden Seals when Gretzky attended his first game at Maple Leaf Gardens as a six-year-old – beat the Oilers in Edmonton 3-1 in game one and 3-2 in game two. After the Oilers won game three in Winnipeg, he came back to win the fourth game 3-2 before stopping twenty-seven of thirty shots in the Jets' clinching 7-3 game-six victory. Just so you know, Dave Semenko scored the last goal in WHA history when he beat Smith late in the third period of that game.

Smith – a.k.a. "The Axe," a.k.a. "Suitcase" – played just one season in the WHA, but the wonder is how the upstarts missed him all those years. In a league that featured such all-star loons from the goaltending fraternity as Gilles Gratton, Al Smith, Andy Brown, Jacques Plante, and Don McLeod, Gary Smith could hold his own with the best of them. He made nine different stops in fourteen WHA and NHL seasons, and left behind a body of work that stands with the greatest eccentrics in the game. In his first NHL start with Toronto in 1965-66, an era when goalies were considered wildmen if they left the crease, Smith skated the puck past centre ice during a nationally televised game. On another occasion, he attempted to punt the puck off the scoreboard at Maple Leaf Gardens. He routinely wore twelve pairs of socks under his skates – "My record is sixteen," he proudly reports – for extra padding. He was yanked in one game in Vancouver when he was a member of the

Canucks, skated off the ice, walked out of the arena, and drove home in his gear. He wore a full-length lynx coat almost everywhere he went. McVie once caught him eating a hot dog on the bench during a game.

Smith freely admits to all this. He says, however, the one about him and former Canucks owner Frank Griffiths's wife, Emily, is fraudulent. At the team's Christmas party one year, the story goes, an over-refreshed Smith was introduced to Mrs. Griffiths, who told the goalie her maiden name was Ballard.

Smith, reportedly, said, "Hey, I've seen your picture on dog-food cans," which led to his trade to Minnesota.

"I wasn't quick enough to think of that line," says Smith. "I don't know why I did those things. It's just the way I was, I guess. But a lot of the stories written about me aren't very flattering. Everything people have read about me is the crazy stuff, and most of it isn't true. I always showed up for the games. If you talk to the guys I played with, you get a different picture."

The picture that emerges, in fact, is that of a goalie who, when he was right, was as good as any keeper in the game. In 1971-72, Smith went 14-5-6 with five shutouts and shared the Vezina Trophy with Tony Esposito in Chicago. Three years later, he carried the Canucks to the Smythe Division pennant and their first-ever playoff appearance, going 32-24-9 in a performance his teammates claimed was deserving of the Hart Trophy.

As luck would have it, McVie had coached Smith in Washington the year before the two men met again in Winnipeg. Prior to that season, McVie had the Axe tested, learned he packed about 250 pounds on his six-foot-four frame, then showed up at his home in Lake Tahoe, where he personally worked him down to 212 pounds. It was a similar story in Winnipeg, where Smith weighed in at about 240. He didn't play for a month. When he did play, "he stood on his head," says McVie. Smith then went 8-2 in the playoffs, and the goalie and coach who'd been through so much in their hockey careers won a championship.

"I love the guy, right," Ferguson says of Smith, his former goalie and racetrack crony. "They broke the mould when they made the Axe. But when he was on his game, he was as good as anyone I've ever seen, and he was on his game in the playoffs that season. He was the reason we won it all."

Gretzky's roommate on the road that final season was Ace Bailey, a checking winger who'd spent ten seasons in the NHL before arriving in Edmonton for his last year as a pro. Bailey had been in Boston during Bobby Orr's early years, and Sather reasoned the veteran would be able to mentor the seventeen-year-old rookie and apprenticing superstar. The two players quickly formed a lasting friendship, proving opposites really do attract.

"I don't know what great judgement went into that," says long-time Oilers scout Lorne Davis, still laughing at hockey's odd couple. "Living with Ace, he'd see all the facets of the game, that's for sure, because Ace was always in trouble. Maybe that's what Wayne learned from him, how to get out of trouble."

There was, for example, the time Ace and the young Great One went out on the town, then came back to Bailey's newly rented house only to find the key didn't work. Ace quickly wrestled a ladder out of the garage and attempted to break in through a window, and just as quickly the police arrived. It seems Bailey and Gretzky were trying to get into the wrong house.

Then there was the time Gretzky threw a dinner party for his pals in the Oilers' hockey department and went out with Bailey, now a scout with the Oilers, to purchase refreshments. Because this was the Wayner, and because this was Edmonton, a parade soon formed behind Gretzky's car that followed them back to his condo. When they got inside, Bailey announced to his colleagues, "You should see the crowd out there. I can't believe it. It's been a couple of years since I've played in Edmonton, but they still remember me."

On yet another occasion, Gretzky lent Bailey his car to drive up to Lloydminster, Saskatchewan, to see relatives when he was pulled over for exceeding the speed limit by a comfortable margin. When the cop asked for the registration, he noticed the driver of the vehicle wasn't, in fact, Wayne Gretzky.

"No," Ace answered quickly. "I'm his best friend. He asked me to break it in for him." And Ace, as always, got out of the jam.

Six years after Gretzky was traded to Los Angeles in 1988, Bailey went to the Kings as a scout, and there he enjoyed another long ride in the game he loved. Ace was one of the leaders of the scouting community, a closely knit confederation of hockey men who live a hard life scouring the game's back country for the next great star. On the road, he'd often find a motel or hotel room with cooking facilities, whip up a meal for eight or ten of his colleagues, then pass the night telling stories, most of which featured himself in a starring role.

"He was such a funny, upbeat guy," says Davis. "Each day was better than the next with Ace. It was a great way to go through life."

On September 11, 2001, Ace Bailey boarded United Flight 175 at Boston's Logan Airport for the Kings' training camp in Los Angeles, the thirty-fourth pro training camp of his career. Flight 175 never made it to Los Angeles. It crashed into the World Trade Center.

Vancouver scout Ron Delorme was watching CNN that day and knew his friend was getting ready to leave for a new season. He was also watching CNN when the crawl went by underneath the talking head: "Hockey scout Garnet Bailey dies on Flight 175."

"It's funny," says Delorme. "I only knew him as Ace."

Which is how everyone, including Gretzky, knew him. Bailey had played with Orr in Boston and watched the great Bruins defenceman struggle with the responsibilities of fame. He always advised Gretzky to sign autographs, to treat fans with respect, to make himself available to the public. It's one of the reasons Gretzky has worn his celebrity as graciously as any superstar athlete in sport. But Bailey also taught him how to be a pro – how to act, how to carry himself – and a bond formed between the game's greatest player and the bird dog. Later on, on those rare occasions when Gretzky slumped with the Oilers, Sather would fly Bailey out to Edmonton from his Boston-area home just to talk with his former roommate. The slumps, it seemed, never lasted long.

Shortly after September 11, Gretzky talked to Bailey's son, Todd, about his father, about their friendship, about the many things the Great One would remember about Ace as long as he lived.

"He was everything to me," Gretzky told him.

On the mantel of the Bailey home was a picture of Todd Bailey, then one and a half, and Gretzky. You sense Gretzky also meant everything to Ace.

# CHAPTER 12

# "The thing people don't understand is the dream and how powerful it is."

T he first merger meeting between the WHA and the NHL occurred after the rebels' first season, when a group led by New York Rangers owner Bill Jennings and Philadelphia Flyers owner Ed Snider sat down with the WHA and offered to take in all twelve teams at $4 million a pop. The only stipulations were that the new league had to drop all its lawsuits and that the merger would be termed "an agreement" to avoid antitrust charges. The original merger movement died quickly and painlessly. But there would be more, many, many more, over the next seven years.

Like the WHA itself, the merger plan would change shapes and sizes continually and make up its own rules more than once before the final terms were agreed upon in March 1979. There were plans to include twelve teams. There were plans to include six teams. There were plans to include four teams. There were plans for two teams, and one that would let the Houston Aeros go to the NHL by itself. The one constant in all the plans was that the majority of the NHL teams wanted some form of accommodation with the WHA while a small but obstinate group of owners – led by Toronto's Harold Ballard, Chicago's Bill Wirtz, and Boston's Paul Mooney – blocked any peace effort. Not coincidentally, those three teams were hit hardest by player defections in the WHA's early years. They would exact some measure of revenge, but the cost of finally bringing the rebels to their knees was fearsome for all concerned.

"The game was to hang in long enough to get into the NHL," says Nelson Skalbania. "I attended at least a dozen merger meetings. It was getting close, but the dollars to keep going to get to the other end – I wasn't prepared to stay that long."

"Some of those meetings were like Russian roulette," says Whalers president Howard Baldwin. "You'd look around the room and you'd go, There's no way that guy's going to make it. There's no way they're going to have a team. But there was a group there you could count on, and enough teams did all right that we could keep the thing moving."

The merger movement really started in earnest when John Ziegler replaced Clarence Campbell as NHL president in 1977. Ziegler, the legal counsel for the Detroit Red Wings, was a moderate, and he could see the war between the two leagues was costing millions. That summer, he and a group led by Baldwin and Bill DeWitt, Jr., of Cincinnati had, as we've seen, an agreement in place that would admit six teams – Cincinnati, Houston, and the four that eventually made it, New England, Quebec, Edmonton, and Winnipeg. Under the terms of that agreement, the six WHA teams would join the NHL intact, play in the same division, and slowly evolve toward a full interlocking schedule with the senior league over five years. In retrospect, that plan made too much sense.

The WHA believed it had a deal. When Benny Hatskin handed the Avco Cup to the Quebec Nordiques in the spring of 1977, he said it would be the last time the WHA championship trophy would be presented and from then on the Nordiques would be playing for the Stanley Cup. At a league meeting, Baldwin told his fellow owners to go home and simply wait for the merger. Then Ballard and Mooney rallied the NHL's anti-merger forces and defeated the Baldwin-DeWitt proposal by one vote.

Infuriated, the rebels vowed to hit back where it hurt the most, by signing under-age juniors. Before Year 7 began, the rebels signed Wayne Gretzky, Mike Gartner, the six Baby Bulls, and others. The Winnipeg Jets also had a glittering array of young talent with the additions of Kent Nilsson and the players they'd purchased from Houston. Mark Howe was still only twenty-three and the Whalers also had young stars like Mike Rogers and Blaine Stoughton. Buddy Cloutier would score 75 goals for the Quebec Nordiques that year. In the end, you couldn't trust the NHL to do the right thing. It was the WHA's young players who ensured the merger would eventually go through.

As you must know by now, it just didn't go through smoothly.

Barry Shenkarow was the Jets' point man on the merger, and the thirty-one-year-old executive spent the WHA's final season chasing down entry into the NHL the way Jason hunted the Golden Fleece. Shenkarow and seven other partners, including team president Michael Gobuty and Bobby Hull, bought the franchise late in the 1977-78 season after the Jets had missed a payroll and amid rumours the team would be sold to Milwaukee. Shenkarow and his colleagues believed their invest-ment was going to be $25,000 each, but after a couple of dropouts it went up to $50,000.

Within a year, he was staring across a boardroom table at Bill Wirtz, Bill Jennings, and Harold Ballard, trying to negotiate his way into the NHL.

"We had no idea what we were getting into," says Shenkarow. "It was hilarious. We'd go anywhere and talk to anybody if we thought it would help. Ultimately, the thing that made it work was Johnny Bassett signing those players."

Shenkarow quickly deduced that he only had to turn a couple of votes to push through expansion. The difficult part was actually convincing the Wirtzes and Ballards of the world of what a keen idea it would be to let Winnipeg, Edmonton, and Quebec into their buildings four times a year. At one point, Shenkarow offered to play the Vancouver Canucks, one of the swing teams, a best-of-three pre-season series for their vote. It didn't happen, but you couldn't blame the man for trying.

"There were some people who weren't going to change their vote," says Shenkarow. "As far as Harold was concerned, Winnipeg didn't exist." He called Charles Bronfman, part owner of the Seagram Company in Montreal and part owner of the Canadiens, to see if he could help with Boston, "but there was no way."

"I was in Detroit at a meeting with all these big shots. They said, 'You told us you're going to expand the Winnipeg Arena. We've got this fax from the mayor that says you're going to get a new rink. What is it?' It was late at night and I went back to my room and called the only guy I knew who'd still be up, [Winnipeg media mogul] Izzy Asper. He said, 'Tell them anything, then once you're in do whatever you want.'"

But Shenkarow and the other WHA teams had just as much trouble with their own people. As the first vote in March drew near, there were a couple of proposals in place and just as many agendas among the rebels. The Oilers and Peter Pocklington didn't have a lot of money, but they had Wayne Gretzky, so they didn't mind a plan that would allow the WHA teams to protect just two players and two goalies. The Jets had a deep, balanced team and would cheerfully have paid more to protect six players. Cincinnati, meanwhile, had decided they'd lost enough money and had the power to hold up the merger if they weren't pieced off to their satisfaction. John Bassett, a WHA guy to the end, knew he wasn't going to get in with Birmingham and did what he could to help his friends.

"In the end, they just wanted our players," said Shenkarow.

The first NHL vote took place on March 8, 1979, and again the WHA believed they had the necessary support – they needed thirteen of the seventeen franchises to vote in favour of the merger – and again they were defeated by one vote. It soon became public that the dissenting votes were from Boston, Toronto, Montreal, L.A., and, of all places, Vancouver. Harold Ballard was jubilant. "I feel so elated," he said. "It's like the North beating the South in the Civil War." At the league meetings in Key Largo, Florida, Ballard had also confronted Emile Francis, the chairman of the GMs committee, who desperately wanted a merger, and said, "Cat, we beat you. If you like those WHA bastards so much, why don't you join them?" Francis then cursed a blue streak at Ballard.

The WHA's response was immediate and direct. Baldwin said the league would sign more under-agers. Bassett said there were six teams in place for the 1979-80 season, the WHA would add two more teams in each of 1980-81 and 1982-83, *and* they'd have a European division in place by 1980-81. Bassett would also sign more kids. He had agreed in principle to a deal with Oshawa Generals star Tom McCarthy. He was after Paul Reinhart, Kevin Lowe, Doug Wickenheiser, and Ray Bourque. He'd signed Craig Hartsburg, Gaston Gingras, Pat Riggin, Rick Vaive, and Rob Ramage to four-year extensions worth $650,000, and even if the Bulls couldn't make it to the next season he'd sell their contracts to the Jets.

It was brave talk and it was largely empty, but the NHL knew its foe had been fighting for seven years and it wasn't going to turtle now. But this time, the rebels would receive some help, and because this is largely a Canadian story we take great delight in reporting that the great merger war was ultimately decided by beer.

Canadians, it would seem, are slow to anger, but when you mess with their hockey teams you've crossed a dangerous line, and so it was with the merger. When word got out that Montreal, which was owned by Molson, and Vancouver, where Molson products were sold, had helped defeat the merger, the public's reaction in Quebec, Winnipeg, and Edmonton – cities where the giant brewery also conducted business – was swift. Aided and abetted by the media, a loose boycott of Molson products, which promised to become a tightly organized boycott, was quickly organized. Just to reinforce the message, bomb threats were received at the Molson plant in Quebec City, and a bullet was shot through the window of the Molson plant in Winnipeg. Molson suits quickly met in Winnipeg and attempted damage control, but Winnipeggers, in particular, weren't going to be placated by a press release.

The vote "was a situation we had no control over," said Morgan McCammon, president of Molson. "We ask for your sympathy, support, and some patience. I have to believe it's possible. I do believe we'll be successful this time."

You could count on it. In the two weeks leading up to the next vote, the Canadian House of Commons unanimously supported a motion urging the NHL to adopt the three Canadian teams. By the time the NHL board reconvened, Montreal and Vancouver had seen the error of their ways. On March 22, the NHL voted 13-4 to accept the merger plan. Ballard, predictably, was apoplectic.

"There are maybe eight or nine players in their league who'll be any good in ours," he howled. "Chicago draws nine thousand for the New York Rangers. What are they going to draw for the Edmonton Oilers? Who the hell are the Edmonton Oilers?"

Others weren't as short-sighted.

"What wasn't there to like [from the NHL's point of view]?" Baldwin says. "It's like you've got this ulcer that's driving you crazy. All of a sudden the ulcer is offering you money and players to go away. It was a pretty good deal for the NHL."

It was all of that. The NHL termed the final agreement an "expansion," because the more accurate term was offensive. The four WHA teams would pay $6 million in franchise fees: $1 million by May 1, $3.625 million by June 1, and the remaining $1.375 million over five years. A $3.5-million indemnification would be paid by the four teams to Cincinnati to fold, and Bassett would take $2.85 million. Each WHA team could protect two goalies and two skaters. All players on NHL protected lists reverted back to their original teams; only forty-five WHA players were not on NHL protected lists. After the NHL teams reclaimed their players, they would protect two goalies and fifteen skaters and the WHA teams could choose from the rest at $125,000 per player. NHL teams could protect another player after they lost a player and they could lose no more than four players.

Oh yes, and the WHA teams would be picking at the end of the junior draft, not at the beginning, as was the custom for expansion teams.

"We had no choice, okay," says Baldwin. "But I'll also say, when you look at it as an expansion, our teams weren't raped that badly. We kept Mark Howe and we made the playoffs that first year. Look at what happened with Edmonton. I know Winnipeg was hurt, but there was nothing else we could do. I don't think we would have made it through another year."

The Jets were hit hardest by the farcical expansion draft that took place that summer. John Ferguson opted to protect Morris Lukowich and Scott Campbell as his two priority selections and hoped to retain Kent Nilsson, Terry Ruskowski, or Rich Preston in the maze of backroom deals that led up to the draft. Montreal, for instance, managed to keep Rod Langway, Pierre Larouche, Rick Chartraw, Bill Nyrop, and Pat Hughes while losing Cam Connor, Alan Hangsleben, Alain Côté, and Peter Marsh. But despite Ferguson's best efforts, his fine team was violated by the NHL. The Jets' GM flew to Atlanta and offered Flames GM Cliff Fletcher $250,000 to stay away from Kent Nilsson. No dice, and two years later Nilsson would ring up 131 points with the Calgary Flames. Fergie then flew to the Bahamas and offered Hawks GM Bob Pulford their first-round pick for Terry Ruskowski. He thought he had an agreement, but when he got back to Winnipeg Pulford called and said the trade was off. Ferguson also tried to use the return of Bobby Hull to Chicago to leverage Ruskowski or Rich Preston back to Winnipeg. The Hawks would reclaim both Hull and Ruskowski but leave Hull off their protected list. Out of spite, as much as anything, Ferguson selected the Golden Jet.

"We were playing in the finals, and by that time word was out about the merger," says Tom McVie, the Jets' coach in the latter stages of Year 7. "I'd look up in the stands and I'd see all the scouts and general managers from the NHL teams. Fergie did his damnedest to arrange deals to keep players, but when we joined the NHL we were a shell of what we could have been."

The Jets would lose Nilsson, Ruskowski, Preston, Barry Long, and Kim Clackson. That wasn't their only problem. Campbell, a big, two-way defenceman who Bill Dineen likened to a young Larry Robinson, came down with asthma and assorted allergies and never panned out. In the 1979 junior draft, likely the richest in NHL history, the Jets managed to pick the only stiff in the first round when they selected Jimmy Mann one spot ahead of Michel Goulet and two ahead of Kevin Lowe. In the expansion draft, the Jets also replaced their stars with players like Gord McTavish, Clark Hamilton, Bill Riley, Al Cameron, and Dave Hoyda.

"I don't know why they didn't take Blue," Boston head coach Don Cherry cackled, referring to his famous pet Staffordshire bull terrier. "They've picked up a lot of other dogs."

"You know, there's enough talent available for us to win the [senior hockey] Allan Cup," said McVie of the Jets' expansion take. "It might be seven games, but if we get home ice in the seventh game, we'd win."

Over the next two seasons, the Jets would ice two of the worst teams in the history of the NHL, winning twenty games

in 1979-80 and just nine in 1980-81, before they drafted Dale
Hawerchuk in 1981 and started the climb toward respectability.

"In five months I went from coaching my best team ever to
my worst team ever," says McVie. "People thought I was a
miracle worker when I went to Winnipeg. But it wasn't like I
got hit in the head and turned stupid the next season. We just
didn't have any players."

Strangely, the other WHA teams didn't fare as badly as the Jets.
The Oilers, of course, protected Gretzky. They subsequently
lost their other priority selection, Bengt Gustaffson, to
Washington on a bizarre NHL ruling. But Sather, along with his
two lieutenants, Barry Fraser and Bryan Watson, also built the
core of a Stanley Cup champion team in that first year. The
Oilers' first three picks in the junior draft were, remarkably,
Lowe, Mark Messier, and Glenn Anderson. In the expansion
draft, they took Lee Fogolin and former wunderkind Pat Price.
Sather also manoeuvred to keep Dave Semenko, Dave Hunter,
and Dave Lumley, all of whom would play a significant role in
the dynasty.

"Barry, Bryan, and I did all the drafting that year," says Sather.
"At that time there weren't any computers, and the information
was very limited, because the league didn't want anyone to
know what everybody else was making. So we went through
each individual contract for five days to find out who was
making how much and who had what left on their deal. We
knew the kind of players we wanted. We were able to make
some good moves."

The Nordiques, for their part, kept defencemen Paul Baxter
and Garry Lariviere as their priority selections but still emerged
from the draft with Buddy Cloutier, Marc Tardif, and Serge
Bernier. New England protected Mark Howe and, in a rare
example of NHL humanitarianism, didn't have to protect his
father or account for Gordie during the expansion draft. They
also managed to hang on to Blaine Stoughton, who'd score 56

goals for them the next season, and Mike Rogers, who'd record 105 points. The Whalers made the playoffs that first season, and in a crucial late-season game went into Toronto and beat the Leafs with Ballard looking on from his bunker.

"I've never gotten so much satisfaction out of a regular-season win," said John Garrett, the Whalers' goalie.

Gordie Howe turned fifty-two that season with the Whalers. He played eighty games and scored 15 goals on the fourth line without any power-play time. Following that year, he met with Baldwin and was finally persuaded to retire.

"He was going to play another year," says Baldwin. "It was the only disagreement I ever had with him. I said, 'Gordie, you've got to shut it down.' He'd *still* be playing. What a remarkable, remarkable man."

Other WHA alums, meanwhile, played with mixed results in the years in and around the merger. Ulf Nilsson rattled off 66 points in his first fifty-nine games with the Rangers before the Islanders' Denis Potvin caught him with a check and broke his ankle. Nilsson would return to Broadway, but he was never the same player.

"I got the shit beat out of me for four years in the WHA and that took its toll," says Nilsson. "The first year in New York was magical, then I broke my ankle. But it was never the same as Winnipeg."

Anders Hedberg, meanwhile, would have some decent seasons with the Rangers, recording three 30-goal campaigns in his seven seasons there, but he also suffered through injuries and was never the force he'd been with the Jets.

"I felt incredibly responsible going to New York for that amount of money, and I put a lot of pressure on myself," Hedberg says.

The WHA players also had to fight a deep-rooted NHL prejudice that first year after the merger. Richard Brodeur, for example, went from being an All-Star goalie in the new league to spending a year in the minors in 1979–80. Two years later he'd carry the Vancouver Canucks to the Stanley Cup final, but he still remembers the feeling of going into the NHL and having to prove himself all over again after spending seven seasons in the WHA.

"Everyone in Quebec was thrilled, because they wanted in the NHL," says Brodeur. "But a lot of us were asking, What now? You looked around our dressing room and you knew a lot of guys weren't going to make it. Whatever we'd accomplished in the WHA didn't matter. It was like I was starting my career over, and a lot of guys were in the same boat."

A lot of those guys also played out of their skulls in the first year out of the merger. Despite Ballard's assertion, eight of the NHL's top twenty-five scorers in 1979–80 were WHA veterans. The first round of the 1979 junior draft also featured ex-WHAers Rob Ramage (first overall to the Colorado Rockies), Mike Gartner (fourth), Rick Vaive (fifth), Craig Hartsburg (sixth), and Goulet (twentieth), all of whom would have long and successful NHL careers.

"I think you can say we were a lot better than the NHL was giving us credit for, but we probably weren't as good as we thought we were," says Harry Neale, which is interesting, because later in the same interview Neale gets a little agitated when the subject of the first year after the merger is raised.

"They said our players weren't good enough," he says. "Well, they were wrong about Mike Rogers. They were wrong about Blaine Stoughton. They were wrong about Robbie Ftorek. Those players were plenty good enough for the NHL."

Mike Gartner spent nineteen seasons in the NHL and is one of nine players in NHL history to score 700 goals in his career. In his playing days he served as president of the NHL Players' Association, and in retirement he became the NHLPA's director of business operations.

Gartner's first year in professional hockey was with the WHA's Cincinnati Stingers in the 1978-79 season, where, as a nineteen-year-old, he scored 27 goals. Gartner had signed a five-year deal with the Stingers worth $750,000, but when the WHA merged with the NHL that contract simply disappeared. Not only that, Gartner was told he was going back in the junior draft and he'd be the property of whoever selected him. In the end, the Washington Capitals drafted him, and Gartner wound up holding out in training camp to get a new contract.

Gartner, the union man, is asked how that would fly in today's NHL. After a pause, he says, "All I can tell you is it wouldn't happen. Let's leave it at that."

Gartner, of course, wasn't the only victim of the merger. Five of the Baby Bulls – Hartsburg, Gingras, Vaive, Riggin, and Ramage – negotiated four-year, $650,000 extensions in the WHA's final year, and those deals, like Gartner's, evaporated. Also like Gartner, all five went into the draft. Their agent, Bill Watters, eventually negotiated settlements for each of them in the $100,000 range, but that was nowhere near what they would have pulled in on the open market. Watters estimates the first-round picks in the 1979 draft lost as much as $250,000 on their contracts from the year before.

"They weren't very happy about it, but Al Eagleson ran hockey in those days," says Watters.

"It didn't really matter, because no one was throwing money around in 1979," says Vaive. "I made good dough in my career and I played thirteen years in the NHL. I've got nothing to complain about."

Others, however, may not be so philosophical. As much as the WHA established new markets and new opportunities for all players, Eagleson and the NHL managed to close those doors following the merger as quickly as the rebels had opened them. In 1979, the NHLPA finally had the leverage to bring its members the rights and freedoms enjoyed by players in other sports. The

NHL owners desperately wanted the $24-million windfall from the four new teams and all those great players, but there was still the threat of charges under antitrust legislation and there would be no merger without the NHLPA's approval.

The Players' Association had a chance to blow up the existing system in 1979 and replace it with meaningful free agency. Five years before the merger, the NHL had replaced the reserve clause with an option clause in the standard player's contract. They also devised a system of free agency in which the compensation required for signing a player was so onerous that, in the five years between 1976 and 1980, 137 players filed for free agency and just twenty-three players changed teams.

Eagleson said all the right things publicly in the months leading up to the league meetings in Nassau that summer, claiming that the Players' Association should get half the $24 million in expansion money. He also floated a new proposal for free agency in which the players in the top third of the league's salary structure would cost draft picks and cash to sign, but the bottom two thirds would be unrestricted.

"In the past, we've been able to work things out with the Players' Association," said Ziegler.

They could work things out to the NHL's satisfaction again, because at the Nassau meetings Eagleson sold his membership down the river. This time, the union's executive director simply abdicated his leadership position and let the players fight it out with the owners. It wasn't much of a fight. The owners trotted out their traditional claims that they were losing money, and this time they could also call on the seven-year war with the WHA as evidence they were being ruined. They told the players the league couldn't support free agency, and if the Players' Association voted to strike it would mean the end of the NHL.

With no help forthcoming from their leader, the NHLPA capitulated. They held the first strike vote in NHL history, but it was defeated 16-1. The owners eventually threw them some trinkets – increased pension payments, increased meal money – in exchange for ratification of the merger. The owners, on the other hand, pulled in $24 million in franchise fees and kept its laughable system of free agency, which in turn allowed them to keep the salaries of their new players depressed. Nine years after the merger, the average hockey salary was $179,000. The average baseball salary at the time was $450,000, and the average basketball salary was $500,000.

In a few months, WHA counsel Don Regan had done more for the players than Eagleson had done in his career. In a few months, Eagleson managed to undo everything Regan had done for the players. And that still wasn't all.

During the life of the new league, members of the WHA Players' Association paid into their own pension fund and were told they would receive full credit for their years in the WHA. That is, if you had seven years toward your WHA pension, you'd get seven years' worth in the NHL. But the final agreement didn't work out that way.

John Garrett, who was the players' rep in Hartford, said approximately one third of the WHA players' pensions was carried over to the NHL. Typically, there was no accounting or no explanation to the players. Eagleson and Ron Roberts, the WHA counsel, simply hammered out a deal and presented it to the players.

Garrett now gets $129 a month for his six years in the WHA. Richard Brodeur paid in the pension plan for seven years and now receives $187 a month. Dennis Sobchuk played five seasons in the WHA and gets a hundred bucks a month.

"I say, 'Let's go to the Dairy Queen,' when I get my cheque," Sobchuk says. "It's the one downer I associate with the WHA. Our league did so many things for the players, and when it was time for a payback, we got nothing."

Eventually, the barriers between the WHA and the NHL broke down. Four seasons after the merger, Wayne Gretzky fulfilled Glen Sather's prophecy when, as captain of the Oilers, he skated around Bill Hunter's Northlands Coliseum with the Stanley Cup. Gartner, the Baby Bulls, Kent Nilsson, and so many other WHA players went on to have distinguished NHL careers. Even Harold Ballard, after a fashion, began to warm to his old enemies.

"I remember we had an NHL meeting at the Breakers and I was with my fiancée, Karen," says Howard Baldwin. "I introduced her to Harold, and he said, 'You're a helluva lot better looking than the broad he had up here last year.' We all laughed."

But over the years, the WHA's legacy has faded from the game, and if it's remembered at all today it's in the thousands of outrageous stories hockey men tell about the league that produced blue pucks and the Miami Screaming Eagles. No one seems to remember the WHA wrestled the game away from a handful of NHL owners and took it to new markets, that it opened the door for Europeans, and that it offered a generation of players their first chance at a real payday. But the men of the WHA remember. That's why they share a bond.

"You think about the characters you met and the great players you played with and against," says Mark Napier. "There's an affinity there to this day. It was like a fraternity. Maybe it's not a fraternity you'd want to join every day, but we were a close bunch."

Al Hamilton, who played in Edmonton with the Oilers for seven seasons, is asked if he had any regrets about joining the rebel league.

"Hell no," he says. "We had an adventure that would be envied by anyone. We changed the game. We saw the league evolve. We had great, great players. It was young and exciting and fun. It was a good seven years."

Those sentiments are echoed by Glen Sather, who came to

the WHA as a journeyman forward in the last days of his career and in two years laid the groundwork for one of the greatest teams in hockey history.

"I don't think it gets the credit it deserves," says Sather. "It helped hockey grow and it opened up a lot of doors for a lot of people, me included. There was always a certain sense of camaraderie among the four teams that made it to the NHL."

After the Winnipeg Jets won the final Avco Cup, Barry Shenkarow took the trophy and placed it in the directors' lounge at the Winnipeg Arena. Sometime later, another version of the Avco Cup appeared in the Hockey Hall of Fame, which, all things considered, is kind of ironic. Shenkarow called the Hall to let them know they had a fake.

"I said, 'That's not the Avco Cup,'" says Shenkarow, who's since donated the real trophy to the Manitoba Sports Hall of Fame. "They said, 'Yes it is.' They didn't want to listen me."

Shenkarow was in his early twenties when the WHA came to Winnipeg, and he watched the town come alive when Ben Hatskin signed Bobby Hull. He was there when Hull, Hedberg, and Nilsson made magic on the ice. He then bought a share of the team and helped get it into the NHL before he became its president. In 1995, in what the NHL termed a "market correction," he sold the team to a group that moved it to Phoenix.

Shenkarow recalls the year leading up to the merger and the frenetic schedule he kept trying to get the Jets into the NHL. When the vote came down in March 1979, he'd been working on it for eighteen months, seven days a week. He was asked how he could have kept up that pace.

"The thing people don't understand is the dream and how powerful it is," he says.

But the men of the WHA understood its power because they chased that dream for seven years. In the end, the league may have died, but you want to believe the dream lives on.

# THE WHA, YEAR BY YEAR

## YEAR 1
## (1972-73)

**Eastern Division**
Cleveland Crusaders; New England Whalers; New York Raiders; Ottawa Nationals; Philadelphia Blazers; Quebec Nordiques

**Western Division**
Alberta Oilers; Chicago Cougars; Houston Aeros; Los Angeles Sharks; Minnesota Fighting Saints; Winnipeg Jets

# YEAR 2
## (1973-74)

### Eastern Division
Chicago Cougars; Cleveland Crusaders; New England Whalers; New York Golden Blades/New Jersey Knights (formerly New York Raiders); Quebec Nordiques; Toronto Toros (formerly Ottawa Nationals)

### Western Division
Edmonton Oilers (formerly Alberta Oilers); Houston Aeros; Los Angeles Sharks; Minnesota Fighting Saints; Vancouver Blazers (formerly Philadelphia Blazers); Winnipeg Jets

# YEAR 3
## (1974-75)

### Canadian Division
Edmonton Oilers; Quebec Nordiques; Toronto Toros; Vancouver Blazers; Winnipeg Jets

### Eastern Division
Chicago Cougars; Cleveland Crusaders; Indianapolis Racers (expansion); New England Whalers

### Western Division
Houston Aeros; Michigan Stags/Baltimore Blades (formerly Los Angeles Sharks); Minnesota Fighting Saints; Phoenix Roadrunners (expansion); San Diego Mariners (formerly New York Golden Blades/New Jersey Knights/New York Raiders)

# YEAR 4
## (1975-76)

### Canadian Division
Calgary Cowboys (formerly Vancouver Blazers/Philadelphia Blazers); Edmonton Oilers; Quebec Nordiques; Toronto Toros; Winnipeg Jets

### Eastern Division
Cincinnati Stingers (expansion); Cleveland Crusaders; Indianapolis Racers; New England Whalers

### Western Division
Denver Spurs/Ottawa Civics (expansion); Houston Aeros; Minnesota Fighting Saints; Phoenix Roadrunners; San Diego Mariners

RIP — Denver Spurs/Ottawa Civics (January 1976); Minnesota Fighting Saints (February 1976)

# YEAR 5
## (1976-77)

### Eastern Division
Birmingham Bulls (formerly Toronto Toros/Ottawa Nationals); Cincinnati Stingers; Indianapolis Racers; Minnesota Fighting Saints II (formerly Cleveland Crusaders); New England Whalers; Quebec Nordiques

### Western Division
Calgary Cowboys; Edmonton Oilers; Houston Aeros; Phoenix Roadrunners; San Diego Mariners; Winnipeg Jets

RIP — Minnesota Fighting Saints II (January 1977)

## YEAR 6
## (1977-78)

Birmingham Bulls; Cincinnati Stingers; Edmonton Oilers; Houston Aeros; Indianapolis Racers; New England Whalers; Quebec Nordiques; Winnipeg Jets

RIP — Calgary Cowboys (May 1977); Phoenix Roadrunners (April 1977); San Diego Mariners (July 1977)


## YEAR 7
## (1978-79)

Birmingham Bulls; Cincinnati Stingers; Edmonton Oilers; Indianapolis Racers; New England Whalers; Quebec Nordiques; Winnipeg Jets

RIP — Indianapolis Racers (December 1978)

# INDEX

© *The Province* (Vancouver)

Ed Willes started his journalism career in 1982 at the *Medicine Hat News*, which is where the idea for this book was born. After four years there he moved on to the *Regina Leader-Post*, then to the *Winnipeg Sun*, where he was the hockey writer for eight years. From 1997 to 1998, he worked as a freelancer in Montreal and ended up writing for the *New York Times*. That summer he was offered the sports columnist job at *The Province* (Vancouver), where he's been ever since. He lives in North Vancouver, B.C., with his wife and two children.